The Depression and the Developing World, 1914-1939

A. J. H. LATHAM

CROOM HELM LONDON

BARNES & NOBLE BOOKS
TOTOWA, NEW JERSEY

© 1981 A. J. H. Latham
Croom Helm Ltd, 2–10 St John's Road, London SW11

British Library Cataloguing in Publication Data

Latham, A.J.H.
  The depression and the developing world, 1914–1939.
  1. Underdeveloped areas – Economic conditions
  I. Title
  330.9'172'4   HC59.7
  ISBN 0-85664-920-1

First published in the USA 1981 by
BARNES & NOBLE BOOKS
81 ADAMS DRIVE
TOTOWA, New Jersey, 07512
ISBN 0-389-20211-8

Typeset in Great Britain by
Pat Murphy, Highcliffe, Dorset
Printed and bound in Great Britain by
Biddles Ltd, Guildford and King's Lynn

CONTENTS

GRAPHS, MAPS AND DIAGRAM

Graphs

Maps

Diagram

TABLES

APPENDICES

PREFACE

This book can be seen as a continuation of my last book *The International Economy and the Undeveloped World, 1865–1914*.[1] As such it argues that the world economy after 1914 cannot be understood without taking into account what was happening in the developing countries of Asia and Africa. In particular it puts forward the view that the cause of the depression lay as much in Asia as it did in America. It also takes the view that development in Asia and Africa was due largely to the capitalistic enterprise of their people in response to the forces of the international market. The topics written about have been chosen because they interested me, rather than to conform with some current fad. No doubt my critics will complain their own tastes have not been catered for, but they are free to write their own book! Just as my last book did not discuss Imperialism, this one does not discuss Colonialism. I leave that issue to those whose hearts burn with a commitment I do not share. But I do include in this book one country which I did not deal with in the last one, the United States colony of the Philippines.

In writing this book I have deliberately kept the style as simple as possible. Writing is about communicating and that is done best with uncomplicated language, particularly when a book may be read by people to whom English is a second or third language. Experience of teaching British and American students suggest that they too prefer to understand plainly what they are reading. Even professional academics occasionally like to be clear what an author is talking about, although often one might not think so.

I am grateful to W. A. Cole who discussed some of the ideas in this book with me and was indulgent about my teaching hours, and to Larry Neal, John McKay, Jeremy Atack, Tom Ulen and Suzan Linz of the University of Illinois, Urbana-Champaign, where I spent a stimulating and congenial semester. I am also grateful to Patrick O'Brian, Christopher Platt, Barry Supple, Mark Elvin, Roger Owen and David Fieldhouse, who provided encouragement in a seminar at St Antony's, Oxford. I owe thanks to Mrs Elaine Davies who typed the manuscript, Tim Fearnside who did the drawings, and Barbara my former wife.

A. J. H. Latham

Preface

Department of Economic History
University College of Swansea

Note

1. A. J. H. Latham, *The International Economy and the Undeveloped World, 1865–1914* (London: Croom Helm, 1978 and Totowa, New Jersey: Rowman and Littlefield, 1978).

INTRODUCTION

The fifty years before the First World War saw the developing world become an integral part of the international economy. The building of the railways was crucial, and from the opening of the first railway in India in 1853, Asia had acquired 47,275 miles in 1913. Nearly three-quarters of them were in India. Africa had 19,886 miles of which over half were in South Africa and Rhodesia. The railways linked economic hinterlands to ports, providing outlets for mining and agricultural exports, and inlets for manufactured imports. As the steam engine revolutionised transport on land, so it did at sea. Steamships connected the railways of the world together by plying between their terminal ports. The Suez Canal helped, in 1869 bringing Asia 4,000 miles nearer to Europe. Besides the physical improvements in transport, a fast way of bringing buyers and sellers into contact across the world was needed. This was provided by the electric telegraph, and by 1871 it was possible to cable London from Shanghai. South Africa was connected to London in 1879 and West Africa in 1886.

To complete the integration of the developing countries into the world market they needed internationally acceptable monetary systems. The monetary innovation of the late nineteenth century was the gold standard by which countries fixed their currencies at a defined gold value. By 1880 most of the western countries were on the gold standard, ceasing to use silver money as they did so. As there was now less demand for silver its value dropped, causing problems for many Asian countries whose currency was still based on silver. From 1872 to 1893 the price of silver nearly halved, and India moved on to the gold standard because of the difficulties of making payments to London in an ever depreciating currency. Most of the other countries of Asia had moved on to gold by 1906 as the price of silver continued to fall, but China remained on silver. In Africa, where traditional monetary mediums were used widely, the colonial authorities gradually introduced monetary systems usually based on the metropolitan unit. In East Africa the rupee was used.

One reason countries adopted the gold standard was to encourage investment from abroad. Britain was the major investor in the developing world, and in the fifty years up to 1914 a quarter of her portfolio investment went to Asia and Africa. That was more than she

15

invested in the United States. On the eve of the First World War Britain had $4,950 million invested in these areas of the developing world, some 65 per cent of total foreign investment there. India and Ceylon received by far the largest share of British investment in Asia, some $1,850 million, and China followed with $600 million. In Africa, South Africa and Rhodesia received $1,750 million, leaving $400 million for all the rest of Africa south of the Sahara. Germany was the next most important investor with $750 million, two-thirds being in her African colonies and the remainder in China. France had $550 million, $200 million in her colonies in Indo-China, $150 million in China, and the rest divided equally between South Africa and her African colonies. Her total investments in Africa and Asia were less than Britain's in China alone. Apart from the $50 million contributed by the United States, all of which was in China, the rest of the world put in $1,300 million. Of this China received $550 million, the Dutch East Indies $550 million and the Belgian Congo $200 million.

It is known that 69 per cent of British international portfolio investment went into social overhead capital, of which the railways were by far the most important single category. Mining and extractive industries took 12 per cent, but manufacturing less than 4 per cent. British investment in Asia and Africa probably followed this overall pattern. In 1910 37 per cent of British investment in India and Ceylon was in railways directly, and of the 49 per cent which was invested in government much was used for railways. In Malaya rubber attracted nearly half of British investment, but the railways were less important as they were financed from the favourable current revenues of the country. More than four-fifths of British investment in China was in government and much of this was used for railways. In South Africa and Rhodesia gold and diamonds attracted capital, more than a third being in mining. Government took over a quarter, much going into railway and transport facilities to serve the mines. An even higher proportion of British investment in West Africa was in mining, more than two-fifths, government taking another quarter largely to provide infrastructure. In other countries not so dependent upon Britain for their foreign capital, the investment pattern seems to have been similar. The Dutch East Indies attracted capital from both the Netherlands and Britain into her plantations, and the government borrowed heavily to provide railways. Siam borrowed from Britain to build her railways and there was other foreign investment in mining. The French provided Indo-China with loans for the railways, irrigation schemes and mines. Her African colonies borrowed to build railways. Railways dominated investment in the German African colonies, and in the Belgian Congo in 1914 half the investment was in railways and a third in mining and related activity. Portuguese Africa too attracted money for railway and port facilities. So the capital flows to the developing world seem to have gone into transport facilities and the mines and plantations which they served.

As communications improved and investment flowed in, the foreign trade of the developing world increased. Rough calculations suggest that exports from Asia and Africa grew at an annual rate of 3.9 per cent during the years from 1883 to 1913, with a rate of 2.0 per cent from 1883 to 1899 and of 6.0 per cent from 1899 to 1913. By the outbreak of war exports were slightly greater than from the United States and Canada. Asia accounted for most of the exports, her exports being more than three times the value of those from Africa. As for imports, Asia and Africa took substantially more than the United States and Canada, but not quite as much as Britain. So the developing world provided 15.5 per cent of world exports in 1913 and 14 per cent of world imports. What was perhaps more important was that the developing world was importing manufactured goods and exporting raw materials. Most of the manufactured goods came from Britain, but most of the raw materials were going to the industrial countries of Continental Europe and the United States. In this way Britain was able to earn enough from her exports to the developing world to pay off the deficits she had with continental Europe and the United States from whom she was buying both manufactured goods and food. Without the surplus from the developing world Britain would have been forced to abandon Free Trade and put on tariffs against imports from Europe and America, which would have severely hit their exports and their growth. The developing countries were able to purchase manufactured goods from Britain because of their surpluses with the United States and Europe. It was a system of trade which benefited everyone. India was the key country in this system, and Britain's surplus of $292.2 million there in 1910 was greater than her deficit of $243.5 million with the United States. Britain also had a surplus of $63.3 million with China. India herself had a massive trade surplus overall, even after her deficit with Britain had been met. She had a surplus with the United States due to sales of jute and with continental Europe due to jute, oilseeds and rice. She also had one with the rest of Asia, and in particular China, where her surplus was due to sales of opium and cotton yarn. China for her part was in deficit with almost every country in the world, and her international accounts were only kept in balance by remittances from Chinese emigrants.

As for the other countries of the developing world Ceylon developed a plantation sector growing tea and coffee, and brought labourers from India to work on the estates. Her own peasants grew copra as an export crop, over and above their own food. Rice had to be imported to feed the estate workers. Malaya had tin mines developed and worked by Chinese immigrants, and there were rubber plantations employing Indian workers. Rice had to be imported to feed all the immigrants, but the Malays grew their own food and copra as a cash crop. Sugar was the key crop in the Dutch East Indies, and there was tobacco, tea, rubber and copra. Peasants and plantations both provided exports, copra in particular being a peasant crop. Siam was a rice exporter, cultivation being in peasant hands, as it was in French Indo-China. Rice exports were growing in these years to feed the plantation hands on the new estates in Asia. So the plantations created opportunities for peasant enterprise not in the countries where the plantations were but in Burma, Siam and French Indo-China where there was surplus land suitable for rice. Rice was also exported to China, and to Europe where it was used for making starch and alcohol. In short, the movement of migrant workers as they seized the economic opportunities created by plantations and mines created a new international market in rice which peasant rice producers soon exploited. South Africa was the leading trading nation in Africa in 1913 providing 63 per cent of the exports of Africa south of the Sahara, and taking 50 per cent of the imports. Diamonds and gold were the key exports, and although the mines were run by Europeans, migrant workers came from all over Southern Africa to work in them. Chinese miners were also used for a short time. So the South African mines relied on the initiative of Africans in seeking opportunities for work. In other parts of Africa there were some plantations but essentially peasant agriculture prevailed. They produced the cotton and maize of East Africa, and the palm products, cocoa and groundnuts of West Africa. In the Congo, Angola and French Equatorial Africa Africans collected the ivory and forest rubber which dominated trade there. Cottons were the most important import in all these Asian and African countries, except the few where rice led. There cottons came second. Britain was the major supplier, which is why the developing world was so vital to her trade. The Netherlands, France and Germany tended to supply their own colonies. Japan began to make inroads in the cotton market at the very end of the period, but the biggest threat to Lancashire's dominance was the development of the cotton industry in India. By the end of the period Bombay yarn had already taken much of the China market from Lancashire, and was supplying Japan.

The migrant flows which began with the establishment of mines and plantations took place against an overall growth of population. Just over half the world's population lived in Asia at the turn of the century but under a tenth in Africa. India's population grew by a fifth between 1871 and 1911, rising from 263 million to 315 million in sudden bursts of growth. Within India there was migration to Burma where the rice economy was expanding, and to Assam tea plantations and Bombay cotton mills. Migrants also left India for plantations in Ceylon and the Straits Settlements. One force behind their migration was the damage done to their handicraft cotton industry by imports from Lancashire. But migration from India in relationship to the entire population was really rather unimportant. Net immigration to Ceylon from 1871 to 1915 was just over one and a quarter million. The impact on Ceylon was such that her population increased by 70 per cent from 2.4 million to 4.1 million, domestic population growth adding to immigration. In Malaya the flow of migrants from India met the flow of migrants from China. Again the outflow made little impact on India, net immigration from India to Malaya being under a third of a million between 1905 and 1913. But it had a big impact on Malaya, whose population was only 2.3 million in 1911. Only 10 per cent of the population were Indians, and the biggest immigrant group were the Chinese who made up 30 per cent of the population. The Chinese tended to work in the mines rather than on the plantations, and preferred to work for employers of their own race. There are no reliable population figures for the Dutch East Indies, but it is clear that there was substantial population growth. The population seems to have nearly doubled from 20 million in 1870 to 37 million in 1905, and was probably greater than this. Chinese migrants came in and there were over half a million in 1905. Chinese also went to Siam, and about a tenth of the population of 7 million was Chinese in 1909. The number of Chinese also increased in French Indo-China, although population estimates there are vague. This migration of Chinese was an important population movement. Apart from Malaya, the Chinese tended to be involved in commerce and in particular the rice trade where they handled transport, milling, and marketing. They seem to have been driven out of China by forces similar to those driving Indians out of southern India, particularly the impact of cotton yarn from Lancashire and Bombay on their handspun cotton industry. The migrants came mainly from the two southern provinces of Kwantung and Fukien. As a proportion of Chinese population the migration was unimportant, although there are no accurate population figures for China. China's population was probably bigger than the 315 million in India in 1911. The alacrity of the Chinese in migrating demonstrates their determination to seize the new economic opportunities which were opening up in these years. Estimates of Africa's population are little better than guesses, although British Africa has better figures than other countries. In 1911 Nigeria had 17 million, South Africa nearly 6 million, and Kenya 2 million. The Gold Coast and Sierra Leone each had over a million. British Africa as a whole had approximately 35 million which was paltry in comparison with the 315 million of India alone. It is likely that the population was growing, and there was some immigration to southern and eastern Africa. Many of these migrants were Europeans but there were also Indians particularly in East Africa. The labourers who came from India to build the railways there returned home, but a community of Indian traders established itself at the communications centres along the railways. The population of the rest of Africa was roughly as large as that in British Africa, some 35 million at the end of the period, 14 million in French Africa, 11.5 million in German Africa, 10 million in Portuguese Africa and the remainder in the Congo.

Per capita income calculations for Asia and Africa in this period are wellnigh impossible, so what estimates there are are little more than guesswork. But it has been suggested that in South East Asia, made up of India, Burma and Siam, *per capita* incomes grew at an annual average of 0.25 per cent between 1860 and 1913. This was despite two severe famines which hit India. In the Far East, made up of the Philippines, Malaya and the Dutch East Indies, *per capita* incomes are said to have grown more quickly at 1.12 per cent per annum. Even in China it is intimated that *per capita* incomes grew at 0.13 per cent, although income per head was the lowest of all the regions in Asia in 1913. Despite population growth there seems to have been advance in *per capita* income. What is more, in 1860 South East Asia, the Far East and China had 64.8 per cent of the world's population and 33 per cent of world income. In 1913 their share of world population had decreased to 56.7 per cent and share of world income to 16.7 per cent. Yet overall national income in the Far East had increased four times, in South East Asia nearly twice, and even in China it had risen by nearly a quarter. Stagnation or regression did not occur even in China. As for Africa there are no estimates. Yet the fact that exports rose, and investment made does suggest that national incomes at least increased there too.

Society in Asia and Africa responded positively to the new economic opportunities of the late nineteenth century. Western capital and enterprise may have built the infrastructure of the developing world, but that infrastructure created many new possibilities for local enterprise. Thus Indians flocked to work in the cotton mills in Bombay, and members of different castes worked side by side in the weaving sheds despite theoretical restrictions against such contact. What is more the mills themselves were owned and operated by Indians. Elsewhere traditional restrictions on migration did not prevent farmers opening new land in the Brahmaputra Valley, or going to the tea plantations in Assam or Ceylon. In Burma the new rice expansion was financed by Indian moneylenders, and whilst the Burmese grew the rice it was transported and milled by Indian labourers. In Ceylon and Malaya immigrant workers lived and worked on estates but the Sinhalese and Malays remained in their traditional agriculture. They had their own food plots and were able to participate in the new opportunities of the international economy by growing cash crops, in particular copra. The coconut was an ancient prop of their economy with a new cash value. In 1913 coconut produce from peasant plots in Ceylon earned 45.5 million rupees in exports, when plantation tea earned only 88 million rupees. In Malaya exports of coconut products from peasant plots rose from 9 million Straits Dollars to 17 million Straits Dollars in the seven years from 1906 to 1912. With opportunities like that economic rationality allowed them to continue their way of life rather than to work in mines and plantations like the less fortunate Indian and Chinese coolies. In the Dutch East Indies the plantation labour force was recruited locally, but sugar land was rented from the villages for a year and a half and then reverted to village crops in order to maintain the fertility of the soil. So it was well integrated into the village economy. Both plantations and smallholders grew tea and rubber, and copra exports from peasant smallholdings trebled between 1910 and 1913. In Siam and French Indo-China the rice export economy depended on the initiative of the rice-growing peasantry. China however remained a problem economy and the Chinese demonstrated their response to economic incentives by migrating. There was some industrialisation in cotton manufacturing and silk manufacturing towards the end of the period under Chinese ownership. In Africa too, traditional attitudes did not prevent Africans taking new opportunities either by migrating to work in the mines in South Africa and Rhodesia, or in growing cotton, maize, cocoa, palm produce or groundnuts.

So the half-century before the First World War saw considerable economic development taking place in Asia and Africa. Western capitalism created a new infrastructure and the capitalistic people of the developing world seized the new market opportunities of wage labour and cash cropping. The surge of progress which resulted was to be maintained during and after the war.[1]

Note

1. A. J. H. Latham, *The International Economy and the Undeveloped World, 1865–1914* (London: Croom Helm, 1978, Totowa, New Jersey: Rowman and Littlefield, 1978).

1 COMMUNICATIONS

Railways and Roads

Railway building had caused a revolution in land communications
before the First World War, and construction continued during the
inter-war years. By 1937 Asia and Africa had over 16 per cent of world
railway mileage as is shown in Table 1.1. In that year a quarter of the
vast Indian railway system had been laid down since 1910, and a
seventh since 1920. Details of the railways in Asia and Africa are given
in Table 1.2.

Table 1.1: World Railway Mileage, 1937

	Total	%	State
Europe	256,824	32.56	139,701
North America	288,771	36.61	24,015
South America	80,742	10.23	35,341
Asia	85,806	10.87	63,222
Australasia	31,891	4.04	30,464
Africa	44,638	5.65	31,526
TOTAL	788,672	100.00	324,269

Source: *Universal Directory of Railway Officials and Railway Year Book*,
(London: 1940–1), pp. 397–8.

The Indian railways predominated, for in 1937 India had 43,021
miles of line out of an Asian total of 63,288 miles, or approximately 68
per cent. China, despite her vast size had only 11,610 miles, having
always lagged behind India in railway construction. Two-fifths of her
network had been built between 1920 and 1930, but here mileage
actually declined in the following years. South Africa had a bigger
system than China, with 16,203 miles, more than a third being built
since 1920 and over a half since 1910. Other British possessions
accounted for another 12,034 miles in Africa in 1937, French
possessions having only 3,853 miles, Belgian possessions 2,550 miles
and Portuguese possessions 2,003 miles. The additional mileage of these
years in the developing world is indicated on Map 1. Probably the
outstanding achievement was the linking of the copper belt in the heart

Map 1: Railways in Africa and Asia, 1913–39

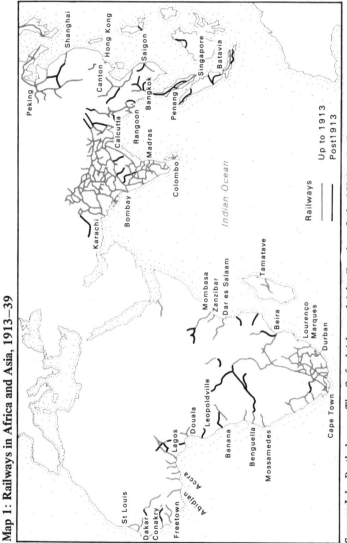

Source: John Bartholomew, *The Oxford Advanced Atlas* (London: Oxford University Press, 1942), p. 20.

Table 1.2: **Railways in Asia and Africa, 1910–37 (miles)**

	1910	1920	1930	1937 Total	1937 %	1937 State
Asia [a]						
Ceylon	578	727	951	951	1.50	951
China	2,139	6,961	11,807	11,610	18.34	10,672
India	32,099	36,735	41,724	43,021	67.97	31,670
Malaya	539	960	1,071	1,068	1.68	1,068
Siam	629	1,431	1,857	2,018	3.18	1,778
Others	–	–	–	4,620	7.29	–
TOTAL	–	–	–	63,288	99.96	–
Africa [b]						
Belgian Colonies	–	–	–	2,550	6.95	–
French Colonies	1,452	2,429	3,096	3,853	10.51	2,874
British Possessions	–	–	–	12,034	32.84	8,485
Portuguese Possessions	–	–	–	2,003	5.46	962
Union of South Africa	7,576	10,107	13,459	16,203	44.21	13,195
TOTAL	–	–	–	36,643	99.96	–

Notes:

[a] China includes Manchukuo, India includes Burma. Asiatic Russia, Turkey in Asia, and Japan are omitted.

[b] Algeria, Sudan, Morocco and Tunis are omitted.

Source: *Universal Directory of Railway Officials and Railway Year Book* (London: 1940–1), pp. 397–8.

of Central Africa to ports on the coast to the west, east and south. The 1930s saw a levelling-off of construction in Ceylon, Malaya and China, but India, Siam, South Africa and French African possessions made considerable additions to their mileage even in this decade. A more detailed breakdown of railway construction in British territories in Asia and Africa is given in Table 1.3.

Inseparable from the story of the development of the railways in this period is the coming of motor transport, which increasingly challenged their economic viability. Comparative international statistics on motor vehicles are not available, but a fair impression of what was happening in the developing world can be gained from the situation in British territories revealed in Tables 1.4 and 1.5. The outstanding feature of these statistics is the very high number of passenger cars in South Africa, more than double the number even of India. What is

Table 1.3: Length of Railway Line in Selected British Territories (miles). (G denotes Government ownership and P Private ownership)

		1913	1922	1923	1924	1925	1926	1927	1928	1929	1930	1931	1932	1933	1934	1935	1936	1937
India	P&G	34,656	37,618	38,039	38,270	38,579	39,049	39,712	40,950	41,724	42,281	42,813	42,961	42,953	43,021	43,118	43,128	43,021
Ceylon	G	605	732	734	742	791	851	895	951	951	951	951	951	951	951	951	951	951
Malaya	G	771	966	982	1,001	1,004	1,004	1,035	1,037	1,037	1,071	1,072	1,067	1,067	1,068	1,068	1,068	1,068
Hong Kong	G	29	29	29	29	29	29	29	29	22	22	22	22	22	22	22	22	22
South Africa	G	8,282	10,985	11,111	11,528	12,052	12,256	12,469	12,647	12,923	13,098	13,151	13,151	13,180	13,225	13,239	13,263	
	P	508	573	566	366	381	368	361	361	361	361	361	357	357	357	357	357	
Rhodesian System																		
South Africa	P	112	112	112	112	112	112	112	112	112	112	112	112	112	112	112	112	112
Bechuanaland Protectorate	P	394	394	394	394	394	394	394	394	399	399	399	399	399	399	399	399	399
S. Rhodesia	P	1,252	1,252	1,252	1,252	1,252	1,252	1,252	1,315	1,302	1,348	1,348	1,360	1,355	1,355	1,355	1,356	1,356
N. Rhodesia	P	506	506	506	506	506	506	506	506	530	571	612	645	644	644	644	644	645
Kenya	G	618	699	741	782	880	1,061	1,137	1,184	1,231	1,282	1,284	1,297	1,295	1,295	1,294	1,294	1,294
Uganda	G	61	67	67	67	67	67	67	209	275	275	332	330	330	330	328	328	328
Nyasaland	P	113	174	174	174	174	174	174	174	174	174	174	174	174	174	313	313	313
Nigeria	G	936	1,126	1,126	1,267	1,265	1,265	1,596	1,625	1,744	1,905	1,905	1,905	1,905	1,905	1,905	1,900	1,903
Gold Coast	G	222	358	394	394	394	475	493	500	500	500	500	500	500	500	500	500	500
Sierra Leone	G	300	338	338	338	338	338	338	338	332	334	311	311	311	311	311	311	311

Source: Statistical Abstracts for the British Empire.

Table 1.4: Number of Passenger Cars in Selected British Territories, 1926–37

	1926	1927	1928	1929	1930	1931	1932	1933	1934	1935	1936	1937
India [a]	34,802	43,537	58,222	68,204	69,924	61,392	–	–	–	–	–	97,872 [b]
Ceylon	8,599	10,410	12,659	14,470	15,119	14,805	14,739	15,046	16,226	17,707	18,950	20,181
Malaya	–	–	–	–	30,108	27,322	23,789	23,103	25,772	27,504	29,273	33,042
Hong Kong	905	1,000	1,148	1,462	1,574	1,822	2,478	2,801	2,988	3,204	3,380	3,665
South Africa	80,000	96,000	113,000	130,000	135,000	138,000	143,000	154,000	185,000	213,000	247,000	282,000
S. Rhodesia	–	–	7,896	–	–	–	–	–	10,289	11,105	12,412	13,100
Kenya	–	–	–	–	–	–	6,670	6,947	7,151	7,554	7,927	8,539
Nyasaland	336	457	595	616	739	736	752	739	741	768	797	847
Nigeria	–	–	2,205	2,412	2,764	2,837	2,835	2,875	2,913	2,984	3,109	4,229
Sierra Leone	230	295	292	378	295	326	326	323	334	347	308	337
Gambia	44	53	76	84	86	87	100	106	117	139	151	174

Notes:

[a] 1926–31 From Wohl and Albitreccia.

[b] 31 March 1938.

Source: *Statistical Abstracts for the British Empire; Statistical Abstracts for British India*: P. Wohl and A. Albitreccia, *Road and Rail in Forty Countries* (London: Oxford University Press, 1935), p. 212.

Table 1.5: Number of Commercial Vehicles and Omnibuses in Selected British Territories, 1926–37

	1926	1927	1928	1929	1930	1931	1932	1933	1934	1935	1936	1937
India[a]	14,156	21,656	31,633	42,492	44,853	36,083	–	–	–	–	–	39,173[b]
Ceylon	3,536	4,007	4,774	5,672	5,774	5,402	5,232	5,153	5,659	6,267	6,643	7,045
Malaya	–	–	–	–	8,969	8,459	7,201	7,333	8,477	9,044	9,567	11,431
Hong Kong	365	348	491	457	439	427	843	919	1,011	1,105	1,024	1,101
South Africa	6,000	9,000	12,000	15,000	17,000	18,000	18,000	19,000	25,000	29,000	35,000	43,000
S. Rhodesia	–	–	699	–	–	–	–	–	1,963	2,431	4,343	4,820
Kenya	–	–	–	–	–	–	1,528	1,616	1,630	1,695	1,800	2,275
Nyasaland	183	306	449	480	528	519	563	524	476	518	534	559
Nigeria	–	–	3,059	3,043	3,243	2,927	2,803	2,903	2,688	2,936	3,545	5,113
Sierra Leone	136	200	208	274	222	197	192	162	156	180	76	86
Gambia	52	74	143	168	174	170	183	173	155	176	202	248

Notes:

[a] 1926–31 From Wohl and Albitreccia.

[b] 31 March 1938.

Source: *Statistical Abstracts for the British Empire*; *Statistical Abstracts for British India*; P. Wohl and A. Albitreccia, *Road and Rail in Forty Countries* (London: Oxford University Press, 1935), p. 212.

more, the number of cars there went on increasing rapidly during the 1930s when other countries saw a levelling-out of numbers. From 1926 to 1937 the number of cars in South Africa rose from 80,000 to 282,000 when there were nearly three times as many as in India. This reflects the buoyancy of the South African economy in this period of rising gold prices, and the higher income-levels there. Malaya had 33,042 cars in 1937 and Ceylon 20,181 but both had experienced a check to the growth of their car population in the early 1930s. Other countries had few cars. The figures for commercial vehicles and omnibuses tell a different tale. India led South Africa, at least up to 1931, although by 1937 South Africa had crept ahead with 43,000 to 39,173. As with passenger cars, numbers of commercial vehicles there went on increasing during the 1930s as South Africa bypassed the depression which the other countries suffered. Malaya and Ceylon came next in 1937 with 11,431 and 7,045 respectively. Nigeria, where there were few passenger cars, followed with 5,113.

There was a definite pattern to the emergence of competition between road and rail in this period, although it was modified according to the circumstances in each area. Initially lines were built inland from the major ports to mines and agricultural districts, and to link important towns. Thus the main trunk lines were laid down, often as in India's case, by the First World War. The next phase was to construct feeder lines to channel more mining and agricultural products into the system. This is when competition from road transport began to make itself felt. Cars, lorries and buses made their first impact in urban areas where their flexibility gave them advantages over railways and where there were good roads and access to petrol. They provided a new outlet to local entrepreneurs to run taxis and bus and lorry services, these developing naturally from the rickshaws, carriages and carts already in service. Gradually motor transport extended into the rural areas, often providing a feeder service to the railways at a fraction of the cost of constructing feeder lines. This was possible in the dry season even where metalled surfaces were not laid down. Then motor vehicles started to compete with the railway feeder lines, and eventually the trunk lines themselves, driving the railways into financial distress. This final stage was reached in the late 1920s by most countries in the developing world, when the depression suddenly superimposed itself upon the plight of their railways.[1]

In India, most of the railway building in these years was the construction of feeder lines to the trunk network completed before the outbreak of the First World War. During the war 165 miles of rail were taken up and requisitioned together with stores and supplies for military purposes in East Africa and Mesopotamia. At the end of the war the Indian railways were in a very run-down condition. Between 1924 and 1932 4,691 miles of track were added to the system, creating a heavy debt burden in subsequent years. The depression brought this phase of expansion to an end, but by the late 1920s the railways were already feeling the effects of competition from motor transport near the cities and where good roads ran parallel to the railways. By 1930 there were about 60,000 miles of metalled roads outside the towns, and another 4,000 miles were added before the war. The number of cars increased from 34,802 in 1926 to 61,392 in 1931 and 97,872 in 1938. Numbers of commercial vehicles and buses saw a similar rise from 14,156 in 1926 to 36,083 in 1931 and 39,173 in 1938.[2]

Burma separated from India only in 1937, and in the 1920s, as in the rest of India, extensions to the trunk network were simply feeder lines. The rapid development of motor traffic made an impact here too, and by 1940 there were 12,500 miles of motor road, some 5,000 metalled. Like their contemporaries in India and elsewhere, Burmans seized the opportunity to run taxis, buses and trucks.[3]

Details of Ceylon's transport developments are rather sparse, although it is clear that 219 miles of line were added between 1922 and 1928, giving a total of 951 miles, with no further additions in the 1930s. That motor transport was making its impact there is obvious from the fact that the number of cars increased from 8,599 in 1926 to 20,181 in 1937, and the number of commercial vehicles and buses virtually doubled from 3,536 to 7,045 in the same period.[4]

In Malaya construction of the railway network linking the principal towns and ports of the country and running through most of the major rubber growing and tin mining districts, was completed in 1931 with the opening of the line up to the east coast. Only about 100 miles were actually added in the 1920s, and the main network had been built previously. Completion of the east coast line coincided with the depression which hit tin and rubber so badly. Revenue fell and passenger traffic decreased, but both had in any case been falling for some years due to buses and long-distance taxis. Freight traffic also declined severely during the depression and never recovered to the 1929 level before the outbreak of war. The first motor vehicles had come to Malaya in 1902 and as the road development programme expanded, many roads were built parallel to the railways, robbing them of their traffic. After 1928 and even during the depression road building continued, particularly in the east coast states and Johore in regions not served by the railways. The effect of the depression in Malaya is nicely revealed in the statistics for motor vehicles, cars dropping from 30,108 in 1930 to 23,103 in 1933, after which numbers picked up again to 33,042 in 1937. As for buses and trucks, numbers fell from 8,969 in 1930 to 7,201 in 1932, recovering slowly to 11,431 in 1937.[5]

Since 1900 there had been a rapid expansion of railways in the Dutch East Indies, and an even more rapid expansion of light private tramways linking in to the main system to serve the needs of planters. During the war construction slowed, but from 1920 onwards it went ahead rapidly, and mileage increased from 1,722 in 1913, to 2,011 in 1920 and 3,535 in 1930. As early as 1907 the government had begun to run motor services, but only after the war did private cars come into general use. In 1922 1,502 cars were imported into Java, and 363 into the Outer Provinces, but in 1925 the number of cars imported into the Outer Provinces equalled that into Java. Then there was a sugar boom, and for two years in succession over 10,000 new cars came into Java. When the depression struck in 1929 car imports fell away, and in 1931 only 3,506 cars came into Java and 397 into the Outer Provinces. So the economic experience of the period is reflected in the figures for the import of private cars. As in other parts of the developing world the coming of the motor vehicle gave the local people a new skilled occupation in which they could exercise their entrepreneurial skills rather than work for Europeans. Buses, trucks and taxis all were operated in this way by local people. Substantial road building took place to accommodate motor traffic, and by 1938 the Dutch East Indies had 32,000 miles of roads with gravel or macadam surfaces, including 7,900 miles that had been tarred.[6]

In the Philippines the same general trends as in other areas are noticeable, although information is very thin. In 1939 the government railway on Luzon had 712 miles of track and there were a further 132 miles of private railway on Panay and Cebu. There were 10,925 miles of road of which 6,127 were first class roads, and in the previous year there were 30,361 motor cars, nearly as many as Malaya, and 18,293 trucks, nearly as many as Malaya and Ceylon added together.[7]

Siam had already made a good start to railway construction by the turn of the century, and by 1910 there were 579 miles open. By 1920 considerable further additions had been made, and the mileage had risen to 1,400. Yet more miles were laid in the 1920s bringing the mileage in 1930 to 1,816. Another hundred or so miles were added in the next decade raising the total in 1940 to 1,945. But road development was negligible, there being in 1938 only 2,122 miles of highways of which 85 miles were first class roads, 93 second class roads and 1,944 third class. Bullock carts were the main form of road transport and there were few motor vehicles. Boats were the alternative form of inter-regional transport to the railways.[8]

On the eve of the First World War there were 962 miles of railway in French Indo-China, excluding the 288 miles of the Yunnan line which were located in China. During the war and up to 1922 there was very little extra development, and only 32 miles of new line were opened to traffic. Then there was substantial building, and by the Second World War the mileage had nearly doubled to 1,807 miles, again not counting the Yunnan line. Passenger traffic was very important as the major exports, rice, corn and coal, usually went by river to the ocean-going vessels. From 1920 competition from motor transport became apparent. The government recognised that improved road transport would unify and develop the territory more quickly than the railway, so by 1936 Indo-China had been provided with 17,091 miles of banked roads passable throughout the year, of which 10,876 were metalled. There were about 350 cars there in 1913, mostly in Saigon and Hanoi, and after 1924 imports increased quickly, 3,000 being imported in 1929. By the end of 1933 there were 17,800 motor vehicles in the country, and the next year 21,876 including 11,411 cars, 3,436 buses and 2,039 lorries. More than half the cars were owned by wealthy Indo-Chinese, the rest by Europeans and Chinese. Buses and trucks were also locally owned, and so were taxis which were kept on the road to the last stage of dilapidation. The opening of each new road would see a burst of keen competition between these local carriers, a triumph of indigenous private enterprise. In 1933 it is estimated that these carriers conveyed between 40 million and 50 million passengers.[9]

Compared with other countries in the developing world, China progressed slowly with railway building. In 1910 when India already had 32,099 miles of line, China had a mere 2,139. By 1920 the mileage had risen to 6,961, but then the political situation deteriorated, and in 1924 the entire railway system was commandeered by the army. The only line which continued to operate for the public was the South Manchuria Railway which was protected by Japanese troops. It connected with the Trans-Siberian Railway and was the most important line in the Far East. Practically all the other railways defaulted on their debts. Later in the 1920s further additions were made to the mileage which stood at 11,807 in 1930. Then the situation was complicated by the Japanese seizure of Manchuria in 1931/2 to form the state of Manchoukuo. There were 3,830 miles in Manchuria in 1930, and more were built, making 5,243 miles in 1937. This was offset by a decrease in mileage in the rest of China, so the Chinese mileage overall, including Manchuria, fell by 197 miles from 1930 to 1937, making 11,610 miles that year. Not only was mileage low in China but the condition of the permanent way and rolling stock was deplorable. There had not been adequate provision for depreciation because of the political and military disorder. Hardly any maintenance had been done since the railways were built. So neglected were the freight cars that merchants preferred the less risky alternative of sending their goods by boat, and the foul conditions in the passenger coaches led travellers also to prefer to go by boat. On some lines nearly 60 per cent of the locomotives were unfit for service in 1930. So the main competition to the railways came from water transport, especially coastal shipping, and to a lesser extent junk shipping on the rivers. Motor transport made comparatively little impact, as Chinese roads were so bad. In earlier times China had an excellent road system, but this had been allowed to deteriorate. Yet there were in 1935 59,886 miles of road in China of which 11,398 was paved. In 1932 China had 41,503 motor vehicles comprising 27,350 private cars, 5,894 buses and 8,259 lorries. This would place China third behind South Africa and India in absolute numbers, but does not take into account the vastness of China and the size of her population. Imports of cars and buses together rose from 2,025 in 1924 to a peak of 4,639 in 1929, after which they fluctuated downwards to a low of 1,350 in 1938, followed by some recovery. Tractors and trucks show a different pattern with 4,142 being imported in 1929, a dip down to 1,227 in 1932 and a rise to 5,932 in 1939.[10]

Turning now to Africa, it was South Africa which dominated transport development south of the Sahara. She already had a substantial railway system of 7,576 miles in 1910, and she added to this having 10,107 miles in 1920, 13,459 miles in 1930 and 16,203 miles in 1937, continuing to build railways even in the 1930s. Unlike most countries South Africa avoided the depression due to the rising price of gold, and this meant that her financial position was sound and she could expand her infrastructure. But as early as 1925 the motor vehicle was making rapid advances, and as is shown in Table 1.4 South Africa led all the countries in Asia and Africa in the number of cars there, rising from 80,000 in 1926 to 282,000 in 1937. Commercial vehicles increased from 6,000 to 43,000 overtaking the numbers in India as they did so. By the early 1930s there were over 71,000 miles of properly constructed motorable roads. So great was the competition from motor vehicles that the railways retaliated by operating motor services themselves. Many Africans operated motor transport services, particularly taxis. In 1926 the General Manager of the Railways was complaining of the competition of the roads, and by 1928 the situation had become acute. Motor transport was not only cheaper than rail transport, but there was less handling of the goods, door-to-door delivery could be made, less time was taken in transit, and better theft control could be exercised over the road haulier than over the railway freight service. Despite improvements in rail services, more competitive pricing, and even government regulation in favour of the railways, the motor vehicle still continued to grow in importance. It eventually became accepted that the motor vehicle would open up the country faster and more efficiently than the railways, because of its greater flexibility of use.[11]

The natural extension of the South African railways was into the Rhodesias, and even in 1913 Southern Rhodesia had 1,252 miles with another 506 in Northern Rhodesia. Just as the Witwatersrand had been the magnet for railway construction in South Africa, so the copper deposits of Northern Rhodesia and Katanga provided an incentive for railway building to the north. By the outbreak of the First World War the railway had been extended from the south right through Northern Rhodesia towards the copper mines near Kambove in the Belgian Congo. Between the wars branch lines were added to connect new areas to the railway system, such as the chrome mines at Umvukwe in Southern Rhodesia. In 1927 lorry services were started to connect agricultural districts to the railheads. In Northern Rhodesia branch lines were built to the Roan Antelope copper mine and to the mine at N'Kana, and a link was built with the Katanga railway system. As in the south, truck services were begun in 1927 to serve neighbouring agricultural districts. By the end of the period the Rhodesias were connected to ports in the south via South Africa, to Biera and Lourenço Marques in the east, and to Lobito Bay on the west via Katanga and the Benguella Railway. In 1937 there were 1,356 miles of line in Southern Rhodesia and 645 in Northern Rhodesia. The extent of motor competition is suggested by the fact that there were 4,820 commercial vehicles and buses in Southern Rhodesia in 1937, rather fewer than in Nigeria, and 13,100 cars, more than three times as many as in Nigeria.[12]

In South West Africa the railway system built by the Germans before 1914 was linked by the South Africans to their railway system during the war for defence purposes. The system was also extended in the north to the port of Walvis Bay, its obvious outlet. In 1939 there

were 1,584 miles of line in the territory, including 98 miles of private
line servicing the diamond fields south of Luderitz.[13]

Kenya and Uganda had been the scene of feverish railway construction before the First World War as a line was built from Mombassa to
Lake Victoria to secure a sound defensive position on the headwaters
of the Nile. After the war the line was extended, reaching Kampala in
1930. Lines were built from Jinja as feeders to bring in the important
cotton crop of the Eastern Province, and other branch lines were built.
Lorry services were introduced to tap the agricultural districts through
which the lines passed. In Kenya the railway mileage increased from
699 in 1922 to 1,297 in 1933, and in Uganda from 67 in 1927 to 332
in 1931, further building then coming to a halt. Motor vessel services
were operated on Lakes Victoria, Albert and Kioga, and on the Nile,
linking to the railway. Roads were improved throughout the territories,
and a motor road was built from Nairobi across Uganda to Mongalla in
the Sudan. Zanzibar had 242 miles of road suitable for motor traffic
by the Second World War. In Tanganyika railway building strategies had
been similar to that in Kenya and Uganda, and two lines were built from
the coast heading for the great lakes of the interior, Lake Victoria and
Lake Tanganyika. These were built by the Germans, and after the First
World War there were only minor branch line additions. As in Uganda
steam boats provided a service on the lakes, and by the outbreak of the
Second World War there were 19,957 miles of road which could take
light motor traffic in the dry season. Although 113 miles of line had
been laid in Nyasaland by 1913 they were not very effective until they
were joined to the port of Biera after the war. By 1935 there were 313
miles of line. At the end of this period there was a good road system of
3,733 miles serving all the principal areas of both African and European
production. There was also a good motor road to South Africa, and
connections to the Great North Road which ran through Northern
Rhodesia, Tanganyika Territory, and Kenya Colony.[14]

On the West Coast Nigeria was the most important British territory,
and by 1912 the line was complete from Lagos to Kano in the north. In
1913 there were 936 miles of line, and this had increased to 1,126 by
1922 with the addition of the Bauchi Light Railway to the tin mines
and the line from Port Harcourt to the coal mines at Enugu in the east.
Another 779 miles were added to reach a total of 1,905 by 1930. The
need for feeder roads for the railways began the transformation of road
transport in Nigeria even before the First World War, from the
beginning providing new opportunities for Nigerian business men. Head
loading began to disappear in face of the influx of bicycles, motor

cycles, and carts constructed on disused motor chassis. Government
road-improvement schemes meant that it was possible to drive from
Ibadan to Port Harcourt by 1925. Trucks were particularly important
in Nigeria, the number of commercial vehicles rising from 3,059 in
1928 to 5,113 in 1937. Mostly these were for carrying agricultural
produce to market. Even in 1937 there were only 4,229 cars. In the
year 1924/5 there were 2,596 miles of road outside the townships
maintained by the government, and in 1937/8 the mileage had increased
to 3,829. But local authorities maintained as many as 22,000 miles of
road in Northern Nigeria as early as 1920, and there were another
3,000 similar roads in the South. As elsewhere, the emergence of motor
transport soon posed grave problems for the railways and in the 1930s
railway finances ran into severe difficulties.[15]

The Gold Coast acquired 136 miles of line between 1913 and 1922,
bringing the total to 358. Further building brought the system to its
inter-war total of 500 miles in 1928. The earliest lines were to the gold
fields, simultaneously opening fertile agricultural areas to world trade
routes through the ports. Roads complemented the railways funnelling
the products of previously inaccessible areas to the railway. In
particular, the spread of cocoa cultivation accompanied the growing
road and rail network. Many villages built their own access roads to the
new road network, which was suitable for light motor traffic in all
weathers and from the early 1920s increasingly tarred. Competition
from Ford trucks on the expanding road system brought financial
problems for the railways of a familiar kind, although lowering of rates
by the railways met with some success. By the end of the period there
were 6,337 miles of motor road.[16]

Sierra Leone had 300 miles of railway in 1913, comprising a line
from Freetown to the Liberian frontier, plus a branch line. There was
very little additional mileage added during the inter-war years. As for
motor vehicles the peak was in 1929 when there were 274 commercial
vehicles, and 378 cars. As for that tiny colony, the Gambia, internal
transport was by steamer or launch. Yet it had from 1933 more buses
and trucks than Sierra Leone, although not as many passenger cars.
There was no railway system.[17]

There was considerable railway building in France's African Colonies
in these years. From 1,452 miles of track in 1910, mileage increased to
2,429 miles in 1920 and to 3,096 in 1930. Another 800 miles were
added in the following years to make 3,853 in 1937. Of individual
colonies, Senegal already had 165 miles from Dakar to St Louis before
the turn of the century, and the line was extended to Keyes on the

Niger, work only being completed in 1923. Later this was continued to Bamako in the French Sudan giving a length of 450 miles. At Bamako the line joined the existing railway to Kalikaro on the Niger, a total distance of 760 miles. In French Guinea there were by 1938 386 miles of railway, running from Konakry to the Niger, most of which had been built by the First World War. There were also 5,297 miles of road. The railway in the Ivory Coast ran inland from Adidjan to Bobo-Dioulasso and there was a total mileage of 494 miles by the end of the period, 301 miles being built after 1912. There was also a network of some 11,130 miles of roads suitable for motor traffic.

By the outbreak of the Second World War there were three railways in Togo, but most of them had been built by the Germans before the First World War. Dahomey had two main railway lines, comprising 178 miles in 1914. Subsequent additions linked the two lines into the interior together with a coastal railway and extended them inland. By the late 1930s the line inland from Cotonou was 257 miles in length and there were at least another 174 miles of line, much of them recent branch lines and extensions. Substantial road building also took place, giving 2,711 miles of carriage road of which 871 were first class. The Cameroons had 193 miles of line built by the Germans in operation by 1914, comprising three separate lines into the interior from Victoria, Douala, and Bonaberi. The Douala line was extended between 1922 and 1927 and a branch line was built, so that by the late 1930s there were 314 miles of railways. There was also a fairly extensive road network of some 3,105 miles. Lastly, in French Equatorial Africa a private line of 102 miles had been opened in 1912 from Mindouli to Brazzaville by the Compagnie Minière du Congo Français. But the main railway was built between 1921 and 1931, a line of 318 miles linking Brazzaville to Point-Noire. In 1938 there were 998 miles of road, and a river port under construction at Brazzaville to facilitate traffic between the Congo and the railway.[18]

Although the Belgian Congo already had 868 miles of line by 1913, there was great activity after the war as the lines were drawn inland as if to a magnet by the huge copper fields of Katanga. The main part of this vast system was the Chemin de Fer du Congo, which was surveyed in 1920 and built between 1923 and 1932. Other important parts of the system were the Bukama-Ilebo and the Tenke-Dilolo lines completed in 1928. Junction between the Katanga and the Benguella Railway was completed in 1931. There was extensive use of lorries and other road transport to augment the newly created rail system, and by 1939 there were 43,923 miles of road.[19]

The Portuguese territories remain, and they were vitally important to the transport structure of Central Africa. In 1937 Angola and Mozambique together had 2,003 miles of line, and it was possible to travel the Benguela Railway right through from Lobito Bay in Angola to the Belgian Congo and Rhodesia, ending at Biera in Mozambique, a distance of 2,920 miles. There was also an extension to Lourenço Marques passing through Rhodesia to Mafeking and from there to Komati Port in South Africa where connection was made with the Lourenço Marques Railway. From Lobito Bay to Lourenço Marques the distance was 3,295 miles. Apart from the Benguela Railway there was in Angola a line from Loanda to the border of the Belgian Congo, whose eventual length was 372 miles although it had partly been constructed before the Great War. As for the Benguela Railway, the first 326 miles were finished in 1913 and by 1928 there were 837 miles complete, taking the line to the frontier. The extension of the line in Belgian territory was not finished until 1931. In the south of the colony there was a line of 64 miles to serve the coffee plantations, the first section opening in 1925. There was also a line of 154 miles running inland from Mossamedes of which 91 miles were built after 1914. Angola also had 17,215 miles of good roads and 20,713 miles of secondary roads by the end of the 1930s. As for Mozambique, it has already been shown how the lines there ran through to serve South Africa, Rhodesia, and indeed connected right across Africa to Lobito Bay by way of the Congo and the Benguela Railway. The Delagoa Bay Railway from Lourenço Marques had 57 miles in Portuguese territory and continued through to Pretoria. The Biera Railway had 200 miles in Mozambique, and linked into the Rhodesian railway system. These lines opened before 1914. But the Trans-Zambesia Railway, 175 miles from Dondo on the Biera Junction Railway to Murraca on the southern bank of the Zambesi was opened for traffic in 1922. On the northern bank of the Zambesi the Central African Railway connected at Port Herald with the Shire Highlands Railway, 45 miles being in Mozambique territory. With the opening of the Lower Zambesi Bridge in 1935, then the longest bridge in the world, these three railways gave a continuous connection between British Nyasaland and the Port of Biera. Mozambique also had 3,970 miles of motor road by the outbreak of the Second World War.[20]

It is clear that railway building continued vigorously until the depression, concluding the vast railway expansion of pre-war days. Yet the emergence of motor transport was beginning to make the railways uneconomic even before the depression came. From 1929 the future lay with the internal combustion engine, and railways all over the developing world saw financial difficulties.

Shipping and the Panama Canal

The Suez Canal and the steam ship marked a fundamental advance in international communications in the late nineteenth century. It was the Panama Canal and the motor ship which were the major innovations between 1914 and 1939. Just as the internal combustion engine was challenging the steam engine on land, where the car and truck competed with the train, so the Diesel ship began to oust the steam ship at sea.

Before 1914 the Pacific had not been a trading ocean, as trade routes to Asia passed through the Suez Canal. But the opening of the Panama Canal in 1914 opened a direct route from Asia across the Pacific by way of the canal to the main industrial area of the United States. Now ships could sail straight from Shanghai and Dairen to New York, Boston and Baltimore. Yet it would be wrong to overemphasise the importance of the Panama Canal in opening up trade across the Pacific. Its most important effect was in bringing the raw-material producing countries of Western South America, Chile, Peru, Bolivia and Ecuador, closer to the heart of United States industry. This was why trade through the canal grew so quickly, for goods bound for Europe from Hong Kong nearly all continued to go by way of Suez, and all from Singapore. By 1929 6,413 ships passed through Panama by comparison with 6,271 through Suez. But between 1929 and 1932 shipping tonnage through Panama dropped by 23 per cent owing to the severity of the depression in the United States, whilst Suez traffic only fell by 15 per cent.[21] The impact of the slump on the Suez Canal is revealed in Graph 1.1.

The routes opened by the Panama Canal were developed by Japanese, Dutch and Norwegian shipping, rather than by British or American ships. The Japanese did very well out of the war, for British ships were involved in the war effort, leaving the Pacific almost a Japanese lake. They were in an ideal position to seize the new opportunities provided by the Panama Canal and also to enter traditional British routes in the Far East and to India. The failure of American shipping companies is more remarkable, as by 1936 88 per cent of imports from the Far East to her main industrial region came through the Panama.[22]

Although there was great destruction of ships during the war, the

Map 2: World Shipping Routes, 1913–39

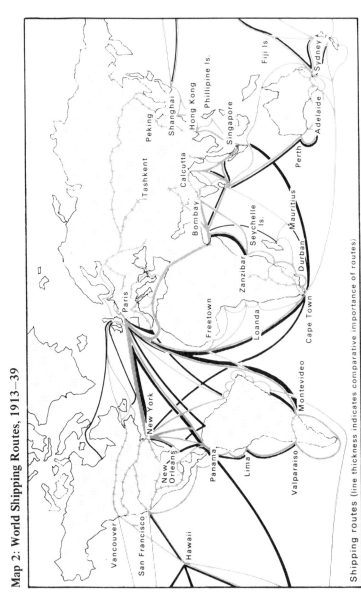

Shipping routes (line thickness indicates comparative importance of routes)

Source: John Bartholomew, *The Oxford Advanced Atlas* (London: Oxford University Press, 1942), p. 20.

Graph 1.1: Suez Canal Traffic, 1914–39

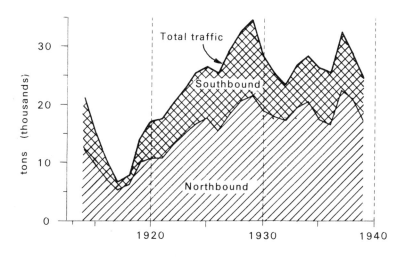

Source: D. A. Farnie, *East and West of Suez: The Suez Canal in History,
1854–1956* (Oxford: Clarendon Press, 1969), p. 753; see Appendix 1.

world's total tonnage in 1919 was greater than in 1914. The United
States had launched a vast shipbuilding programme when they entered
the war, at a time when British shipyards and those of many other
countries were working at full stretch. The Japanese shipyards even had
orders from Britain, and Japanese shipowners were laying down vessels
as fast as they could. World shipbuilding capacity probably increased
by two and a half times. Tonnage continued to increase even after the
end of the war, because German companies rebuilt their fleets which
had been confiscated and transferred to the allies. Freight rates boomed
between 1919 and 1920, then fell alarmingly as shown in Graph 1.2.
Yet fleets continued to expand because only the most up-to-date
vessels could earn profits and because the increased use of petroleum
meant that more tankers were needed. At the same time many countries
introduced subsidised national shipping lines. Britain, still the world's
leading shipping nation, did not add much to the overexpansion of
fleets, laying down tankers but scrapping many obsolescent ships.
Between 1919 and 1931 British tonnage remained at about its pre-war
level, whilst the combined fleets of other countries rose to 75 per cent
above their 1914 size. Up to 1934 British shipowners, helped only by
their efficiency and accumulated reserves, struggled against the

Graph 1.2: Shipping Freight Index, 1920–37

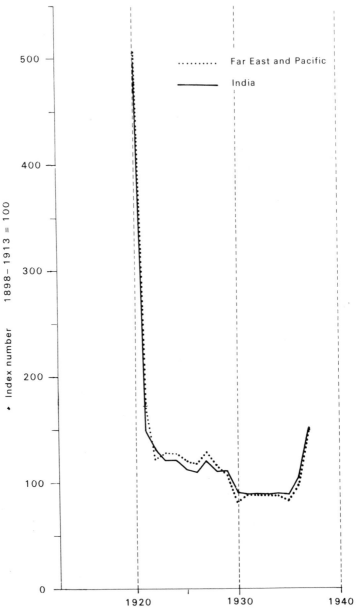

Source: *The Economist*, 26 February 1938, p. 484; see Appendix 2.

subsidised national shipping lines of South Africa, Canada, Australia, the United States, Japan, Italy, Germany and Russia. Reserves were drained and often depreciation was not covered. Then signs of collapse became apparent and tramp tonnage was laid up in every estuary in Britain as the subsidised national lines moved into direct competition with the tramps by picking up grain, sugar, rice, maize and other bulk cargoes wherever they could. In 1935 the British Government was forced to provide assistance for tramp voyages which would otherwise be unprofitable. Even though five million tons of shipping were scrapped worldwide between 1931 and 1937, world tonnage increased by 40 per cent but trade by only 30 per cent. The impact of these years on the British Mercantile Marine is shown by the fact that in 1939 it had 26 per cent of the world's tonnage, whereas in 1914 it had 41 per cent.[23]

Technically there were great improvements in propulsion. There was the British Parsons steam turbine, perfected in 1901, which enabled large horsepowers to be generated in less space, increasing cargo capacity and making high speeds and smooth action possible. Then there was the German Diesel engine, first put into a successful ocean-going vessel by the Danish in 1912. During the war a vast amount of machinery was made for both naval and mercantile vessels, but the circumstances allowed little time for trying out new ideas. After the war there were further innovations in steam practice, and whole fleets of motor ships were constructed. By 1937 about a fifth of world tonnage was powered by oil engines, and motor ships and oil-fired steamships together made up half the world's tonnage.

Table 1.6: Steam Ships and Motor Ships, 1922–37

	Steam reciprocating engines	Steam turbines	Internal combustion engines
	Gross tons	Gross tons	Gross tons
1922/3	51,653,324	8,149,165	1,540,463
1926/7	50,040,978	9,137,675	3,493,284
1931/2	50,225,758	9,065,610	9,431,433
1936/7	42,605,474	9,108,812	12,290,599

Source: E. C. Smith, *A Short History of Naval and Marine Engineering* (Cambridge: Babcock and Wilcox, 1937), p. 304.

The decision between steam or steam turbines and internal combustion engines depended to a degree upon availability of fuel. Coal was cheaper than oil and for this reason British owners tended for many years to be influenced in favour of steam, having access to prime Welsh steam coal. Harrisons of Liverpool who were active in the Indian and South African trades, built and maintained throughout the inter-war years a fleet consisting overwhelmingly of coal-fired triple-expansion engines. Cheap coal was available to them both on the Mersey and in Calcutta and Natal where much of their business lay. What is more, the greater reliability of the well-tried triple-expansion engine meant almost no likelihood of breakdown at sea, which would have meant grave complications to a company with such a large network of scheduled liner services. Oil made space available for dry cargo which had previously been needed for coal bunkers, as it could be carried in deep tanks in space not usable for dry cargoes. But this advantage was outweighed for many owners by the fact that Diesels were still experiencing teething troubles and their initial cost and depreciation was higher than for steam engines. Only those companies without access to cheap coal on their routes were likely to prefer oil, although Alfred Holts of Liverpool became convinced that there were advantages in oil, and built up a Diesel fleet.[24]

Before 1914 the shipping routes of the world were controlled to a large extent by shipping conferences. This was certainly true of the routes to Asia and Africa. The main shipping lines on a particular route agreed to charge the same freight rate, and to share the trade between them according to an agreed division. Outsiders were excluded by allowing merchants a percentage rebate payable after a fixed number of months, which they could only claim back if they continued to ship with conference lines. It was in the Calcutta trade that the deferred rebate was first used, and up to 1914 the British dominated this route. One German line gained entry in 1907 but only with loading rights from Middlesborough, and of course they were excluded during the war. After the war German, Scandinavian and Dutch lines joined the conference in a small way, their participation being formalised in agreements made in 1925 and 1926. Whilst the conference operated as before, there were several mergers between British companies, unification adding to co-operation as a means of controlling the market. The British India Steam Navigation Company merged with the Peninsula and Orient Steam Navigation Company, and the Ellerman Line merged with the Hall Line. But there continued to be an informal division between lines operating from the East Coast of Britain and those from the West Coast. There was no formal agreement between lines on the Bombay-Karachi route, but the rates on the outward trade were set by reference to the Calcutta trade, and the deferred rebate was operated. Although there was agreement that the outward rate from Britain and from the Continent should be the same, in practice Continental rates were lower. During the 1920s there were complaints that the British lines were not carrying enough cargo to Bombay and Karachi to justify their share of the earnings pool, so a minimum number of sailings were specified to qualify for each month's share-out. In the homeward trade the conference organisation was much looser, and from Calcutta there was no agreement as to which line would serve which port, although Continental lines did not carry cargoes destined directly or indirectly to Britain. There was no rebate in the homeward trade, and whilst rates were supposed to be the same to Britain and the Continent, they were actually lower to the Continent. From Madras only certain 'choice' items were regarded as conference items, and the British lines tried to keep these for themselves. One French line was allowed to carry 'choice' items to Marseilles at conference rates, and German and Scandinavian lines operated regular services from Madras in 'non-choice' cargo. Trade from Bombay and Karachi remained open in the inter-war years, and an attempt to organise a conference in the 1920s failed. This was because there were merchants powerful enough there to charter vessels for themselves if they thought freight rates too high. Although Bombay and Karachi were free ports, regular lines usually sailed to the ports of discharge agreed from other Indian ports. During the 1930s an Indian line was admitted to the Bombay-Karachi conference, the Scindia Navigation Company of Bombay, which had one ship belonging to a cotton manufacturer. It was a small but significant development for the future.

In the Indian trade as a whole it is clear that Britain's share of the tonnage fell severely before 1929. The decline in the German share between 1913 and 1920 was taken up by American and Japanese ships, and during the 1920s the Germans re-entered the trade, mainly at the expense of the British. But the British share grew again in the 1930s, as Table 1.7 shows.[25]

The Ceylon Conference in these years was troubled by disputes over deferred rebates, but a Government Commission was split in its views and no action was taken. In 1937 a group of coconut-product exporters pressed the Government to make the deferred rebate illegal, but no action was taken before the outbreak of war.[26]

In the Far Eastern Trade the conference was re-established in 1918

Table 1.7: **Shipping at Indian Ports, 1913–38**

	1913	1920	1929	1936	1938
British	73.0	76.7	67.0	64.8	70.4
Others	27.0	23.3	33.0	35.2	29.6

Source: S. G. Sturmey, *British Shipping and World Competition* (London: Athlone Press, 1962), p. 128.

and the German lines were re-admitted in 1921. But after the short post-war boom trade was poor and there were many attempts to break the conference rules from Belgian and German ports. Illicit rebates were offered and low rates charged or cargoes underweighed or undermeasured. German shipowners found the conference rules particularly limiting and wanted to fix their own rates. They were only allowed to do so for goods which were produced exclusively in Germany. When the Japanese lines made a similar request in 1922 they were turned down. In 1930 a penalty scheme was brought in to deal with undermeasuring, undercharging and kickbacks, and in 1931 an earnings pool on the outward trade was set up to counter undercharging completely. Outside competition was usually solved by admitting the newcomer to the conference. This meant existing members had to accept smaller shares of a trade which was declining for much of the period. On the recommendation of the Imperial Shipping Committee the contract system was introduced in 1931 as an alternative to the deferred rebate. This was copied from the South African trade and it meant that a shipper could contract to use conference vessels for a fixed period such as twelve months, for which he was charged a lower rate roughly equivalent to the rebate. The shipper gained by not having large sums held by the shipping companies. In the Philippines homeward conference the contract system had been used from 1920 because the rebate system was illegal under American law.[27]

On the Bombay–Japan Conference, the Austrian and Italian companies retired from the trade during the war, leaving in 1919 the British Peninsular and Orient, and the two Japanese companies the Nippon Yusen Kaisha and the Osaka Shosen Kaisha. In 1925 a third Japanese line joined the trade, the Kokusia Kisen Kaisha, and revisions of the conference agreement that year and in 1935 reduced the P & O's share to 20 per cent even though her ships were only half full. The Japanese could operate their ships at 10–15 per cent cheaper than the British, and they also received a government subsidy. Because the Japanese liner companies were integrated with trading companies in vertical combines, they could negotiate from a position of great strength in the conference. As rates in this conference were fixed by majority rule the Japanese lines could force the P & O to accept the rates agreed between the Japanese lines and their Japanese importers. On the Calcutta–Japan Conference the Japanese also provided aggressive competition for the British owners, although rates were fixed according to usual conference practice.[28]

Six British lines and one American line participated in the Straits–United States Conference which controlled the important trade from the Straits Settlements to industrial North America. Another American line had an understanding with the conference. The conference had an exclusive contract with the Rubber Association and merchants who were not members of the association were charged a higher rate. But one of the Japanese Mitsui companies bought and shipped rubber, and in 1934 Mitsui Bussan Kaisha and its affiliated 'K' line were admitted to the conference. Their share of the trade grew from 10 per cent to 35 per cent in September 1935 and by early 1936 it reached 50 per cent before starting to decline as the other conference lines introduced lower rates. Growing anti-Japanese sentiment in the Chinese trading community in Malaya also worked against them. By late 1937 the Japanese share was down to under 12 per cent, then the situation in China drew their remaining vessels from this route.[29]

The Japanese increased their share of the Java–Japan Conference by offering low rates. But in a new rate war in 1933 the Netherlands Line struck back with the encouragement of the Netherlands East Indies Government, local shippers, and Dutch firms in Japan. The government allocated certain ports of entry for foreign goods and restricted Japanese imports and shipping. There were negotiations with the Japanese and the trade was split about equally between the lines of the two countries. Tension however continued. [30]

The South African trade was of chief importance in Africa. Here the conference system had been dealt a severe blow in 1911 when it was made illegal for mail contracts to be given to lines which offered rebates. The Union Castle, who held the mail contract, had to give up the deferred rebate and the other members of the South African Conference followed. The Agreement system was now adopted, by which the South African Trade Association promised to use conference lines, and the conference provided regular services and stable rates. After the brief post-war boom, rates fell, particularly on homeward cargoes of wool and other primary products. As there was fierce competition for the higher value cargoes like metals, Harrisons of

Liverpool worked out a plan for combining copper from Biera with sisal from East Africa, so combining high deadweight with bulk. After the war the two German lines Woermann and DOAL were readmitted to the conference, and the Dutch Holland–Afrika Line were allowed to join after a period of competition. There were many other attempts by outside lines to break into the South African market, notably by Blue Star Line and Sir Robert Thomas's British and Continental South African Line, but the conference remained in control throughout the inter-war years. The South African Government continued to play an active role in shipping matters, in 1929 signing a five-year agreement with the Union Castle which governed rates between South Africa and the Continental European ports. In 1933 the government made an agreement with two Italian lines by which they maintained services to the Mediterranean ports, and East and West Africa in return for a subsidy of £150,000 each year. The government did a similar deal in 1934 with Swedish and Norwegian lines. Overseeing all shipping matters a Shipping Board was set up in 1929 by the government, and ship-owners had to supply details of all rates to and from South Africa and give 21 days notice of all changes. The conference lines sought to introduce differential-contract rates in 1935 because of serious non-conference completion. But the Board recommended instead that import duties be introduced to prevent cheap iron and steel flooding into the country carried by these outsiders and harming Union producers. The Board took further steps to control shipping in 1937 when every shipowner was required to provide the Board with a copy of any agreement they had made with any other shipowner.[31]

The deferred rebate continued in the West African trade throughout the inter-war years, but there were big changes in this trade, especially in the relationship between shipowners and merchants. This culminated spectacularly in 1931 in the bankruptcy of the Royal Mail Steam Packet Company to which Elder Dempster belonged, and the imprisonment of Lord Kylsant, its Chairman, on the grounds of issuing a false prospectus. Lever Brothers, the other company in the dispute, bought six ships in 1916 to ship palm kernel oil from their mills at Lagos and Opobo, and though they lost three through enemy action during the war, they bought the Niger Company in 1920 which increased their fleet still further. They also continued using Elder Dempster. John Holts, another merchant company, used their own ship and shipped by Elder Dempster as well. In 1919 the Holland Steamship Company began regular services between the Continent and West Africa, with a link to Britain so that British traders could use the service. From 1920 the service operated under the name of the Holland West Africa Line, with sailings from Hamburg, Amsterdam, Rotterdam and Antwerp. In 1921 a German combination of the Woermann Line, the Hamburg–America Line and the Bremen–Africa Line, called the Deutscher Afrikadienst, re-entered the West, South and East African trades. This Dutch and German competition came at the time of the post-war slump, and Elder Dempster answered it by reintroducing the deferred rebate in 1922. After a rate war, the West African Shipping Conference was set up again in 1924 under the name of the West African Lines Conference with the three British, Dutch and German members. There was minor competition from French, Italian and Danish lines, whilst the Danish and American Bull Line retired defeated. But on the increasingly important North America–West Africa route the Bull Line and other American lines got a hold, alongside Elder Dempster. Under the new conference agreement Elder Dempster could load and discharge on the Continent, but the Continental lines could not do the same in Britain, except for embarking and discharging passengers at Southampton. Ports of call in West Africa were allocated to particular lines. The deferred rebate was only used on the outward voyage but shippers had to use conference vessels for the homeward cargo. Rates to and from the Continent were to be the same as to and from Britain. As soon as the conference was set up again it raised rates, homeward freights rising by about 70 per cent.

Meanwhile during the 1920s amalgamations were taking place between the West African merchant firms. The African and Eastern Trading Corporation had resulted from the amalgamation of the numerous trading companies operating on the coast. In 1928 it merged with the Niger Company as the United Africa Company, a direct subsidiary of Lever Brothers. In the shipping world a similar process was taking place in Britain with Elder Dempster Company being linked to Lord Kylsant's Royal Mail Company with world-wide interests. Between 1928 and 1931 Lever Brothers took on Lord Kylsant in a bitter battle between UAC and Elder Dempster operating in the conference. Levers were unwilling to accept the high rates charged by the conference and the conference view that UAC would lose its rebate if it used its own ships for part of its trade. So in 1929 UAC simply refused to renew its contract with Elder Dempster and chartered vessels to carry the cargo which their own ships could not handle. Overnight Elder Dempster lost 40 per cent of their West African trade. This started a chain of financial collapse, which in 1930/1 put the Royal Mail Company in the hands of the Official Receiver, and Lord

Kylsant in gaol. The African Steam Ship Company and the British
Steam Navigation Company, which had operated the West African
service since the middle of the nineteenth century, were wound up, and
after separation from the Royal Mail Group the Elder Dempster assets
were put under the control of a newly formed company, called the
West African Lines Company. UAC and the conference now came to
terms, and although there was a large increase in freight rates, UAC
was able to continue using both their own ships, and conference vessels,
without losing their rebate. UAC continued to charter ships, many of
them Scandinavian, during the 1930s, and they built up their own fleet
with modern lifting gear and tanks for palm oil. Obviously the
conference disliked this, and an uneasy peace lasted until the war. What
made things worse for the conference was that UAC absorbed or
bought control of many of the remaining trading companies in West
Africa, such as G. B. Ollivants in 1933, and the Swiss Trading Company
on the Gold Coast in 1936. Their business could now be channelled
through UAC's growing fleet. John Holts, the next biggest British firm
in the West African Trade, also used their own ships to carry more and
more of their cargo and were not penalised by the conference for doing
so.

Since 1914 Japan had begun to ship directly with raw material
suppliers, and in 1926 Osaka Shosen Kaisha opened a regular service
between Japan and East and South Africa. They extended this to West
Africa in 1934, but withdrew in 1937 after the outbreak of war with
China.[32]

These years saw the Pacific opened to international trade with the
opening of the Panama Canal, and the arrival of the Diesel ship as a
serious alternative to the steam ship. At the same time British
dominance of sea lanes and shipping conferences took some severe
knocks from German, Dutch and Japanese competitors. Even in
Britain herself the traditional autocracy of the shipping magnates took
a nasty blow from the uncompromisingly tough northern soap
manufacturers Lever Brothers.

Telecommunications and Aeroplanes

The perfecting of the submarine cable had made it possible to connect
Asia and Africa into a world-wide telegraph service before the First
World War. There was nothing so dramatic in the inter-war years, but
progress continued in the development of telecommunications. To a

large extent this was the provision of extra telegraph cables and the
filling-out of domestic networks. There was also considerable expansion
of telephone systems, this nineteenth-century invention coming into
common usage in the developing world in these years. In 1932 the
South African telephone system was linked directly to the British
telephone system by radio. The level of sophistication of telecommunications gauged the economic development of the various countries.

India and South Africa make an interesting comparison, India having
in 1939 9,879 telegraph offices, nearly three times as many as South
Africa which had only 3,420. But South Africa had more than twice
as many telephones with 190,195 to India's 82,378. The Dutch East
Indies had a surprisingly large number of telephones too with 45,033,
although she only had 1,813 telegraph offices. As for other countries,
they mostly had adequate telegraph systems, linking their main towns
to each other and to the international system. Telephone provision
was less extensive and tended to be concentrated in the wealthier and
more urbanised countries. Malaya had a very good telegraph and
telephone system throughout, and Siam had 675 telegraph stations in
1939, the Philippines 552 and Ceylon 325. Even China had an adequate
telegraph system, necessary for administering that vast region.
Telephones were not used much, because income levels were too low
for most people to own one. Telephones, like cars, were a good pointer
to individual wealth. French Indo-China fared better than China proper,
with a good telegraph system and 9,087 telephones. South Africa led in
Africa, and the direct radio link between the telephone system and that
in Britain put it ahead of any other Asian or African country. But by
1929 Nigeria had quite and extensive telephone system augmenting the
telegraph network, and in 1939 the Gold Coast had 286 telegraph
offices and 2,627 telephones. By contrast the great expanses of the
Belgian Congo had 76 telegraph offices and 1,704 telephones, and
South West Africa 64 telegraph offices and 2,012 telephones. In the
French colonies and Angola and Mozambique telecommunications were
more rudimentary.

The 1930s saw the arrival of radio as a means of communication in
the developing world. It was cheap, because it did not need lines
laying; and it was more reliable, because there were no wires which
could be cut during civil disorder. On the eve of the Second World War
India had 72,282 licences, but the Philippines had 29,175 and as many
as 105 radio stations, reflecting American influence. The Dutch East
Indies also used radio extensively and had 70 stations. Elsewhere radio
was at a much lower level, although a basic system of radio

communication was being built up. Radio communication was also becoming essential to service the growth of air transport.[33]

The major step in air travel for the developing world came in March 1929, only months before the Wall Street crash, when a weekly service was opened by Imperial Airways from Croydon, London, to Karachi. The journey was by air to Paris, train to Brindisi, air to Cairo and Basra on the Persian Gulf and on to Karachi. Later in the year the service was extended to Delhi and in 1933 it was carried through to Singapore by way of Calcutta and Rangoon. The British airline Imperial Airways also pioneered a route from Cairo down the East Coast of Africa to Cape Colony and Natal. This passed over a continuous run of British territory and apart from passengers there was a good demand for mail services, existing mail provision being irregular and slow. In March 1931 regular flights went as far as Kisumu on Lake Victoria, then they were scheduled to Nairobi in Kenya and on to Northern Rhodesia. Early in 1932 regular flights opened to Johannesburg and Cape Town. So within five years of the first journey to Karachi, regular services were operating over the length of Africa, and by way of India to Singapore and on to Australia. During the remaining years before the war the number of flights increased and the time of the journey was shortened. A regular service to Hong Kong began in 1936.

West Africa was a little later getting a regular air service, but the first scheduled service to West Africa left Khartoum for Kano in February 1936. In October that year the service was carried southwards through Kaduna, Minna and Oshogbo to Lagos. Next year Accra was added to the route. When Bathurst in the Gambia was included it was found to be unprofitable and this link was closed in 1939.

Other colonial authorities were setting up air links to their possessions, the French operating a service from Saigon to Marseilles and the Dutch from Bandoeng in Java to Amsterdam. This last service was run in 1938 three times a week, by the Royal Dutch Airline. Other internal flights in the Dutch East Indies were run by the Netherlands East Indies Airways, linking the leading towns of Java, Sumatra, Borneo, Celebes and Singapore. Manila in the Philippines was served by Pan American Airways on its trans-Pacific air route which began in 1935. Even in China air transport had made a tentative beginning, in 1929 a regular air route starting between Shanghai, Nanking and Hankow. 1931 saw a service being set up between Mukden, Peking, Tientsin and Shanghai. These routes were linked to international routes by arrangements with Imperial Airways, the French service from Saigon and the Dutch service from Bandoeng. In Africa, the Belgians operated flights in the

Congo between Leopoldville, Boma and Stanleyville, and between Banningville and Lusambo. In 1935 a weekly air service began between Elizabethville, Leopoldville and Brussels.[34]

Air transport remained in the pioneering state at the outbreak of war. Regular services there were, conveying a few passengers and urgent mail. But rail and ship remained the major conveyor of international transport, just as telegraphs remained the most important form of telecommunication. The transformation of communications by motor, air, telephone and radio in the developing world had begun but was very far from complete. Meanwhile, London still remained a vital centre of communications by telephone, telegraph, radio and air. This was partly a legacy of the past, and partly due to her continuing role as the head of a widespread empire.

Notes

1. J. N. Sahni, *Indian Railways: One Hundred Years* (New Delhi: Ministry of Railways, 1953), pp. 25–6; N. Sanyal, *Development of Indian Railways* (Calcutta: University of Calcutta, 1930), pp. 367–9; Dhires Bhattacharyya, *A Concise History of the Indian Economy, 1750–1950* (Calcutta: Progressive Publishers, 1972), pp. 156–9; D. R. Gadgil, *The Industrial Evolution of India in Recent Times, 1860–1939*, 5th edn (Bombay: Oxford University Press, 1971), pp. 341–6; F. V. de Fellner, *Communications in the Far East* (London: P. S. King, 1934), pp. 134, 230–3; Lim Chong Yah, *Economic Development of Modern Malaya* (Kuala Lumpar: Oxford University Press, 1967), pp. 276–82; J. S. Furnivall, *Netherlands India: A Study of Plural Economy* (Cambridge: University Press, 1944), pp. 330–1; Charles Robequain, *The Economic Development of French Indo-China* (London: Oxford University Press, 1944), pp. 98–101, 105; R. O. Ekundare, *An Economic History of Nigeria, 1860–1960* (London: Methuen, 1973), pp. 142–4, 146–9; *Economic Development in a Plural Society: Studies in the Border Region of the Cape Province* D. Hobart Houghton (ed.) (Cape Town: Oxford University Press, 1960), pp. 196, 201–3; R. Horowitz, 'The Restriction of Competition Between Road Motor Transport and the Railways in the Union of South Africa', *South African Journal of Economics* 5 (1937), pp. 145–6, 148; P. R. Gould, *The Development of the Transportation Pattern in Ghana* (Evanston, Illinois: Northwestern University, 1960), pp. 37–8, 44, 159, 162–3; Paul Wohl and A. Albitreccia, *Road and Rail in Forty Countries* (London: Oxford University Press, 1935), pp. 209–11, 219–20, 223–4; G. Walker, *Traffic and Transport in Nigeria: The Example of an Underdeveloped Tropical Territory* (London: HMSO, 1957), pp. 62–73, 81–4, 88–106, 139–47, 158–66.

2. Sahni, *Indian Railways*, pp. 25–6; Sanyal, *Development of Indian Railways*, pp. 367–9; Bhattacharyya, *Indian Economy*, pp. 156–9; Gadgil, *Industrial Evolution of India*, pp. 341–6; Wohl and Albitreccia, *Road and Rail*, pp. 209–15; J. N. Westwood, *Railways of India* (Newton Abbot: David & Charles, 1974).

3. J. S. Furnivall, *Colonial Policy and Practice: A Comparative Study of Burma and Netherlands India* (Cambridge: Cambridge University Press, 1948), pp. 185–6.

4. *Statesman's Year Book, 1940* (London: Macmillan, 1940), p. 96.

5. Chong Yah, *Modern Malaya*, pp. 272–82.

6. Furnivall, *Netherlands India*, pp. 329–31; *Statesman's Year Book, 1940*, pp. 1165.

7. *Statesman's Year Book, 1940*, p. 670; Department of Overseas Trade, *Economic Conditions in the Philippines Island, 1933–4* (London: HMSO, 1935), p. V.

8. Ingram, *Economic Change in Thailand*, pp. 85–6, 276; *Statesman's Year Book, 1940*, pp. 1343–4.

9. Robequain, *French Indo-China*, pp. 92–101, 104–6, 111–12; Wohl and Albitreccia, *Road and Rail*, pp. 223–4.

10. de Fellner, *Communications in the Far East*, pp. 97–8, 100–2, 107–8, 134–5, 227–9, 230–3; Wohl and Albitreccia, *Road and Rail*, pp. 226–30; P. H. Middleton, *Railways of Thirty Nations: Government Versus Private Ownership* (New York: Prentice Hall, 1937), pp. 230–8; Liang-lin Hsiao, *China's Foreign Trade Statistics, 1864–1949* (Cambridge, Mass: Harvard University Press, 1974), p. 55.

11. *Economic Development in a Plural Society*, pp. 180, 196, 201–3; Horowitz, 'Restriction of Competition', pp. 145–6, 148; *The Oxford History of South Africa*, Monica Wilson and Leonard Thompson (eds) (Oxford: Clarendon Press, 1971), vol. II; *South Africa, 1870–1966*, pp. 20–1; Wohl and Albitreccia, *Road and Rail*, pp. 248–52; Middleton, *Railways of Thirty Nations*, pp. 108–10.

12. Lionel Weiner, *Les Chemins de Fer Coloniaux de l'Afrique* (Bruxelles: Goemaere, 1930), pp. 433–64; S. H. Frankel, *Capital Investment in Africa: Its Course and Effects* (London: Oxford University Press, 1938), p. 249.

13. *Statesman's Year Book, 1940*, p. 461; Weiner, *Chemins de Fer Coloniaux*, pp. 408–25.

14. Weiner, *Chemins de Fer Coloniaux*, pp. 465–70, 471–86, 487–508; *Statesman's Year Book, 1940*, pp. 210–13, 217, 263.

15. Ekundare, *Economic History of Nigeria*, pp. 134–6, 142–4, 146–9; Walker, *Traffic and Transport in Nigeria*, pp. 62–73, 81–4, 88–106, 139–47, 158–66.

16. Gould, *Transportation Pattern in Ghana*, pp. 34, 37–8, 40–4, 50–6, 58–62, 66–74, 159, 162–3.

17. *Statesman's Year Book, 1940*, pp. 245, 251.

18. Weiner, *Chemins de Fer Coloniaux*, pp. 82–118; *Statesman's Year Book, 1940*, pp. 930, 942–4, 947–8.

19. Weiner, *Chemins de Fer Coloniaux*, pp. 187–293; Simon E. Katzenellenbogen, 'The Miner's Frontier', in *Colonialism in Africa, 1870–1960*, vol. 4; *Economics of Colonialism*, Peter Duigan and L. H. Gann (eds), (Cambridge: Cambridge University Press, 1975), p. 393; *Statesman's Year Book, 1940*, p. 723; André Huybrechts, *Transports et structures de développement au Congo: Étude de progrès économique de 1900 à 1970* (Paris: Mouton et IRES, 1970), pp. 30–33; S. E. Katzenellenbogen, *Railways and the Copper Mines of Katanga* (Oxford: Clarendon Press, 1973).

20. Weiner, *Chemins de Fer Coloniaux*, pp. 143–186; *Statesman's Year Book, 1940*, pp. 1237–8.

21. D. A. Franie, *East and West of Suez: The Suez Canal in History, 1854–1956* (Oxford: Clarendon Press, 1969), pp. 576–8, 582; F. V. de Fellner, *Communications in the Far East* (London: P. S. King & Son, 1934), pp. 42, 278–9, 287–9, 315–25; W. A. Radius, *United States Shipping in Transpacific Trade, 1922–1938* (Stanford: Stanford University Press, 1944), pp. 3–4, 44–57.

22. S. G. Sturmey, *British Shipping and World Competition* (London: Athlone Press, 1962), pp. 39–41, 133–4; Radius, *Transpacific Trade*, pp. 37–8, 57–8, 119–20.

23. C. Ernest Fayle, *A Short History of the World's Shipping Industry* (London: George Allen & Unwin, 1933), pp. 293–8; R. H. Thornton, *British Shipping* (Cambridge: Cambridge University Press, 1939), pp. 95–102. Daniel Marx, Jr, *International Shipping Cartels: A Study of Industrial Self-Regulation by Shipping Conferences* (New Jersey: Princeton University Press, 1953), pp. 31–2; Francis E. Hyde, *Shipping Enterprise and Management, 1830–1939: Harrisons of Liverpool* (Liverpool: Liverpool University Press, 1967), pp. 124, 148, 161–2; Sturmey, *British Shipping and World Competition*, pp. 37–41, 61–7, 85–6, 108; Radius, *Transpacific Trade*, pp. 157–9.

24. E. C. Smith, *A Short History of Naval and Marine Engineering* (Cambridge: Babcock and Wilcox, 1937), pp. 303–5, 330–1; Marx, *International Shipping Cartels*, pp. 31–2; Sturmey, *British Shipping and World Competition*, pp. 82–4; Hyde, *Shipping Enterprise*, pp. 149–52, 171–3; V. D. Wickizer, Shipping and Freight Rates in the Overseas Grain Trade: *Wheat Studies*, 15 (1938), pp. 50–3.

25. B. M. Deakin and T. Seward, *Shipping Conferences: A Study of Their Origins, Development and Economic Practices* (Cambridge: Cambridge University Press, 1973), pp. 27–9; Hyde, *Shipping Enterprise*, pp. 131–2, 136–8; Sturmey, *British Shipping and World Competition*, pp. 127–8.

26. Marx, *International Shipping Cartels*, pp. 101–3.

27. Deakin and Seward, *Shipping Conferences*, pp. 34–6.

28. D. L. McLachlan, 'The Conference System Since 1919', *Business History*, 4 (1961), pp. 56–7; Marx, *International Shipping Cartels*, pp. 80–1.

29. Marx, *International Shipping Cartels*, pp. 81–2.

30. Ibid., p. 82.

31. Marx, *International Shipping Cartels*, pp. 90–3; Hyde, *Shipping Enterprise*, pp. 134–6, 138–43; M. Murray, *Union Castle Chronicle, 1853–1953* (London: George Allen & Unwin, 1953), pp. 155, 160, 182–3.

32. McLachlan, 'The Conference System', p. 57; Charlotte Leubuscher, *The West African Shipping Trade, 1909–1959* (Leyden: A. W. Sythoff, 1963), pp. 29–58; P. N. Davies and A. M. Bourn, 'Lord Kylsant and the Royal Mail', *Business History*, 14 (1972), pp. 103–23; P. N. Davies, *The Trade Makers: Elder Dempster in West Africa, 1852–1972* (London: George Allen & Unwin, 1973), pp. 209–89; Murray, *Union Castle Chronicle*, pp. 186–190; Ernest Hieke, G. L. Gaiser, *Hamburg-Westafrika: 100 Jahre Handel mit Nigeria* (Hamburg: Hoffman und Campe Verlag, 1949), pp. 95–115.

33. *Statesman's Year Book, 1940*, pp. 96, 134–5, 185–6, 191–2, 210–11, 213, 217, 223, 242, 243, 247–8, 251, 263, 444–5, 461, 669–70, 723, 773–4, 906, 930, 942–3, 948, 1165, 1237–8, 1343–4; de Fellner, *Communications in the Far East*, pp. 255–7, 277, 339–42; Bhattacharyya, *Indian Economy*, p. 169; Ekundare, *Nigeria*, pp. 154–5; Furnivall, *Netherlands India*, p. 331; G. L. Lawford and L. R. Nicholson, *The Telecon Story* (London: The Telegraph Construction and Maintenance Co., 1950), pp. 174–5.

34. R. E. G. Davies, *A History of the World's Airlines* (London: Oxford University Press, 1964), pp. 170–200; Howard Robinson, *Carrying British Mails Overseas* (London: George Allen & Unwin, 1964), pp. 287–9; David Jones, *The Time Shrinkers: The Development of Civil Aviation between Britain and Africa* (London: David Rendel, 1971), pp. 206–7, 214, 218, 232–6; Davies, *The Trade Makers*, pp. 289–93; Robin Higham, *Britain's Imperial Air Routes 1918–1939: The Story of Britain's Overseas Airlines* (London: G. T. Foulis & Co, 1960), pp. 109–81, 203–228; *Statesman's Year Book, 1940*, pp. 671, 723, 774, 1166; de Fellner, *Communications in the Far East*, pp. 239–40; H. L. Smith, *Airways Abroad: The Story of American World Air Routes* (Wisconsin: University of Wisconsin Press, 1950), pp. 31–6; M. R. Dhekney, *Air Transport in India* (Bombay: Vora & Co., 1953), pp. 32–3, 54–81.

2 MONEY AND CAPITAL

Money

The late nineteenth century saw the gradual establishment of a truly international currency system, the gold standard. When India went on to gold in 1893 she gave the lead to the remaining countries in Asia on the silver standard to move to gold. By the First World War only China, French Indo-China and Hong Kong remained on silver. In Africa currencies were placed on the gold standard as the colonial authorities introduced metropolitan-type money. But this flowering of the international gold standard was to have only a short period of bloom. The First World War dealt it a severe blow, and despite attempts to restore it during the 1920s it limped to ultimate collapse in the international financial crisis of 1931.

The position of sterling was central to the entire issue. The king-pin in the gold standard system of the late nineteenth century, it never really recovered this position after the war. The outbreak of war brought severe risks to shipping, making the movement of gold necessary to the gold standard system impossible. Sterling rose from its traditional level of $4.86 to $5.00 to begin with, but then settled to $4.76 where it was pegged by the British authorities. After the war this level was maintained, but the cost of support was so great that it was abandoned in 1919 and the export of gold prohibited. The British still had as their primary aim a return to gold and policy over the next few years was directed to this end. Gradually the exchange rate recovered from its low of $3.40 in February 1920 to $4.63 at the end of 1922, making a return to gold at the traditional rate of $4.86 a practical possibility. It was achieved on 29 April 1925. There was no real dispute as to whether sterling should return to gold or not, but some urged the rate should have been lower. Keynes in particular argued that the rate was too high and would hold back exports and the recovery of the British economy. Certainly the British economy did continue to be depressed in consequence of low exports and the government had to deflate to lower prices to retain some international competitiveness. Gold nonetheless trickled out day by day.[1]

By 1930 sterling was in grave difficulties. The gold reserves were low, and the Bank of England allowed interest rates to fall, discouraging foreigners from holding sterling. It was also felt that London was too heavily committed financially to the agricultural debtor countries, many of them in the developing world. These countries were in grave difficulties due to the agricultural depression. India and Ceylon both floated substantial loans in London between 1928 and 1931. In the early part of 1931 sterling continued weak, but bank rate was not raised to protect it for fear of depressing still further the domestic economy. In May a major Austrian bank, the Credit Anstalt, failed spectacularly, bringing a loss of confidence in neighbouring financial centres. This resulted in a run on German banks, which had to be closed two months later. Now there came a run on London and the sterling exchanges sharply depreciated on 15 July 1931. What made the situation particularly difficult for London was that she had £70 million short-term assets trapped in Germany where the banks were closed. The Macmillan Report estimated that there was a short-fall between London's short-term foreign assets and its liabilities, and the May report suggested a substantial internal budget deficit, both contributing to the decline in confidence. In August there was a change in government and the new government introduced a tough budget in September to try to come to grips with the situation. The budget made wage cuts in the public sector, and there was a strike by Royal Navy personnel at Invergordon which was reported internationally as a mutiny. Confidence in London's political and economic stability evaporated, the outflow of funds could not be staunched, and sterling was effectively taken off the gold standard and devalued on 21 September 1931. The sterling crisis of 1931 was the final phase of a more prolonged international financial crisis which had been building up since at least 1928 due to the collapse of world agricultural prices which caused severe problems in many developing countries to whom Britain was the major creditor. This situation was aggravated by a demand for increased liquidity by other major creditor countries, particularly France and the United States. It was the withdrawal of funds by these two countries which provoked the crisis in Germany and Austria.[2]

With the abandoning of gold the pound fell from $4.86 with remarkable speed. Within days it was down 25 per cent to $3.75, and by December the rate had fallen to a low of $3.25, some 33 per cent below the old par, the average for the month being $3.47. The authorities made no attempt to intervene in the market or even to maintain orderly conditions. As many of the world's currencies were linked to sterling, the international monetary system was in chaos. Twenty five countries followed Britain off gold, particularly empire countries, many of whom were in the developing world, and also countries in Scandinavia, Eastern Europe and trading partners such as Argentina, Egypt and Portugal. Canada held her dollar halfway between sterling and the US dollar and the Union of South Africa resisted depreciation, along with the US dollar, the German mark and the remaining gold bloc. By the end of 1932 another seven countries had left the gold standard, including South Africa which came off at the end of the year to re-align with sterling. In April 1933 the United States also left the gold standard, unhinging the other major international currency. In January 1934 the dollar was stabilised at 59 per cent of its former parity. The pound was then loosely linked with the dollar at about the previous dollar parity and most other countries began to keep their exchange values stable. France, which had only returned to the gold standard in 1926 after a period of severe depreciation, clung to gold until 1936, but it left her price levels too high internationally and the collapse of her external position forced her to devalue. Britain, France and the United States signed a tripartite agreement not to alter exchange rates without consultation and this remained the basis of the international monetary system until the war.[3]

Sterling was easily the most important currency for the developing world, as it was the basis of the currency in Empire countries such as India, Ceylon and Malaya, and even Siam, which was outside the Empire. In Africa sterling was the basis of the currency of all Britain's possessions. Britain was also the major trading partner and source of capital for many of these countries, sterling providing the basis of exchange.

In India the Chamberlain commission had been set up in 1913 to review the existing currency arrangements. This included John Maynard Keynes as one of its members, and it recommended that the gold exchange standard be adopted, gold not being put into circulation. The silver rupee was to continue as the normal medium of exchange. But during the war Indian exports rose considerably due to war needs abroad and at the same time London had to make payments to India to meet the costs of war in the East. The inflow of funds pushed up the money supply and the government had to buy silver to coin into rupees. This pushed up the price of silver, which rose from 2s 3¼d per standard ounce in 1915 to 3s 7d in 1917. At this price the silver value of the rupee rose above its face value and the exchange value of the rupee rose inexorably as the value of silver continued to increase. The continued rise in the sterling value of silver was due to the depreciation of sterling and in 1919 because of exceptional demand from China. From 1s 5d in August 1917 the rupee reached 2s 4d in December 1919.

The Babington Smith Committee recommended in February 1920 that the rupee should be linked to gold rather than to sterling which was depreciating. It was declared equivalent to 2s gold, and sovereigns were made legal tender at Rs 10 each. This rate proved difficult to maintain as the post-war boom gave way to a recession in which Indian exports fell whilst her imports continued to increase. There was a flood of remittances to Britain as people feared a fall in the exchange rate and early in 1921 the rupee fell below 1s 3d sterling or 1s gold. By presenting a balanced budget for 1923—4 the circulation of currency was reduced and the rate of exchange slowly recovered to 1s 6d or 1s 4¾d gold. It was decided that without making any public announcement of policy the rate be sustained at that level. When sterling returned to gold in 1925 at pre-war parity the Hilton Young Commission recommended that India should do likewise, the rupee remaining the medium of exchange at 1s 6d. When Britain was forced off gold again in 1931 India followed, the sterling—rupee rate remaining at 1s 6d until the war. The depreciation of the rupee meant gold could be sold in London at an appreciated price, so there was a substantial export of gold from 1931—7 which helped her tide over the continuing adverse balance of payments resulting from the collapse of agricultural export prices.[4]

The currency situation in Ceylon was greatly influenced by the situation in India, as it had been through history. Ceylon was the first British territory with a 100 per cent reserve system, rupee notes being issued against Indian silver rupees from 1884, silver coin being kept in the reserve up to at least half the value of currency notes in circulation. After the turn of the century the Currency Board issued and redeemed notes against rupees or sovereigns, although they had the discretion to refuse to issue notes against sovereigns when it seemed inadvisable to add to the gold portion of the currency reserve. During the war the circulation of notes increased considerably as a shortage of silver rupees developed owing to the currency situation in India. When the Paper Currency Ordinance was amended to enable the issue of currency against credits at the Bank of England, the currency situation needed no further attention. Thus, unlike many countries in Europe and the developing world, Ceylon, like most British colonies with a similar currency system was not confronted with any special monetary problems in the inter-war years. The value of the Ceylon rupee was maintained at the same level as the Indian rupee, so its exchange value shared the vicissitudes of that currency in these years. When the rupee followed sterling back on to the gold standard in 1925, the Ceylon rupee maintained parity with it, and when the rupee followed sterling off gold in 1931 so did the Ceylon rupee, to become a simple sterling exchange standard.[5]

Malaya had a currency system similar to that of Ceylon in many respects, although parity was maintained against sterling rather than the rupee, the rate being one dollar to 2s 4d from 1906 through the inter-war years. The Currency Board exchanged any amounts of Straits Settlements currency notes against sterling, to maintain par. Reserves were kept to 100 per cent of the value of the currency, but liquid reserves to only half the value. Because the Straits dollar was maintained against sterling, it did not suffer the problems of the rupee during the war and early post-war years and Malaya enjoyed comparative freedom from monetary instability through the inter-war years. In 1938 a currency agreement was made between the Straits Settlements and the other Malay States, as the Straits currency circulated in their area. This enabled them to share the profits resulting from the successful investment policies of the managers of the reserves.[6]

In the Dutch East Indies the currency had been placed on the gold standard as early as 1877, following the Dutch decision two years previously. There was a currency union between the mother country and the Netherlands Indies, both countries having the same standard and the same gold and silver coins, although the small change in the Indies was a different shape. This union facilitated the flow of capital to the Dutch East Indies. Thus the monetary history of these islands followed that of the Netherlands, the guilder representing 0.6048 grams of fine gold. It was temporarily abandoned during the war, being restored in 1925, the day that sterling returned to its pre-war parity. From then on a gold exchange standard operated, gold coins ceasing to circulate. From 1926 to 1929 the system operated well, but from 1930 to 1936 both the Netherlands and the Netherlands Indies ran into difficulties, particularly after the devaluation of sterling in 1931 left guilder prices uncompetitive internationally. But it was not until September 1936 that gold was abandoned and the guilder devalued, following the situation in France. The devaluation promoted economic recovery in the Netherlands and the Indies.[7]

For many years the Philippines had what was in effect a gold standard system, parity being maintained with the dollar by dealings with various approved banks in the United States where the Insular Treasurer kept deposits. The Gold Standard Fund was maintained at a minimum of 15 per cent of the circulating currency and the note issue was covered by reserves of more than 100 per cent. When the dollar was

allowed to depreciate in 1933 the peso followed, and the Gold Standard
Fund became the Exchange Standard Fund. The peso was worth half a
dollar both before and after the depreciation.[8]

Siam, which had previously been on the silver standard, adopted a
sterling exchange standard in 1902, the rate finally being fixed with
the baht worth 1s 6.46d. Notes were backed by 100 per cent reserves,
and during the war their circulation increased considerably, although
silver coins continued to circulate. The rise in the price of silver
however led to coins being melted down and smuggled from the
country. When the war ended an unprecedented rise in the price of rice
led to substantial exports and a consequent demand for baht. The last
reserves of silver were coined and released and the paper currency then
declared inconvertible. As silver prices continued to rise, the remaining
silver coinage was protected from smuggling by increasing the exchange
rate to 2s 1.15d in 1919. Then the rice crop failed and the export of
rice was prohibited, leading to a fall-off in the demand for baht and a
rise in the demand for sterling. As treasury holdings had been purchased
at the old rate and now were converted at the new rate a substantial
loss accrued to the treasury. In 1923 the exchange rate was dropped
again, now to 1s 9.81d. This stimulated exports which were recovering
after the rice failure. The rate remained stable until the baht went on to
the gold standard in 1928, with the baht defined as 0.6627 grams of
gold, which confirmed the exchange rate as it stood. When Britain
devalued and left gold in September 1931, the baht stayed on a gold
basis until May 1932 when the link with sterling was re-established at
the former rate. This was maintained until the Japanese invasion. Thus
apart from a six month period the exchange rate of the baht remained
steady from 1923 to 1941. This gave Siam a considerable measure of
stability whilst many of her neighbours suffered from the monetary
and balance of payments problems of the time.[9]

French Indo-China suffered from considerable currency instability,
having broken her tie with silver in 1902 without adopting a fixed
exchange rate. During the war the exchange rate of the piastre was
pushed up by the rise in the value of silver. At the end of the war a
crisis developed as the supply of paper money persistently increased,
but the exchange commission refused to allow the necessary purchases
of silver to back it. An attempt was made to solve this problem by
freeing the export of rice, which had been prohibited during the war
and by compelling exporters to turn over to the Bank of Indo-China
one fifth of the gold or silver value of their exports in exchange for
banknotes. This decree met a storm of protest and was withdrawn on

30 December 1919 only 13 days after it was introduced. In January 1920 fiat currency was established. The Government General determined the limit of the issue and also the piastre's rate of exchange against the franc. In effect the piastre became a floating currency and despite discussions about stabilising the piastre against gold nothing was done. The 'closed vase' regime continued to operate, with the export of piastres prohibited and no obligation to convert silver into piastres. Thus, when the balance of trade was favourable and foreigners were unable to obtain piastres with silver the exchange rate rose high above parity; and when the balance of trade was unfavourable the exchange rate fell as specie could not be exported to settle the account. The value of silver fell from 3s 6½d an ounce in London at the beginning of 1921 to 1s 9¼d by the end of 1929, a drop of a half. The piastre, although not directly linked to silver, fell with it and from 27 francs in 1926 it had dropped to under 10 francs by the end of 1929. Thus on 31 May 1930 the piastre was fixed at 0.655 grams of gold, equivalent to 10 francs. The trade piastre was withdrawn from circulation on 31 December 1931 and the notes of the Bank of Indo-China became the normal means of exchange. Many felt that the exchange rate was too high and pressure built up in favour of a devaluation. In September 1936 the French monetary crisis ended in the devaluation of the franc and the Bank of Indo-China guaranteed to convert its notes into francs on the basis of 10 francs to the piastre. This provisional agreement remained in force until the Second World War.[10]

China's monetary affairs before the First World War had been rather chaotic and China remained on the silver standard whilst many other countries switched to gold. Thus, during the 1920s the exchange value of the haikwan tael fell with the fall in silver. China's exports benefited from this falling exchange rate and silver flowed into China until 1931. Then political disturbances in Shanghai and Jehol Province, together with the general trade depression and a decline in remittances from overseas Chinese, brought this brief period of prosperity to an end. By 1933 there was a net export of silver and this became a flood the following year after the London Agreement of 1933 and the United States Silver Purchase Act of 1934 raised the price of silver. Now a change was forced upon the Chinese Ministry of Finance and in November 1935 a decree was made giving China a managed standard currency, with banknotes full legal tender. The value of the Chinese dollar was set at US $0.30 or 1s 2½d sterling, which was 20 per cent lower than the rate at which the exchanges had operated since 1934. The new rate was 40 per cent below the silver par. The move to a

managed currency was supervised by a British expert and the control of
the currency issue was put in the hands of the Central Bank which was
to become independent of the Ministry of Finance. At the same time
the government was to re-organise its finances to eliminate the need to
borrow for currency purposes which led to inflation. But the Central
Bank did not become independent and the government proved unable
to reform its finances. Budget deficits were responsible for the
subsequent note expansion, only half of which represented notes issued
for silver, all of which was surrendered by the public. Even before the
Japanese invasion the note issue was leading to inflation, and the actual
invasion triggered off a run on the government banks. The exchange
rate fell by a half between March 1938 and March 1939, and in March
1939 the Sino-British Stabilisation Fund was set up with funds
advanced by the Bank of China, the Bank of Communications and two
British banks, the Hong Kong and Shanghai, and the Chartered Bank of
India, Australia and China. But the Fund could not stop the Chinese
dollar from continuing to fall after war broke out.[11]

The neighbouring British colony of Hong Kong was affected by
these changes in China, to whom the colony was an entrepôt. Up to
1935 the British dollar was the currency unit and its value declined
with its silver content, keeping in line with the Chinese currency. Thus
Hong Kong too suffered an outflow of silver after 1934, forcing change.
Thus, in 1935 Hong Kong moved to a managed currency on the sterling
exchange standard, the currency fund being maintained in sterling.
Dollar notes were put into circulation, the exchange rate being
1s 3.375d.[12]

The years before the First World War saw most of the countries in
Africa adopting monetary systems based on the domestic currency of
their colonial authority. In South Africa sterling had circulated
alongside boer rix dollars, but in 1911 the currency system was unified
on a sterling basis, British and Transvaal coins were legal tender, bronze
up to 1s, silver up to 40s and gold to any amount. When war broke out
it was announced that minting would take place in the country if
necessary. An embargo was placed on the export of specie, but gold
remained in circulation and the banks continued to redeem notes
against gold. After the war coin was smuggled from the country due to
the disparity between sterling and gold. By the Currency and Banking
Act of 1920 the Treasury was authorised to issue gold certificates which
would be legal tender. Whenever the market price of gold exceeded
£3 17s 10½d per standard ounce, the redemption of gold certificates
could be suspended, and in fact they were declared irredeemable until

June 1925. In May 1925 the Union returned to the gold standard
following the British decision and the gold certificates again became
convertible. By March 1926 they had all been redeemed. In 1931 when
Britain left the gold standard South Africa decided to remain on it and
for sixteen months endured the competition of countries whose
currencies had been devalued. But at the end of 1932 the government
was forced to resign, and a coalition government came into power
which abandoned the gold standard. Immediately the economy began
to recover, spurred on by the gold-mining boom due to the high price
of gold. After a brief period when the South African pound was left to
depreciate, it was stabilised at par with sterling in January 1933, a
situation which was maintained until the war.[13]

Nyasaland and Northern Rhodesia used only British coin until 1933,
but in that year Southern Rhodesian currency was declared legal tender.
Bank notes issued by local branches of the Standard Bank of South
Africa and Barclays DCO were also current. Par was maintained with
sterling.[14]

British West Africa saw some important currency innovations,
although the system was based on sterling. The West African Currency
Board was set up in London in 1913, and it covered the territories of
the Gambia, Sierra Leone, the Gold Coast and Nigeria. The Board
managed the new silver shilling coinage, coinage profits going to set up
a fund to meet the eventuality of a mass conversion of shillings into
sterling. In 1916 notes were issued on par with sterling, and par with
sterling was in fact maintained throughout all the vicissitudes of
sterling in the inter-war years. In East Africa a currency board similar to
the West African one was set up in 1919. The problem in East Africa
was that when British traders and missionaries first entered the area
they did so from India and areas where the rupee was the currency, and
this became the legal tender as British rule was established. So prevalent
was the rupee in this area that the German Government in Tanganyika
also introduced a coin equal in weight and fineness to the Indian rupee
as the basic currency unit. At the end of the First World War the
currency situation was unstable because of the position of the rupee,
which had risen from its pre-war value of 1s 4d to over 2s and was
fluctuating violently due to the rise in silver. As there was little trade
between East Africa and India, but a great deal between East Africa
and neighbouring sterling-based countries, the government decided to
stabilise the rupee against sterling in East Africa at 2s. The Indian rupee
coin was replaced by a local token coin issue in Kenya, Uganda and
Tanganyika, now a mandated British territory. The Board's operations

ran into difficulties as they had a substantial amount of rupee notes printed only to meet local pressure for a standard coin of a florin equal to 2s sterling and divided into 100 cents. By the time a quantity of this new coin and equivalent notes had been issued the sterling exchange value of the rupee fell considerably below the 2s at which it was still pegged in East Africa. So it was decided to make the standard coin a shilling, equal to 1s sterling, divided into 100 cents, and withdraw the short-lived florin and florin/cent currency. The demonetisation of the florin cost the Board a great deal, but much greater losses were incurred in withdrawing the Indian rupee at 2s and presenting it to the Government of India for exchange at a substantially lower figure. A loss was also made in withdrawing the German heller and rupee coinage at 2s and selling it for bullion. There was also a loss on the small local Kenya and Uganda rupee currency which was in existence before the Board was created. The low point in the Board's history came in 1932 when circulation of currency reached its lowest level. Like the West African currency, parity with sterling was maintained throughout its ups and downs in the inter-war years, once the new currency had replaced the rupee. Both the West African and East African currency was really sterling in a different place from the United Kingdom, having the same internal and external purchasing power as sterling. Both currency boards exchanged on demand local currency for sterling in London, and sterling for local currency in London at a fixed rate.[15]

In the French African colonies the situation was somewhat different. In 1901 the Banque d'Afrique Occidentale was given the privilege of becoming the sole bank of issue for French West Africa. The Bank had to ensure that the currency circulating in French West Africa was freely convertible with the franc and to maintain a specified ratio between reserves and currency. It also had to make a financial contribution to the metropolis and the colonies. French Equatorial Africa was also part of this currency area as all legislation applying to Senegal was applicable in the Gabon. This system operated right through to 1945, the par value of the currency mirroring the fortunes of the franc. Thus it depreciated until the franc was stabilised in 1926, and depreciated again in 1936 when the franc left gold and was devalued. In 1937 the franc was devalued a second time.[16]

As for the Belgian Congo, the Belgian franc was the basis of the currency from 1908. The Bank of the Belgian Congo, a private bank, was given the authority to issue notes, but it had to share the profits with the metropolis. The charter giving Belgian currency validity in the colony assigned the profits of any coinage struck for the Congo to the colonial revenue. Thus the Congo franc followed the Belgian franc in depreciating severely prior to stabilisation against gold in 1927, and in devaluing with the Belgian franc devaluation of March 1935, a devaluation of 28 per cent. The devaluation proved a stimulus to the economies of Belgium and the Congo.[17]

In the Portuguese colonies of Angola and Mozambique the metropolitan unit, the escudo, had been introduced. Portugal devalued with sterling in 1931 because as Britain was a major trading partner the sterling–escudo rate was of crucial importance.[18]

So the developing world experienced considerable currency confusion in the inter-war years, adding to the difficulties of the depression.

International Capital Movements

The 1914–18 war severely disrupted the pattern of international investment. Previously Britain had been the major international lender, followed by Germany and France, as was shown on p. 16 in the Introduction. But to meet the costs of the war these countries sold many of their foreign securities. Britain sold about $4,000 million of her foreign investments, about two-thirds of which were United States securities, mostly railway bonds. These were obtained by the British Government from private investors in exchange for War Loan and then sold. Thus the United States obtained full ownership of her railways, the money being used by the British Government to buy munitions supplied by America. Apart from these sales of stock, Britain also suffered losses as her investments in Central and Eastern Europe and the Near East were wiped out, a sum of some $600 million being involved. France sold about $700 million of her investments, but she lost over $4,000 million in Europe and the Near East. German investments were either liquidated or given up, so that by the end of the war this major international investor had been virtually removed from the scene. Britain and France had had their investments diminished by between $4,000 and $5,000 million dollars each, about a quarter of Britain's pre-war investments, and about half of French pre-war investment. At the same time the United States had emerged as the major international creditor nation, both by buying back the American securities which the French and British were selling, and also by buying large quantities of French and British securities and making other substantial investments abroad. A debtor country when the war broke out, she emerged from the war with net foreign investments on private account of several thousand million dollars, plus inter-governmental credits amounting to some $10,000 million.[19]

The decline in Britain's position as an international lender, and the rise of the United States, did not affect Asia and Africa much immediately, as Britain's investments there survived the war intact. Although the United States was now the major international lender, her attentions were largely restricted to Europe, Canada and Latin America, leaving Britain the principal creditor in both Asia and Africa in the inter-war years.[20]

International investment in Asia and Africa soon resumed after the war, as is shown in Table 2.1. During the 1920s Britain continued to export capital, despite the difficulties the British economy experienced in these years. After 1930 Britain became an importer of capital in most years, and this was matched by an outflow of capital from many parts of Asia and Africa, South Africa being a notable exception. India imported capital during most of the twenties, except 1923 and 1925, but 1931 and the following years saw an outflow of capital until 1937 and 1938 when again she received capital. The Netherlands Indies lost capital in the years 1925 to 1927 inclusive, received an inflow until 1933, and lost capital again from then on. China imported capital from 1928 to 1930, and again in 1933, but suffered an outflow afterwards. South Africa imported capital throughout the 1920s and 1930s, except for 1932 and 1933, but she was in a unique position as a gold producer. What is clear is that the whole pattern of international investment suffered a severe reversal after 1930.[21]

Britain being the major investor in Asia and Africa it is of some interest to examine her investments there in 1930 and 1936, just before and just after the big reversal of investment (Table 2.2).

Although these figures are not directly comparable, they may be taken to give a reasonable picture of the situation. Whilst the percentage of British investment going to the particular areas indicated remained much the same, there was an overall reduction in the amounts invested. India and Ceylon stand out as the most important investment area in the developing world, with South Africa coming next with about half the investment made in India and Ceylon. The biggest change in Britain's overall investment position since 1914 was the decline in the importance of the United States as an area for British investment as a result of war-time liquidations. The dominance of India and Ceylon and South Africa as investment areas in Africa and Asia reflects their

Table 2.1: Capital Movements, 1919–38[a] ($ million)

Year	UK	China[b]	India[c]	Netherlands Indies[d]	S. Africa
1919	–	–	–	–	–
1920	−881	–	–	–	–
1921	–	–	–	–	–
1922	−682	–	–	–	–
1923	−700	–	−17	–	+5
1924	−380	–	+71	–	+34
1925	−261	–	−69	−171	+20
1926	+126	–	+177	−31	+72
1927	−385	–	+120	−41	+26
1928	−569	+93	+67	+10	+46
1929	−574	+95	+37	+73	+65
1930	−112	+110	+92	+62	+32
1931	+313	–	−86	+28	+19
1932	+179	–	−25	+18	−76
1933	–	+83	−130	+12	−90
1934	+35	−37	−65	−51	+55
1935	−158	−48	−33	−55	+9
1936	+90	−109	−127	−77	+22
1937	+277	–	+120	−101	+66
1938	+269	–	+99	−53	–

Notes:

[a] Net inward (+) or outward (−) capital movement, measured by estimated deficits or surpluses on account of goods, services, and gold.

[b] The Chinese figures from 1933 to 1936 inclusive exclude Manchuria and Kwantung; the balances for Manchuria and Kwantung were as follows: 1934, +55; 1935, +61; 1936, +39 and 1937, +79.

[c] India: Fiscal years beginning 1 April.

[d] Netherlands Indies: Excluding re-investments of profits earned in the country by firms other than Netherlands firms.

Source: United Nations, *International Capital Movements during the Inter-War Period* (New York: Lake Success, 1949), Table 1, pp. 10–14.

similar importance at the outbreak of the First World War.[22]

An analysis of the categories of investments into which these funds had been directed gives some insight into the use of British investment in these areas (Table 2.3).

Table 2.2: British Investment in Asia and Africa, 1930 and 1936

Country	1930		1936	
	£ millions	%	£ millions	%
India and Ceylon	540	14.4	438	13.5
Malaya[a]	108	2.8	84	2.5
China	47	1.2	41	1.2
South Africa	263	7.0	248	7.6
British West Africa	46	1.2	37	1.1
Total	1,004	26.9	848	26.1
World Total	3,726	100.0	3,240	100.0

Notes:

[a] Including non-British in 1930, but not in 1936.

Source: Royal Institute of International Affairs, *The Problem of International Investment* (London: Oxford University Press, 1937), p. 142; R. M. Kindersley, 'British Overseas Investments in 1931', *Economic Journal*, 43 (1933), p. 200; R. M. Kindersley, 'British Overseas Investments in 1935 and 1936', *Economic Journal*, 47 (1937), p. 657.

Table 2.3: Categories of British Investment in Asia and Africa, 1930 and 1936[a]

	India & Ceylon		Malaya		South Africa	
	1930	1936	1930	1936	1930	1936[b]
Government and Municipal	56.9	58.4	3.7	7.1	52.6	41.5
Railways	19.6	19.1	–	–	8.9	8.4
Public Utilities	2.6	1.5	3.7	4.7	1.3	2.4
Mines	3.0	2.7	7.4	8.3	22.3	29.0
Miscellaneous	17.6	18.0	85.1	79.7	14.7	18.5
Total	99.7	99.7	99.8	99.8	99.8	99.8
100% £ millions	£458	£438	£108	£84	£224	£248

Notes:

[a] The 1930 figures are based on an 85% sample and the 1936 figures on a 96.31% sample. The figures were not compiled on exactly the same basis.

[b] Including Rhodesia.

Source: Royal Institute of International Affairs, *The Problem of International Investment* (London: Oxford University Press, 1937), p. 143; R. M. Kindersley, 'British Overseas Investments in 1931', *Economic Journal*, 43 (1933), p. 201; R. M. Kindersley, 'British Overseas Investments in 1935 and 1936', *Economic Journal*, 47 (1937), p. 658.

These figures suggest that a very high proportion of British investment in India and Ceylon had gone into government and municipal investment, between 50 and 60 per cent. Railways were the next most important item with nearly 20 per cent. Mines and public utilities followed a long way behind. In Malaya mines dominated the investment scene, followed by public utilities and government and municipal. A very high proportion, in the region of 80 per cent, was classified as miscellaneous. As for South Africa, government and municipal investments dominated, with approximately 50 per cent, although both mines and railways were important. Mining was the only category in which commercial investment abroad appreciably increased during the depression, notably in Rhodesia where the copper mines were expanding and in South Africa where gold-mining operations were extended. Of British world investment in mines in 1936 some £72 million, 43 per cent of the total, was accounted for by South Africa and Rhodesia.[23]

After the reduction in investment in Asia and Africa which took place during the 1930s, the distribution of international investment there on the eve of the Second World War is shown on Table 2.4. If the situation in 1938 is compared with the situation in 1914, various interesting points emerge. With the repatriation of so much investment during the 1930s the overall level of world investment was not all that much above the situation in 1914, at $54,950 million compared with $45,450 million. As regards the major investor, Britain's world investment in 1938 stood at $22,900 million compared with $20,000 million in 1914. Her investments in Africa and Asia had, however, increased from $4,950 million to $6,600 million. Of this increase Asia received nearly all, the investment in Africa hardly increasing, although there was some redistribution of Britain's assets there, investment in Rhodesia and South Africa actually declining by something in the region of $500 million. Investment in India and Ceylon by contrast almost doubled from $1,850 million to $3,050 million, and the proportion of British investment in Africa and Asia going to India and Ceylon also increased from 37.4 per cent to 46.2 per cent. Investment in Malaya more than doubled from $150 million to $400 million, and investment in China rose from $600 million to $850 million. But it is clear that the overall increase in investment in Africa and Asia was largely accounted for by the increase in India and Ceylon, $1,200 million out of $1,650 million. It must, however, be remembered that all these figures are just very crude approximations to show rough orders of magnitude. Other changes which are worth noting are the

Table 2.4: Foreign Investment in Asia and Africa, 1938 ($ million)[a]

	Britain	%[b]	France	Germany	Netherlands	Belgium and Luxemburg	USA	Others	World	%
Asia										
India and Ceylon[c]	3,050	47.6	—	—	—	—	50	—	3,100	25.4
Siam	100	1.5	—	—	—	—	—	100	200	1.6
Indo-China	—	—	400	—	—	—	—	100	500	4.0
Malaya	400	6.2	—	—	—	—	—	250	650	5.3
Dutch E. Indies	200	3.1	50	—	1,900	—	50	150	2,350	19.2
Philippines	50	0.7	—	—	—	—	150	150	350	2.8
China	850	13.2	100	150	50	100	250	1,100	2,600	21.3
Asian total	4,650	72.6	550	150	1,950	100	500	1,850	9,750	79.9
Africa										
South Africa and Rhodesia	1,250	19.5	50	—	—	—	50	—	1,350	11.0
Brit. E. Africa	150	2.3	—	—	—	—	—	—	150	1.2
Brit. W. Africa	200	3.1	—	—	—	—	—	—	200	1.6
French W. & Equatorial Africa	—	—	150	—	—	—	—	—	150	1.2
Belgian Congo	50	0.7	—	—	—	350	—	—	400	3.2
Portuguese Africa	100	1.5	—	—	—	—	—	100	200	1.6
African total	1,750	27.3	200	—	—	350	50	100	2,450	20.0
Total	6,400	100.0	750	150	1,950	450	550	1,950	12,200	100.0
World total	22,900								54,950	

Notes:

[a] To the nearest $50 million.

[b] The percentages do not add up to the totals because of rounding.

[c] Including Burma.

Source: William Woodruff, *Impact of Western Man. A Study of Europe's Role in the World Economy, 1750–1960* (New York: St Martin's Press, 1966), pp. 156–7. Table IV/4.

disappearance of Germany as an investor of much significance, and the considerable importance of the Netherlands, most of whose investments were in the Dutch East Indies. Indeed the Dutch East Indies were the third most important investment area in the developing world, after India and China, and much more important than South Africa and Rhodesia, taking $2,350 million against $1,350 million. This was a change from 1914 when they were the fourth most important investment area, a long way behind South Africa and Rhodesia. Investment had more than trebled there since 1914 and her proportion of investment in Asia and Africa had risen from 9.8 per cent in 1914 to 18.9 per cent in 1938. Of other Asian countries India and Ceylon took $3,100 millions and China $2,600 million. As for Africa, all the investment there added together, some $2,650 million or 21.2 per cent of the total, did not exceed the investment in the Dutch East Indies by much. The decline in the proportion going to South Africa, 10.8 per cent in 1938 against 24.9 per cent in 1914, reflects the increased capacity of that economy to provide for its own capital requirements, and the consequent paying off of much of her external debt.[24]

How then did the recipient countries use this capital inflow? It has already been shown that in India, where British investment predominated, capital went heavily into government funds and municipal loans. On the whole this investment was used productively and not dissipated. India experienced some difficulties in 1931 at the time of the sterling crisis, but default was avoided, and the situation improved subsequently. This was due to the fact that the rupee was maintained on the sterling standard and that the high price of precious metals called out large supplies from hoards in India, which increased her foreign balances. Since most of the obligations of the government of India were trustee securities in Britain, the Indian Government was able to carry out favourable conversion operations in London and borrow cheaply on short term. Railways had been a major outlet for capital in India before the First World War and they continued to be so afterwards, so that by 1930, 18 per cent of total railway mileage had been laid since 1913. Further mileage was added during the 1930s, so that by 1937 21 per cent of the existing mileage had been laid since 1913. Of investments in private industry, over half was in trading and manufacturing industries, and there were further amounts in banking and loan companies and insurance companies. There were also investments in steamships, railway and other transport, and in tea plantations and mines. There was a tendency for direct investment to increase and portfolio investment to decline, as the government encouraged firms having rupee capital and a number of Indians on the board of directors. Another feature of the inter-war years was that Indians themselves began to put up much of the capital required in trade and industry and by 1934 they owned practically all the cotton mill shares, over half the jute shares, nearly all the iron and steel interests, and over half the national debt. Utilities, transport, mining, plantations and banks remained for the most part under foreign capital and control.[25]

Burma was separated from India in 1937. On the eve of the First World War she had already become the world's leading rice-exporting region, and her potential for oil, rubber and certain metals was only just being recognised. It was into these new developments that foreign capital went after the war, most of the capital being British. Oil led, but silver and lead were important, and there was investment in zinc, copper, iron and nickel too, and also in tin and tungsten. Teak, of which Burma was the world's leading producer, also received foreign capital, but rubber was of minor importance. Foreign funds also went into trade and banking, and into plant to process local raw materials and foodstuffs, such as rice mills, sawmills, cotton gins and mills, oil refineries, sugar factories, rubber factories, soap, rope and cement works. Of these, rice mills were by far the most important. There were some Chinese investments in estates and primitive tin smelting. On the eve of the Second World War 34 per cent of foreign business investment was in oil and 32 per cent in mining.[26]

In Malaya the First World War was a period of prosperity, her industries booming and her balance of payments favourable, leading to a revenue surplus which yielded sufficient sums to meet the capital needs of development. But over-ambitious plans were laid placing a heavy debt burden against future revenues, which fell as tin and rubber prices collapsed in the immediate post-war depression. Thus loans were raised from London, a pattern of events similar to that in the Dutch East Indies. But unlike the Dutch East Indies and French Indo-China, further heavy debts were not incurred to sponsor budget deficits during the subsequent major depression. Instead Malaya did not embark on policy requiring new loans after 1930, but sought only two small local loans to redeem or replace loans contracted in previous years. She reduced her indebtedness by 25 per cent between 1930 and 1937, a considerable contrast to some other countries in South East Asia in this period. By 1937 two-thirds of the public debt was locally owned. The government received considerable income from mineral royalties, forest reserves for development, telegraphs, telephones and railways. The railways, 19 per cent of which had been built since 1913, were government built, owned and controlled, using current revenue and treasury surpluses. So most capital investment from abroad was private investment in business and industry, making nearly 80 per cent of the total. In 1936 52 per cent was in rubber companies, 13 per cent in tin companies, and 9 per cent in miscellaneous companies, including trading companies, smelting companies, breweries, collieries, electricity and power concerns. Britain was the major investor, contributing over 70 per cent of total business investment. There were minor investments by the Americans, Dutch, French and Japanese, Japanese investment dating only from after the First World War, being directed to the iron mines. The iron mines in Malaya were financed by Japanese capital, run by Japanese management and the ore exported almost exclusively to Japan. Overall, investment increased during the twenties but declined somewhat during the thirties. The Chinese are said to have had about $200 million invested in Malaya on the eve of the Second World War, and they certainly formed a majority in the colony, with 2.2 million people. Tin mines were the main item of Chinese investment, but after the First World War rubber plantations also became important outlets of Chinese investment, besides numerous minor enterprises.[27]

The Dutch East Indies were a major destination for foreign capital and one of the features of the inter-war years was her increasing importance as an investment area. Not surprisingly, Dutch capital predominated, and of private business investments, oil led with 18 per cent. Rubber followed with 17 per cent and sugar with 15 per cent. Other agricultural investments took 13 per cent and there were smaller investments in railways and trams which took 5 per cent, shipping which took 3 per cent, public utilities 3 per cent and miscellaneous investment 9 per cent. Less than half the foreign investment in rubber was Dutch and peasant smallholdings cultivated a greater rubber acreage than all the foreign countries put together. In coffee and tobacco the Dutch interest was greater than that of other countries, but was again exceeded by peasant holdings. Cinchona and the production of quinine was exclusively in Dutch hands, as was the palm oil industry. The British had major investments, particularly in oil and rubber, and also merchandising, banking and agricultural exports, such as sugar, coffee and tea. There were some minor German investments, in plant for making railway equipment, and plantations; and there was Japanese investment in sugar, tea, oil palm and rubber. Of total foreign business investment in 1937, the Dutch owned 73 per cent, the British

14 per cent and the US 6 per cent, most of American investment being in rubber and oil. Apart from private business investment, portfolio investment took 37 per cent of the total in 1937. The government had always played an active role in the economy of the Indies, and government loans were used for railway and harbour construction, and irrigation. Right up to the Second World War, government and private enterprise operated side by side. The government was particularly prominent in tin mining, and teak, chinchona and salt were government monopolies. The government was active also in oil and owned and operated over half the railways. During the depression the government also sought loans in order to stimulate the economy with public works. As elsewhere in South East Asia, the Chinese were active throughout the economy and their total investment would probably make them the third most important foreign investor. They were active in almost every branch of economic activity, including rubber, sugar, tin-mining and the retail trades.[28]

Foreign investment in the Philippines was at a rather low level, and portfolio investment was of minor importance, rising from 10 per cent of the total in 1914 to 22 per cent in 1930, from which it fell to 16 per cent in 1935. Direct investment predominated, and the US provided 51 per cent of the total in 1936. But the level of US investment was much less than British investment in Malaya, or Dutch investment in the East Indies. American investment was especially concerned with gold mining, but there was also investment in iron, copper, manganese and chromium, mining taking 23 per cent of total American direct investment. Public utilities were the next most important area of investment, taking 19 per cent. These included radio companies, a cable company, a telephone company and gas and electricity companies. There was also investment in water and transport. Although agriculture was the main economic activity of the islands, there was little investment from abroad. But in the sugar industry American capital was second in importance to peasant holdings, about one-third of the sugar centrals being controlled by US capital. Twelve per cent of American direct investment was in sugar. Another 12 per cent was in plantations of coconuts, hemp and rubber. Merchandising took a further 10 per cent, followed by a full range of minor investments in lumber, transportation, coconut producers, general manufactures, engineering, embroidery and miscellaneous activities. Spanish investments followed American investments in importance, contributing 28 per cent of direct investment in 1936, largely in gold mining and the manufacture of cigars and cigarettes. The Spanish also followed the Americans in their investment in sugar, and had other investments in coconuts and their processing, and also public utilities. British investments were small, contributing only 11 per cent, mainly in banking, lumber and the import–export business. The Japanese had been traditionally active in fishing and hemp growing, coconuts and shoe-making, but their investments increased in the 1930s, especially in textiles, mining, and merchandising, where they came to rival the Chinese. This was because successive boycotts by the Chinese of Japanese goods after the First World War had demonstrated to the Japanese the need to control their own outlets. The largest field of Japanese enterprise was, however, hemp cultivation, but they also had interests in timber, corn and rice, and holdings in manganese and copper. They contributed 8 per cent of direct investment in 1936. The Chinese were active in many spheres of economic life, as elsewhere in South East Asia, and they predominated in the retail trade. Indeed, their investments probably made them the next most important foreign investor after the Americans. They owned 75 per cent of the rice mills in the islands and were active in ware-housing, marketing, shoe-making, cordage and lumber.[29]

Britain was the major investor in Siam, and also her leading market. She was the chief holder of her foreign debt and the largest foreign investor in her businesses. Indeed Siam was part of the sterling bloc from 1932. Unlike the Dutch East Indies and Indo-China, foreign public debt fell during the depression, and Siam was more cautious in her financial policy than neighbouring colonial countries, who had no independence and therefore nothing to lose. Siamese securities were almost exclusively in the hands of British subjects and Malayan residents, but direct investment was greater than portfolio investment as elsewhere in South East Asia, increasing from 38 per cent of the total in 1914 to 72 per cent in 1938. Siam was essentially a rice-producing country, its rice cultivators poor, converting whatever savings they had into hoards. So foreign capital came in to develop raw material resources, such as tin, rubber and timber. Banking communications and public utilities were also financed with foreign capital, mainly British. The majority of the tin-dredging firms were Australian, although there were three large British concerns. The Chinese continued to operate small primitive workings. After tin, teak was the most important location for foreign investment, with the British putting in two-thirds of the total, the Danish also having substantial interests. Rubber contributed a third of Siam's international trade, but it was mainly in the hands of small Chinese and Malay planters, not foreign plantations. Rubber was a recent innovation in Siam, developing only after the First

World War. At the time of the Thai revolution in 1932/3 industrialisation was not much advanced. Trams, river-boats and railways were built and run by foreigners, as were teak mills. Soap, matches, cigarettes and cement were manufactured locally, and also ice and mineral waters. The Chinese were very active and owned two large teak mills. Probably Chinese business interests equalled the entrepreneurial investments of all other foreigners in the country added together. They owned rice mills and some sawmills, and were active in tin-mining, sugar and rubber. They dominated internal trade including the rice trade, which was Siam's chief economic activity.[30]

French Indo-China was bedevilled with currency problems in the inter-war years, both the French franc and the Indo-Chinese piastre fluctuating considerably. From the outbreak of the war in 1914 to 1931 the inflow of loan funds to the country was at a standstill except for two small loans in 1921 and 1926. Up to 1924 there was depression in the colony, followed by a boom up to 1930, this partly fuelled by the flight into the piastre as the franc depreciated. Investment in this period went initially to rubber, but later mining, trade, banking and real estate. Between 1931 and 1938 there was an investment policy of 'Mise en valeur' based on M. Albert Sarraut's ideas, put forward in his book *La Mise en Valeur des Colonies Françaises* of 1923. He advocated substantial spending on public works and general economic expansion, in order to promote a large expansion of production and private investment as in the British, Belgian and American colonial areas. These ideas were put into practice when the slump came and substantial loans were authorised to ameliorate conditions during the slump. More than 60 per cent of the loans raised in 1931—5 from France went into railway construction, particularly the completion of the Trans-Indo-China line between Tourane and Nhetrang. The remainder was used for irrigation, highways, and sanitation. In those years 1,490 miles of railways were built, 8,700 miles of roads and also many modern bridges. The government participated in the Bank of Indo-China, developed electricity supplies, air companies and made advances to cultivators of rubber and coffee. The policy in fact proved something of a disaster, particularly in respect to the railways which tended to duplicate existing sea and river communications and did not even cover their running expenses in consequence. Portfolio investment dominated foreign investment in this period and private direct investment declined sharply. This decline was assisted by the fact that both the franc and the piastre were now threatened by devaluation, so there was no longer a flight to the piastre. Utilities and manufacturing came to the fore in this period, while agriculture and mining lagged. But none the less, 33 per cent of French business investment was in agriculture, due to the expansion of rubber in the twenties and thirties. Only 3 per cent of Indo-Chinese rubber was in the hands of peasant producers and French Colonial Corporations dominated. The planters there were supported by the government during the depression and therefore survived, in contrast to the plight of planters in Ceylon and the Dutch East Indies. Other agricultural investment was in tea, coffee, coconuts, sugar cane and coffee, and funds also went into teak, and forest products like rattan, cinnamon, lacquer, camphor and pulp. Mining production increased four times during the inter-war years, coal predominating, then tin, zinc, tungsten and gold. There was also investment in plant to process raw material, for example rice milling, sugar refining, soap, vegetable dyes, tea, coffee, silk, cotton and rubber. Cement from Indo-China was exported all over the Far East, where it was prized for its quick drying properties. Most of the foreign investment came from France, in the region of 97 per cent. This contrasts with the situation in the Dutch East Indies and the Philippines where 70 per cent and 50 per cent respectively of the investment came from the colonial power. Although there was a small amount of British investment in trading firms and banks, the Chinese were the second most important capitalists. They monopolised the rice trade and owned 80 per cent of the rice mills. They also controlled about half the semi-wholesale trade in other commodities, corn, silk and tropical products. They were also involved in the multifarious activities common to the Chinese all over South East Asia, particularly pepper plantations, retail business, tanneries, sawmills, soap and match factories and mechanical workshops. They were less prominent in tin and rubber production than in Thailand, Malaya, or the Dutch East Indies.[31]

In China railway construction was the largest outlet for foreign investment before the First World War, and there was also investment in coal mines. But from 1912 to 1926 was the Peking Government period, a time of political chaos and civil war, and to solve their serious financial difficulties the government borrowed abroad. Direct business investment for goods for domestic consumption also increased, both to offset falling imports, and to beat the upward revision of the Chinese tariffs. Japanese investment in textiles was important, and also in banking. When the National Government was founded in 1927 it avoided foreign loans until 1936 and in 1937 substantial railroad loans were contracted from foreign sources. Direct business investment made little progress, although Japanese investments in Manchuria witnessed an increase after Manchuria had been taken over by Japan in 1931. In China proper the new field of commercial aviation was developed by foreign investors, with the United States and Germany participating prominently in co-operation with the Chinese Government.

The progress of foreign investment in China is shown in Table 2.5.

Table 2.5: Foreign Investment in China, 1914–36

Types of Investment	1914	1931	1936
	%	%	%
Direct investment	67	78	77
Obligations of Chinese Government	33	22	22
Loans to private parties	–	–	1
Total	–	100	100
Total US $ millions	1,610.3 (100%)	3,242.5 (100%)	3,483.2 (100%)

Source: Chi-ming Hou, *Foreign Investment and Economic Development in China, 1840–1937* (Cambridge, Mass.: Harvard University Press, 1965), p. 14.

From this it is clear that foreign direct investment became increasingly dominant as time went on, so that by 1931 78 per cent of total foreign investment in China was direct. As the same time, borrowing by the Chinese Government declined proportionately. Foreign borrowing by private individuals and firms remained negligible. Government loans were mainly used for building railways, indemnity payments and general administrative payments, and very little went into industrial development. A breakdown of foreign direct investment in China by industry is given in Table 2.6. This shows that foreign business capital in China was primarily used in transportation, especially railways, and fields associated with foreign trade, including banking and finance. Manufacturing also attracted a fair amount, and an increasing proportion over the years. Cotton textiles were particularly important here. Coal and iron mining however received little, and there was virtually no investment in agriculture or plantations.

The principal foreign investors in China are indicated in Táble 2.7. As can be seen, Britain continued to be the most important investor in China in these years. Most of her investment was direct, as was the case with other countries, taking 66 per cent in 1914 and 81 per cent in 1930. Loans to the Chinese Government constituted 34 per cent and 19 per cent of investment in these years. Of the direct investment in 1931 half was in fields directly associated with trade, including the

Table 2.6: **Foreign Direct Investment in China by Industry, 1914–36**

Industry	1914	1931	1936
	%	%	%
Import–export trade	13	19	16
Banking and finance	--	8	20
Transportation	31	23	25
Manufacturing	10	14	19
Mining	3	4	1
Communications and public utilities	2	4	5
Real estate	9	13	9
Miscellaneous	28	11	2
Total US $ millions	1,067.0 (100%)	2,493.2 (100%)	2,681.0 (100%)

Source: Chi-ming Hou, *Foreign Investment and Economic Development in China, 1840–1937* (Cambridge, Mass.: Harvard University Press, 1965), p. 16.

import-export business, general trading, banking and finance, and transport, principally shipping. The remaining half was spread amongst real estate, manufacturing, public utilities, mining and miscellaneous. Geographically 77 per cent of British investment in China in 1929 was in Shanghai, 9 per cent in Hong Kong and 14 per cent in the rest of China.

Japan's investment in China increased rapidly after the First World War when she acquired much of Germany's former interests. By 1936 her investments had even overtaken Britain's. Most of her investment was concentrated in Manchuria, her interests there originating in her defeat of Russia in 1905. In 1930 63 per cent of her investment was in Manchuria, mostly direct investment in the South Manchuria Railway Company, and Shanghai took another 25 per cent. As already indicated, Japanese direct investment concentrated on railways, but import-export business was important and manufacturing investment grew rapidly between 1914 and 1930. Mining was also important, and public utilities, banking and finance, and real estate all received capital. Investment in agriculture was negligible. Although most Japanese investment was direct investment, there were some loans to the Chinese Government for political purposes in the era of the Peking Government, 1912–27.

Russian investment was mainly in the Chinese Eastern Railway and nearly all located in Manchuria and Outer Mongolia. French, Italian, Belgian and Dutch investment was more than half in loans to the

Table 2.7: Foreign Investment in China by Country, 1914–36

Country	1914	1931	1936
	%	%	%
Great Britain	37	36	35
Japan	13	35	40
Russia	16	8	–
United States	3	6	8
France	10	5	6
Germany	16	2	4
Belgium	1	2	1
Netherlands	–	–	–
Italy	–	1	2
Scandinavia	–	–	–
Others	–	–	1
Total US $ millions	1,610.3 (100%)	3,242.5 (100%)	3,483.2 (100%)

Source: Chi-ming Hou, *Foreign Investment and Economic Development in China, 1840–1937* (Cambridge, Mass.: Harvard University Press, 1965), p. 17.

Chinese Government. But the French also placed direct investment and provided railway loans, particularly for the Yunnan Railway, which took about a sixth of French investment in 1931. A peculiar feature of French investment was that about a fifth was represented by property held for income by Roman Catholic missions. In 1914 Germany had been the third largest investor, but the First World War liquidated most of her assets in China, most of which were concentrated in Shantung Province, especially the Tsingtao-Tsinan Railway. US investments were rather insignificant.[32]

In Africa, the pattern of investment for the continent was dominated by South Africa. As has already been noted, Britain was the major investor there, concentrating largely on government and municipal loans. Much of these loans went into railway building, 37 per cent of the railways in existence in 1931 having been built since 1931. In 1930 60 per cent of foreign capital in South Africa was in government loans. The remainder was in municipal securities, railways and mines. The majority of private listed capital went into mining, particularly gold mining, and smaller amounts went into commerce, agriculture, industry, land, and financial and investment companies. Britain was the principal source of foreign funds, but small amounts were furnished by the Netherlands and the United States. Since gold was one of the most important of South Africa's exports, little difficulty was experienced during the depression in meeting the service payments on external debts. Helped by a devaluation of the South African pound, a phenomenal increase in the price of gold and a credit policy designed to prevent internal inflation, South Africa had a surfeit rather than a shortage of foreign balances. These were used to pay off a large part of the external debts, but even then there was a surplus and inflation came to be feared by the South African monetary authorities. So South Africa's position was unique, for other parts of the British Empire were all debtors on capital account.[33]

Details of investment in the rest of Africa are not good. In South West Africa, by far the largest amount of private listed capital went into mining and exploration work associated with it. In Southern and Northern Rhodesia there was a high proportion of private listed capital, due to the fact that for many years it was administered by the British South Africa Company, which raised the money for the Rhodesian railway system. Mining dominated private investment, including the capital in finance, land and exploration companies. There were smaller amounts in commerce, agriculture and industry. Base-metal mining was the basis of all economic development in Northern Rhodesia and between 1927 and 1936 about £25 million was made available for the copper industry there. Nigeria experienced about an equal inflow of public and private capital. Most of the private capital was invested in trading companies, which gradually amalgamated into large concerns of which the United Africa Company stands pre-eminent. Capital invested in tin mining was appreciable, but did not rank with the trading companies. In the Gold Coast private listed capital went into gold mining, and later, tin mining. Turning to East Africa, private listed capital in Kenya was invested in agricultural estates, particularly sisal and coffee plantations. This was augmented by direct investment brought in by the settlers there. Tanganyika had received much listed capital before the war when it was a German possession, but after the war investment went into agriculture and plantation activities. In the 1930s mineral exploration and mining grew in importance. Estimates of capital invested in the Belgian Congo are marred by the difficulties due to the fluctuations in the Belgian currency and the scattered nature of much of the data. But an official estimate of capital invested there in 1932 suggests that 38 per cent was in railways, 20 per cent in mining and 10 per cent in agriculture. Much of the other investment in real estate, finance and building was in enterprises connected with mining and railway expansion, the railways themselves being built to serve the mines. As regards government capital, this rose after 1928, as the government guaranteed interest and dividends in many of the companies engaged in mining, exploration, transport and industrial or agricultural activities. The system of attracting private capital via concessions accounted for only a small proportion of government capital. For the French colonies investment estimates were difficult because of non-listed capital and changes in the value of the franc. The largest part of investment in the French African colonies took place after the First World War. The situation in the Portuguese colonies was even worse, but the poverty of Portugal meant that investment in her African colonies was small, and nationalistic policies after the war restricted inflows of capital from elsewhere. None the less a considerable amount of the capital in the Portuguese territories was British, and raised in London for railway and harbour works. Portuguese private capital developed plantations in Mozambique.

Looking at investment in general in Africa, government borrowing was fairly high as a proportion of capital in each territory in many cases, ranging from 24 per cent in Mozambique to 85 per cent for Nyasaland, with the higher figures in British East Africa, rather than Southern or West Africa, although South West Africa and Sierra Leone also had high percentages. French territories also showed high figures for public capital, but French West Africa had only 54 per cent. The ratio was only 25 per cent for the Belgian Congo owing to the concession and guarantee system which characterised the development of that territory. The Portuguese territories also had low percentages of public capital. It is worth noting that over half the public listed capital in British territories was listed in railways.

Another feature of African investment is that the substantial economic development that took place after the First World War took place at a time of high interest rates. This placed a particular burden on many countries, particularly those dependent on raw materials and foodstuffs whose prices fluctuated considerably. When export prices fell it became increasingly difficult to meet the interest payments, particularly on the government loans which had financed much of the development. Those countries with high proportions of private capital fared better, as falling prices led to falling profits and therefore decreased dividends.

Lastly, it is clear that mining drove on economic development in much of Africa, and capital tended to concentrate in the mining territories: South Africa, South West Africa, Southern Rhodesia, Northern Rhodesia and the Belgian Congo. The Gold Coast and Nigeria also had substantial mining interests. Much of the capital raised went to provide the railway and harbour facilities needed by the mines. In Mozambique the development of mining in the Rand and the Rhodesias led to the building of the Biera Railway and the Biera Junction Railway, and accompanying harbour works. In Angola, the main railway, the Benguella line, was largely built with British capital and was intended to serve the copper belts of the Belgian Congo and Northern Rhodesia.[34]

In summary it may be said that after the war the pattern of investment in the developing world continued much along the pattern established before the war. Britain remained the key investor and capital went into railways, mines, oil and plantations. But the depression changed the situation considerably and Britain became an importer of capital, pulling money out of many of the countries of the developing world. Meanwhile, these years saw increased provision of capital by the capitalists of the developing world themselves, particularly in India and South Africa.

Notes

1. D. E. Moggridge, *The Return to Gold, 1925: The Formulation of Economic Policy and its Critics* (Cambridge: University Press, 1969); J. M. Keynes, *The Economic Consequences of Mr. Churchill* (London: Hogarth Press, 1925).

2. David Williams, 'London and the 1931 Financial Crisis', *Economic History Review*, 15 (1962–3), pp. 518–25.

3. Charles P. Kindleberger, *The World in Depression, 1929–1939* (London: Allen Lane, Penguin Books Ltd, 1973), pp. 48–52, 162–7, 207–61; W. Arthur Lewis, *Economic Survey, 1919–1939*, 8th imp. (London: Unwin University Books, 1966), pp. 63–71; League of Nations, *International Currency Experience: Lessons of the Inter-War Period* (Princeton: League of Nations, 1944), pp. 116–20; M. Wolfe, *The French Franc between the Wars, 1919–1939* (New York: Columbia University Press, 1957).

4. Dhires Bhattacharyya, *A Concise History of the Indian Economy, 1750–1950* (Calcutta: Progressive Publishers, 1972), pp. 204–11; B. R. Tomlinson, 'Britain and the Indian Currency Crisis, 1930–2', *Economic History Review*, 32 (1979), pp. 96–7.

5. H. A. de S. Gunasekera, *From Dependent Currency to Central Banking in Ceylon: An Analysis of Monetary Experience, 1825–1957* (London: G. Bell & Sons, 1962), pp. 77, 137–61.

6. Lim Chong-Yah, *Economic Development of Modern Malaya* (Kuala Lumpur: Oxford University Press, 1967), pp. 222–30; Frank H. H. King, *Money in British East Asia* (London: HMSO, 1957), pp. 11–13; G. L. M. Clauson, 'The British Colonial Currency System', *Economic Journal*, 54 (1944), pp. 18–19.

7. C. P. Kindleberger, *The World in Depression, 1929–39* (London: Allen Lane, Penguin Books Ltd, 1973), pp. 247–61; *The Lessons of Monetary Experience: Essays in Honor of Irving Fisher*, A. D. Gayer (ed.) (London: George Allen & Unwin Ltd, 1937), pp. 237–58.

8. Department of Overseas Trade, *Economic Conditions in the Philippine Islands, 1933–34* (London: HMSO, 1935), pp. 4–5.

9. James C. Ingram, *Economic Change in Thailand, 1850–1970* (Stanford: Stanford University Press, 1971), pp. 152–62.

10. Charles Robequain, *The Economic Development of French Indo-China* (London: Oxford University Press, 1944), pp. 142–49.

11. Frank H. H. King, *A Concise Economic History of Modern China, 1840–1961* (New York: Praeger, 1969), pp. 135–40; King, *Money in British East Asia*, pp. 106–7.

12. King, *Money in Britain East Asia*, pp. 107–8; Clauson, 'British Colonial Currency System', pp. 19–21.

13. E. H. D. Arndt, *Banking and Currency Development in South Africa, 1652–1927* (Cape Town and Johannesburg: Juta & Co., 1928), pp. 122–4; D. Hobart Houghton, 'Economic Development, 1865–1965', in *The Oxford History of South Africa*, Monica Wilson and Leonard Thompson (eds), vol. 2 (Oxford: Clarendon Press, 1971), pp. 31–2; G. de Kock, *A History of the South African Reserve Bank, 1920–1952* (Pretoria: Van Schaik, 1954), pp. 3–213.

14. Clauson, 'British Colonial Currency System', p. 14.

15. Ibid., pp. 2–13; Ida Greaves, *Colonial Monetary Conditions* (London: HMSO, 1953), pp. 10–12; J. B. Loynes, *The West African Currency Board, 1912–1962* (London: West African Currency Board, 1962).

16. Michel Leduc, *Les Institutions Monétaires Africaines des Pays Francophones* (Paris: A. Pedore, 1965), pp. 11–25; A. G. Hopkins, *An Economic History of West Africa* (London: Longmans, 1973), pp. 207–8; Kindleberger, *World in Depression*, p. 255; Lewis, *Economic Survey*, pp. 32–3.

17. Kindleberger, *World in Depression*, pp. 251–2; Roger Anstey, *King Leopold's Legacy: The Congo under Belgian Rule, 1908–1960* (London: Oxford University Press, 1966), p. 109; A. B. Keith, *The Belgian Congo and the Berlin Act* (Oxford: Clarendon Press, 1919), pp. 199–200; Lewis, *Economic Survey*, p. 47; R. H. Meyer, *Bankers' Diplomacy: Monetary Stabilisation in the Twenties* (New York: Columbia University Press, 1970), pp. 16–41.

18. Kindleberger, *World in Depression*, pp. 251–2.

19. Arthur L. Bowley, *Some Economic Consequences of the Great War* (London: Thornton Butterworth Ltd, 1930), pp. 98–9; Gerd Hardach, *The First World War, 1914–1918* (London: Allen Lane, Penguin Books, 1977), pp. 289–90; League of Nations, *The Course and the Phases of the World Economic Depression* (Geneva: 1931), p. 29; Cleona Lewis, *America's Stake in International Investments* (Washington D.C.: The Brookings Institution, 1938), pp. 117, 119; Douglas C. North, 'International Capital Movements in Historical Perspective', in Reymond F. Mikesell (ed.), *U.S. Private and Government Investment Abroad* (Eugene, Oregon: University of Oregon Books, 1962), p. 26; United Nations, *International Capital Movements during the Inter-War Period* (New York: Lake Success, 1949), pp. 4–5.

20. Royal Institute of International Affairs, *The Problem of International Investment* (London: Oxford University Press, 1937), pp. 181–2.

21. United Nations, *International Capital Movements during the Inter-War Period* (New York: Lake Success, 1949), pp. 10–14.

22. Royal Institute of International Affairs, *The Problem of International Investment* (London: Oxford University Press, 1937), p. 142; William Woodruff, *Impact of Western Man: A Study of Europe's Role in the World Economy, 1750–1960* (New York: St Martin's Press, 1960), pp. 154–5, Table IV/3; Eugene Staley, *War and the Private Investor: A Study in the Relation of International Politics and International Private Investment* (Chicago: University of Chicago, 1935), pp. 12, 535–6.

23. R. M. Kindersley, 'British Overseas Investments in 1935 and 1936', *Economic Journal*, 47 (1937), p. 659.

24. Woodruff, *Western Man*, pp. 156–7, Table IV/4.

25. Royal Institute of International Affairs, *International Investment*, pp. 261–2; Nural Islam, *Foreign Capital and Economic Development: Japan, India and Canada. Studies in Some Aspects of Absorption of Foreign Capital* (Rutland, Vt.: Charles E. Tuttle Co., 1960), pp. 169–92; A. K. Banerji, *India's Balance of Payments: Estimates of Current and Capital Accounts from 1921–22 to 1938–39* (New York: Asia Publishing House, 1963), pp. 148–200; Woodruff, *Western Man*, p. 126; A. K. Bagchi, *Private Investment in India, 1910–1939* (Cambridge: Cambridge University Press, 1972).

26. H. G. Callis, *Foreign Capital in South East Asia* (New York: Institute of Pacific Relations, 1942), pp. 88–95.

27. Ibid., pp. 48–58.

28. Ibid., pp. 27–38.

29. Ibid., pp. 10–24.

30. Ibid., pp. 59–70.

31. Ibid., pp. 71–85.

32. Chi-ming Hou, *Foreign Investment and Economic Development in China, 1840–1937* (Cambridge, Mass.: Harvard University Press, 1965), pp. 9–21; C. F. Remer, *Foreign Investments in China* (New York: Macmillan, 1933), pp. 81–102, 117–48, 239–663; Royal Institute of International Affairs, *International Investment,* pp. 263–6; Yu-Kwei Cheng, *Foreign Trade and Industrial Development of China: An Historical and Integrated Analysis through 1948* (Washington: University Press, 1956), p. 46.

33. Royal Institute of International Affairs, *International Investment*, pp. 262–3.

34. S. Herbert Frankel, *Capital Investment in Africa: Its Course and Effects* (London: Oxford University Press, 1938), pp. 148–215.

3 INTERNATIONAL TRADE

In the years before the First World War a complex network of international trade came into being. Countries no longer tried to be in surplus or balance with each of their trading partners. Instead they allowed deficits to grow with some partners which they offset by surpluses with others. This system of multilateral trade was to suffer a severe setback between the wars.

Despite the problems from which the international economy suffered, the share of the developing countries in world trade grew noticeably. Lamartine Yates's analysis indicates that Africa's share of world exports increased from 3.7 per cent in 1913 to 5.3 per cent in 1937, and Asia's from 11.8 per cent to 16.9 per cent. As for imports, Africa's world share rose from 3.6 per cent to 6.2 per cent in this period, and Asia's from 10.4 per cent to 14.1 per cent. These estimates are shown in Table 3.1 and Table 3.2. Apart from the marked increase in the proportion of world exports and imports attributed to Africa and Asia, it is worth noting that the United States' and Canada's share of world exports grew from 14.8 per cent to 17.1 per cent, whilst the British Isles' contribution fell from 13.1 per cent to 10.6 per cent. The most severe fall was in North West Europe's share, down from 33.4 per cent to 25.7 per cent, reflecting the difficulties which that region experienced in those years. As for imports, the United States' and Canada's share rose from 11.5 per cent to 13.9 per cent, and so did the British Isles' share, from 15.2 per cent to 17.8 per cent. But North West Europe's share was down from 36.5 per cent to 27.8 per cent. In 1937 Asia's contribution to world exports almost equalled that of the United States and Canada, and her share of world imports was marginally greater. Africa and Asia together were markedly more important in world trade than North America.

But the fact that Africa and Asia increased their share of world trade at the expense of North West Europe does not reveal the shock which the multilateral payments system received in those years. Crucial to the web of international payments was the relationship between Britain and the developing world. Before 1913 Britain had large trade deficits with both the United States and continental Europe, which she was only able to sustain because of the surplus she earned with the developing world, particularly India. The developing world in its turn

Table 3.1: World Exports by Geographical Region, 1913–37 (%)

	1913	1928	1937
United States and Canada	14.8	19.8	17.1
British Isles	13.1	11.5	10.6
North West Europe	33.4	25.1	25.8
Other Europe	12.4	11.4	10.6
Oceania	2.5	2.9	3.5
Latin America	8.3	9.8	10.2
Africa	3.7	4.0	5.3
Asia	11.8	15.5	16.9

Source: P. Lamartine Yates, *Forty Years of Foreign Trade: A Statistical Handbook with Special Reference to Primary Products and Underdeveloped Countries* (London: George Allen & Unwin, 1959), Table 6, p. 32.

Table 3.2: World Imports by Geographical Region, 1913–37 (%)

	1913	1928	1937
United States and Canada	11.5	15.2	13.9
British Isles	15.2	15.8	17.8
North West Europe	36.5	27.9	27.8
Other Europe	13.4	12.5	10.2
Oceania	2.4	2.6	2.8
Latin America	7.0	7.6	7.2
Africa	3.6	4.6	6.2
Asia	10.4	13.8	14.1

Source: Yates, *Forty Years of Foreign Trade*, Table 7, p. 33.

earned surpluses with the United States and Europe which enabled it to meet its deficit with Britain. India also earned a surplus on her trade with the rest of Asia. After the war this pattern re-established itself, as is shown in the League of Nations' publication *The Network of World Trade*.[1] In 1928 Britain continued to have substantial trade deficits with the United States and Europe, and also with the recently settled regions comprising Canada, Australia, New Zealand, South Africa, Argentina and the temperate regions of South America. It was only with the tropics, made up of India, Ceylon, South East Asia, Central Africa and tropical Latin America that she had a surplus. But the surplus with these countries had declined since 1910 and covered much less of her deficits. Then Britain's surplus with India alone was greater

than her deficit with either the United States or continental Europe.[2]
Now her surplus with India of $64 million fell far short of her deficit of
$582 million with the United States and $618 million with continental
Europe. Even if her surpluses with South Africa, Central Africa, South
East Asia, China and Japan were added in, they still fell far short of her
deficits. This is shown in Table 3.3. The same table reveals that the

Table 3.3: British Balance of Trade, 1928 and 1938 ($ of 1928 millions)

Countries	1928			1938		
	Imports	Exports	Balance	Imports	Exports	Balance
North Africa	164	84	−80	57	32	−25
South Africa	134	175	41	66	132	66
Central Africa	140	156	16	61	53	−8
Northern America	288	188	−100	234	71	−163
USA	918	336	−582	341	83	−258
Latin America	709	400	−309	295	132	−163
India, Burma, Ceylon	382	446	64	198	118	−80
South East Asia	133	142	9	60	51	−9
Japan, Korea, Formosa	38	70	32	27	6	−21
China	129	143	14	74	57	−17
USSR	105	23	−82	56	50	−6
Continental Europe	1,935	1,317	−618	749	486	−263
Ireland	222	222	−	67	77	10
Australasia	498	383	−115	348	171	−177
Total	5,795	4,085	−1,710	2,635	1,520	−1,115

Source: League of Nations, *The Network of World Trade* (Geneva: League of
Nations, 1942), p. 167.

situation had deteriorated further by 1938. For the most part imports
and exports from and to all regions had fallen in dollar terms. But what
was even more significant is that the old surplus areas of Central Africa,
South East Asia, China and Japan were now deficit areas, leaving only
South Africa as a surplus area for Britain. As these figures do not take
into account gold, they disguise the fact that Britain actually had a
deficit with South Africa as well due to gold purchases. This turn
round in Britain's trading position was a crucial part in the story of the
impact of the depression on the international trading network and
accounts for much of the disintegration of trading relations which
marks these years.

Diagram 1 shows the pattern of multilateral balances of merchandise trade for 1928 and 1938. It is striking that the values of most of the settlement flows have decreased between these years. But the only flow actually to have reversed is that between Britain, and India, South East Asia, Central Africa, etc. As already discussed, the surpluses which Britain earned there before the First World War and in the 1920s have now completely disappeared and been replaced by a deficit. Britain was now in deficit with all the regions she traded with.

British trade balances with major regions are shown on Graph 3.1 in order to examine more closely what was happening to Britain's international trading position. It shows that Britain had a substantial trade deficit with the United States and also with Latin America throughout these years. She had a temporary surplus with industrial Europe during reconstruction there from 1919 to 1924 and afterwards a deficit. India, having been a deficit area during the war, yielded a surplus until 1930, after which there was generally deficit. As for the rest of Asia, this too normally produced a deficit after 1924. Only Africa seems to have continued to provide a surplus, however small, throughout the period. This is something of an illusion, as the figures do not include gold bullion transactions, South African gold sales to Britain rendering the entire African account negative. What is clear is that Britain no longer earned vast trading surpluses in the developing world, and what small surpluses she did earn there in the 1920s for the most part disappeared in the 1930s. The disappearance of Britain's trading surpluses clearly adversely affected her ability to sustain purchases from North America and continental Europe, and her capacity to sustain large capital outflows. The king-pin of the international economy had broken.

India was the vital country in the re-orientation of multilateral settlements in the inter-war years. Graph 3.2 shows India's balance of trade. Exports show a peak in 1919/20, with a fall to 1921/2 then a rise to the inter-war peak in 1924/5, followed by decline almost continually to the trough of 1932/3. There was some recovery later in the 1930s. Imports show their inter-war peak in 1920/1, followed by modest levels in the 1920s, and much lower levels after 1929/30. The net effect of exports and imports are revealed by the line showing India's trade surplus. This shows India to have continued to enjoy her usual trade surplus during the war years, but to have had a substantial deficit in 1920/1 when imports soared, sucked in by the export boom of the previous year, and re-equipping after the dislocation of the war. Recovery from the deficit was swift, and by 1925/6 India was

Diagram 1: Multilateral Balances of Merchandise Trade, 1928, 1938

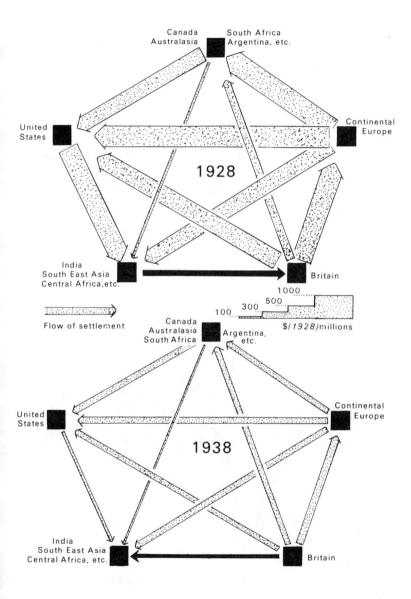

Source: League of Nations, *The Network of World Trade* (Geneva: League of Nations, 1942), pp. 78, 90.

Graph 3.1: British Trade Balances with Major Regions, 1913–38

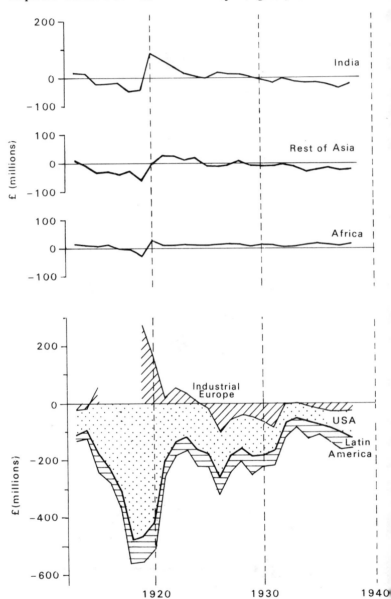

Source: B. R. Mitchell and Phyllis Deane, *Abstract of British Historical Statistics* (Cambridge: Cambridge University Press, 1971), pp. 315–27; see Appendix 3.

Graph 3.2: Indian Trade Balances, 1913–39

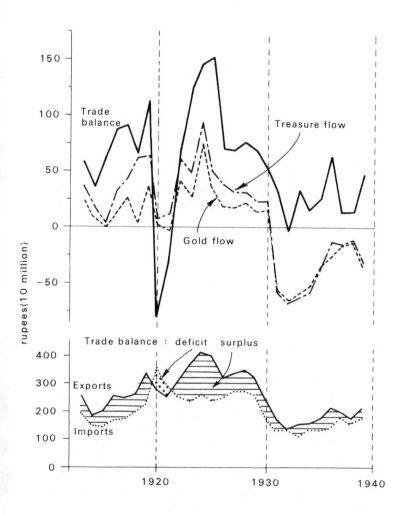

Source: *Statistical Abstracts for British India*; see Appendix 4.

experiencing her biggest trade surplus of the inter-war years. But the decline in her exports eroded this, with decline down to 1932/3 when the surplus was reduced almost to nothing. There was some recovery during the rest of the 1930s. The movement of treasure into India moved in sympathy with the trade surplus and from 1930/1 became very heavily adverse. Gold flows followed the overall treasure pattern. Clearly, the outflow of gold after 1930/1 marks a crucial change in India's international trading position, as the outflow of treasure was in marked contrast to the situation since at least the middle of the nineteenth century.[3] The explanation for this phenomenon is that agricultural prices had fallen drastically, forcing the Indian peasants to draw upon their hoards of gold and silver. These had been amassed in the prosperous years as a safeguard against leaner times. These leaner times had now come, and encouraged by rising gold prices as the rupee depreciated with sterling, the hoards were being opened and changed into cash. The gold sales cushioned the impact of the depression on India by helping to maintain purchasing power.[4]

Graph 3.3 shows India's trade balances with major regions. The decline in her deficit with Britain stands out, mirroring the picture revealed by the British figures. During the war the deficit with Britain fell considerably, but increased during the re-equipping boom of 1920/1. From then on the deficit decreased continually, with a check in the mid-1920s, and by 1931/2 had nearly been eliminated. The figures for the later 1930s are affected by the separation of Burma from India in 1937/8. With other major regions, India enjoyed surpluses of which those with America, Europe and Asia were particularly important. The American surplus was largely due to sales of jute and jute manufactures, and the surplus with Europe due to sales of jute, oil seeds, hides and skins, raw cotton and rice. The Asian surplus is worth further examination as it was so important to India and the rest of Asia. Details of the Asian surplus are shown on Graph 3.4. Just before the war Japan took over from China with Hong Kong as the largest surplus area, and this was due to her increasing purchases of raw cotton. Japan retained the leading position during the early 1920s, China with Hong Kong coming next. Ceylon was another area which yielded a good surplus because of rice sales to feed the Indian plantation labour force there. But all these areas reached their maximum levels in the mid-1920s and then began to fall away, several years before the international crisis of 1929. In the early 1930s the Japanese balance actually became negative, with some recovery later. Java was the only persistent deficit area, resulting from India's imports of sugar. This deficit was cut in the 1930s as measures were taken to restrict sugar imports.

The commodities which featured in India's exports have been examined by Venkatasubbiah and his breakdown is given in Table 3.4. One commodity missing from the pre-war list is opium, following the

Graph 3.3: Indian Trade Balances with Major Regions, 1913–39

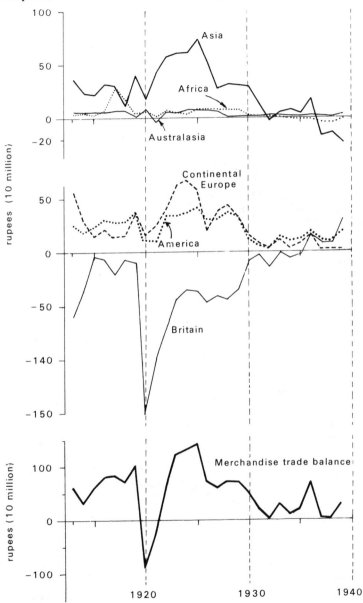

Source: *Statistical Abstracts for British India*; see Appendix 5.

Graph 3.4: Indian Trade Balances with Asia, 1913–39

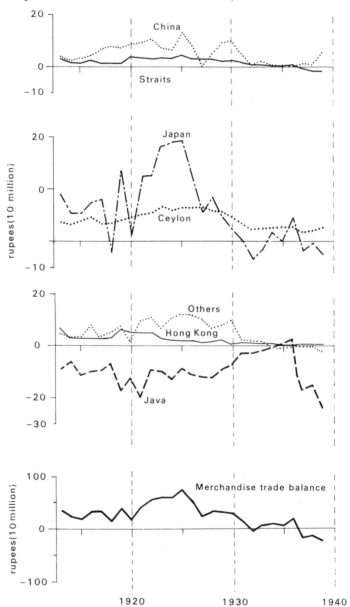

Table 3.4: Indian Exports, 1910/11 to 1939/40

	1910/11 1913/14	1914/15 1918/19	1919/20 1923/4	1924/5 1928/9	1929/30 1934/5	1934/6 1939/40
	%	%	%	%	%	%
Cotton: Raw	14.8	15.6	22.6	21.0	19.4	17.8
Cotton: Manufactures[a]	4.9	5.4	6.0	2.8	2.3	3.5
Rice	12.2	8.8	8.6	9.9	9.8	3.5
Wheat	6.2	4.8	1.3	1.7	0.2	1.0
Hides & Skins: Raw	4.6	4.6	3.3	2.3	2.4	2.4
Hides & Skins: Dressed or Tanned	1.9	3.3	2.1	2.3	3.1	3.3
Jute: Raw	10.5	6.0	6.8	9.1	7.4	8.5
Jute: Manufactures[b]	9.2	18.6	15.1	16.2	15.4	17.2
Seeds	11.1	5.6	8.0	8.0	8.4	7.7
Tea	5.9	8.1	7.3	8.7	11.3	12.6
Others	18.7	19.2	18.9	18.0	20.3	22.5
Total	100.0	100.0	100.0	100.0	100.0	100.0

Notes:

[a] Including twist and yarn.

[b] Including twist and yarn.

Source: H. Venkatasubbiah, *Foreign Trade of India: 1900–1940: A Statistical Analysis* (Bombay: Oxford University Press, 1946), Table B.

closing of the Chinese market in 1917. Raw cotton was the leading export, but jute manufactures ran a very close second, emphasising India's nascent industrialisation. Rice was less important than previously, but usually third in rank. After the separation of Burma in 1937 rice exports fell heavily, of course. Raw jute vied with seeds in importance and tea continued to grow in significance. Wheat exports declined, reflecting increased population growth and domestic consumption, and the difficulties of the international wheat market in these years. As Vera Anstey noted, it is very significant that the percentages of manufactures in India's exports went on increasing as they had done since before the turn of the century. There was also an increase in exports of processed hides and skins, wool, metals and oil seed products. India became more and more an exporter of manufactured and semi-manufactured goods, and less and less an exporter of raw materials and foodstuffs as she continued the process of industrialisation she had long since begun.[5]

Britain was the major destination for Indian exports, as Table 3.5 shows. Whilst the percentage of exports to Britain declined in the 1920s, it recovered again in the 1930s particularly following the introduction of Imperial Preference after the Ottawa conference of 1932. Europe's share of India's exports fell, largely reflecting economic and political difficulties in Germany. The position of the United States also declined, because of the depression from 1929. In Asia, Ceylon's share was maintained, but China and Hong Kong together took a declining proportion, and Japan's share fluctuated downwards. Of the various commodities, raw cotton went predominantly to Japan and by the 1930s she was taking half of India's raw cotton exports. Britain by contrast took less than a tenth, although Imperial Preference raised this a little. China and Hong Kong had been the main market for Indian cotton manufactures in the years just before and just after the war, but in the 1920s exports there fell considerably, as did the total amount of cotton manufactures exported. Her remaining overseas markets for cottons were Ceylon, the Straits Settlements, and other smaller countries in Africa and Asia, mostly in the British Empire. As for rice, Ceylon's importance as a purchaser increased, and the Straits Settlements remained important, as she too needed suitable rice for the Indian plantation workers. Germany, Britain, Austria, Hungary, Java, China and Japan all took rice, the last three according to the product of their own rice harvest. As for wheat, Britain continued to be the leading consumer right through the period. Raw hides went to Germany and skins to the United States, whilst Britain was the leading purchaser of 'manufactured' dressed and tanned hides and skins. Raw jute went to Germany, the United States, France and Britain, whilst the United States led the jute cloth market and Australia was the main purchaser of jute sacks. Seeds went to a variety of markets with Britain taking most linseed, and France and Germany groundnuts. Not surprisingly, Britain bought most tea.[6]

The main features of India's imports are shown on Table 3.6. They were affected by the imposition of protective tariffs from 1921 after India was granted fiscal autonomy. Year by year the tariffs surrounding the Indian economy were hoisted to exclude the import of goods which could be produced in India. Whilst many of these duties hit British exports to India, the introduction of Imperial Preference in 1933 favoured British and Empire products by allowing such products a small reduction in the overall high tariff levels.[7] Despite the move to protection, cotton manufactures remained the leading import item throughout, although their proportion declined consistently. Imports

Table 3.5: Destination of Indian Exports, 1913/14 to 1938/9

	1913/14	1918/19	1923/4	1928/9	1933/4	1938/9
	%	%	%	%	%	%
Britain	25.1	25.7	22.0	24.4	27.8	33.3
Germany	10.3	−	7.5	10.1	6.4	5.7
France	6.5	3.6	5.1	5.0	6.1	2.9
Italy	2.8	3.6	3.3	4.0	3.5	3.0
Belgium	5.4	−	3.7	3.4	3.0	3.3
Netherlands	1.5	−	1.3	2.5	3.1	0.8
United States	7.7	13.0	11.4	11.2	7.3	10.1
Ceylon	3.7	4.1	4.0	4.7	4.9	2.9
Straits Settlements	3.7	2.5	2.5	2.8	2.6	1.4
Hong Kong	3.8	1.7	2.2	0.6	1.0	0.5
China	4.9	1.8	4.5	1.4	2.6	1.1
Japan	7.7	14.6	13.4	9.0	10.5	10.0
Others	16.9	29.4	19.1	20.9	21.2	25.0

Source: Venkatasubbiah, *Trade of India*, pp. 31–59.

Table 3.6: Indian Imports, 1910/11 to 1939/40

	1910/11 1913/14	1914/15 1918/19	1919/20 1923/4	1924/5 1928/9	1929/30 1934/5	1935/6 1939/40
	%	%	%	%	%	%
Cotton: Manufactures[a]	36.2	35.5	28.0	28.3	18.6	11.0
Hardware, machinery, railway plant	10.0	7.7	15.6	10.2	10.9	12.4
Iron, steel, brass, copper	10.8	8.4	11.0	10.8	8.8	7.6
Oils	2.5	2.7	3.1	4.1	5.4	8.1
Sugar	8.9	9.9	7.8	7.1	4.6	0.8
Silk: manufactures	1.9	1.9	1.6	1.4	1.8	1.1
Wool: manufactures	2.2	1.2	1.0	1.8	1.7	1.5
Others	27.5	32.7	31.9	36.3	48.2	57.5
Total	100.0	100.0	100.0	100.0	100.0	100.0

Note:

[a] Including twist and yarn.

Source: Venkatasubbiah, *Trade of India*, Table A.

of hardware, machinery and railway plant also held up fairly well, and
so did iron, steel, brass and copper. Oils became more important as
motor transport spread. Where protective tariffs seem to have been
particularly effective was in reducing imports of sugar from Java. Silk
and wool manufactures provided a steady percentage of imports,
although they were proportionately of little importance. The
percentage of sundry items included as 'others' increased reflecting the
diversification of India's imports as the years went by.[8]

Britain remained the main supplier of imports to India as she had
been in the nineteenth century, as shown in Table 3.7. Yet the long

Table 3.7: Origin of Indian Imports, 1913/14 to 1938/9

	1913/14	1918/19	1923/4	1928/9	1933/4	1938/9
	%	%	%	%	%	%
Britain	63.0	54.3	60.1	47.7	36.8	29.9
Germany	6.4	–	5.1	6.1	7.8	8.8
France	1.3	1.0	0.8	1.7	1.5	0.9
Italy	0.9	1.1	0.9	2.7	3.0	1.5
Belgium	1.8	–	2.7	3.0	2.5	1.1
Netherlands	0.9	0.4	0.9	1.9	1.2	0.8
United States	3.2	7.8	5.6	8.1	8.4	7.4
Ceylon	0.4	1.6	0.6	0.7	1.3	0.9
Straits Settlements	1.9	3.4	1.9	2.3	2.1	2.1
Java	5.9	7.7	5.5	5.9	2.8	0.2
Hong Kong	0.6	0.9	0.6	0.4	0.4	0.1
China	1.2	1.3	1.2	1.7	2.2	0.6
Japan	2.5	12.1	6.2	7.1	15.4	12.8
Others	10.0	8.4	7.9	10.7	14.6	32.4

Source: Venkatasubbiah, *Trade of India*, pp. 31–69.

decline in her share of the Indian market continued, whilst Japan's
rose. Japan remained, however, a much less important supplier than
Britain and the increase in her share of the market was less than
Britain's decrease. Germany was the third most important supplier
except for the period of the war, and Java came next until restrictions
were put on her sugar in the 1930s. The United States became
increasingly important because of petroleum. Of particular imports
Britain remained the leading supplier of hardware, machinery and
railway plant, but the United States supplied increasing amounts of

machinery and Germany competed strongly in hardware. Britain faced competition from Belgian iron and steel and German brassware, whilst retaining her overall lead. The United States was originally the main supplier of petroleum, but from the late 1920s imports rose from Persia and Burma in the late 1930s. Sugar was a Javanese speciality until the protective legislation and silks came from Japan throughout. Even in woollen manufactures Britain faced competition from Italy, Germany, Japan and France.[9]

The most dramatic story concerns the decline in Britain's sales of cottons to India. Lars Sandberg has demonstrated that contrary to widely held beliefs, Japanese competition was not the principal reason for the drop in Britain's cotton sales to India. The real reason was the development of the Indian domestic cotton industry, and the tariffs which surrounded it. It was not until the 1930s that Japanese cotton imports overtook imports from Britain, but by then total imports of cottons had in any case fallen away considerably. Even before the First World War output of factory-produced cotton manufactures was growing rapidly in India and handloom production was also increasing. During the war the difficulties of shipping from Britain gave a boost to Indian production. Graph 3.5 tells the story of the situation from 1919/20. Factory production, total imports and imports from Britain all rose until 1927/8. The following year saw a fall in both factory production and imports from Britain. Whilst recovery took place in factory production which was then sustained well through to 1935/6, imports from Britain fell away severely, and so did total imports. The graph makes it quite clear that it was domestic factory production which was the chief cause of the fall in imports from Britain, not the rise in imports from Japan. The protective measures adopted played their part, and also the boycott of British cottons launched by the Congress Party in 1930. Imperial Preference in the 1930s did little to increase Britain's share of the market, but it did help keep Japanese cottons out, the rate on Japanese cottons reaching 50 per cent in 1935. Whilst it is clearly established that the domestic industry was the main gainer from the fall in imports of British cottons, it is worth noting that in fact market expansion for manufactured cottons as a whole in India came to a halt about 1927/8. From that year total sales of domestic factory production and imported cottons added together fluctuated severely on a downward path. There were obviously constraints operating in the domestic market which had their effect on imports regardless of factory production and the tariff level. These constraints were clearly a reflection of the depression, like the outflow of gold, to which they are related.[10]

Graph 3.5: Indian Factory Production and Imports of Cotton Cloth, 1919–35

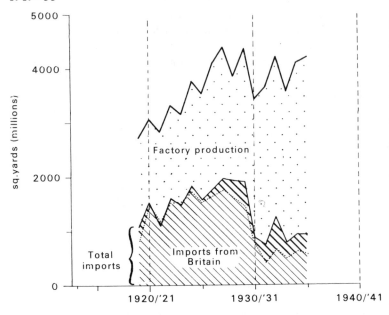

Source: Lars G. Sandberg, *Lancashire in Decline; A Study in Entrepreneurship, Technology, and International Trade* (Columbus: Ohio State University Press, 1974), p. 183; see Appendix 7.

In the years before the First World War China with Hong Kong had provided India with a large trade surplus, which went a long way to cover her deficit with Britain. But by the outbreak of war Japan had already emerged as India's most important Asian trading partner, and was to remain so until 1929/30. Yet China was still a vital part of the Asian economy and it was there that much of the rivalry between Japan and Britain was played out. In the previous century China had provided Britain with a surplus on her trade directly, quite apart from indirectly through her deficit with India. Now Britain's position in the China market was jeopardised both by the growth of industrialisation in China itself and Japanese competition.

China not including Hong Kong continued to be in deficit as before the war. This is shown on Graph 3.6. Imports exceeded exports every year. Exports reached their inter-war peak in 1929, but imports did not

Graph 3.6: Chinese Trade Balances, 1913–39

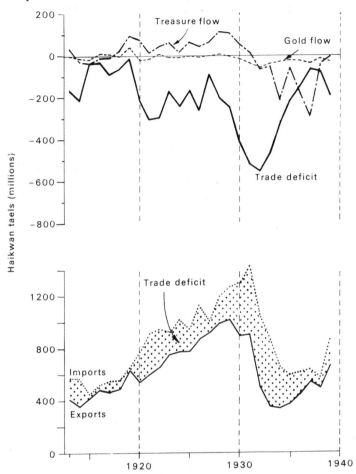

Source: Liang-lin Hsiao, *China's Foreign Trade Statistics, 1864–1949* (Cambridge, Mass: Harvard University Press, 1974), pp. 22–5, 128; see Appendix 8.

do the same until 1931. Exports hit their 1930s low in 1932 but imports not until 1938, although the figures were affected by the Japanese invasion of Manchuria. From the last six months of 1932 Manchurian figures are no longer included in the total and were treated as 'foreign' as 'Kwantung Lease Territory'. The pattern of the trade balance shows 1919 to be the year in which the overall deficit was smallest, followed by severe deficits both in the 1920s and 1930s. The years 1931 and 1932 were particularly bad. Despite the permanently adverse trade balance, there was a treasure inflow during the 1920s, and it was not until 1932 that a treasure outflow began. The inflow was due to remittances by Chinese emigrants and presumably the outflow in the 1930s was linked to a cessation of remittances as the depression bit into the incomes of overseas Chinese. Net gold investments show there to have been an outflow of gold in most years, with an increase in the outflow after 1929. It must, however, be noted that all the treasure figures are seriously distorted to an unknown extent because of smuggling.[11]

A look at Chinese trade balances with major countries, Graph 3.7, will show that China in deficit with Britain throughout the period. She was also heavily in deficit with Japan. There was a deficit with the United States in most years after 1919 and with Hong Kong until 1931. 'Others' showed a positive balance in the 1920s, but it fell heavily after 1927 and became adverse in 1931. The various commodities exported from China are given in Table 3.8. Silk and silk goods which had been the leading items before the war continued to lead until the mid-1930s but their share declined. Tea came next but was much less important than previously. Soya beans and bean cake became the leading exports

Table 3.8: Chinese Exports, 1913–36

	1913	1916	1920	1925	1928	1931	1936
	%	%	%	%	%	%	%
Silk and silk goods	25.3	22.3	18.6	22.5	18.4	13.3	7.8
Tea	8.4	9.0	1.6	2.9	3.7	3.6	4.3
Beans and bean cake	12.0	9.3	13.0	15.9	20.5	21.4	1.3
Seeds and oil	7.8	8.4	9.1	7.9	5.8	8.4	18.7
Egg and egg products	1.4	2.6	4.0	4.3	4.4	4.1	5.9
Hides, leather, skins	6.0	6.0	4.3	4.0	5.4	4.1	5.7
Ores and metals	3.3	6.3	3.2	2.9	2.1	1.6	7.7
Coal	1.6	1.2	2.3	2.6	2.9	3.0	1.6
Cotton yarn and cotton goods	0.6	0.8	1.4	2.0	3.8	4.9	3.0
Cotton: raw	4.0	3.6	1.7	3.8	3.4	2.9	4.0
Others	29.6	30.5	40.8	31.2	29.6	32.7	40.0
Total	100.0	100.0	100.0	100.0	100.0	100.0	100.0

Source: Yu-Kwei Cheng, *Foreign Trade and Industrial Development of China. An Historical and Integrated Analysis through 1948* (Washington D.C.: University Press, 1956), p. 34.

Graph 3.7: Chinese Trade Balances with Major Countries, 1913–39

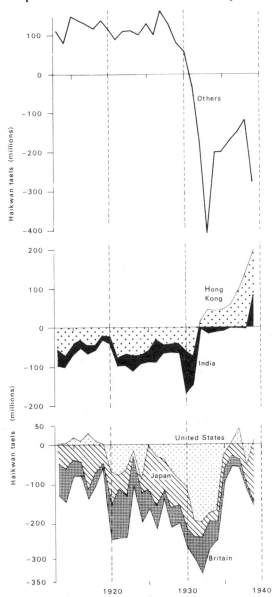

Source: Liang-lin Hsiao, *China's Foreign Trade Statistics, 1864–1949* (Cambridge, Mass.: Harvard University Press, 1974), pp. 22–5, 138–64; see Appendix 9.

by the late 1920s, but the Japanese invasion of Manchuria and the creation there of the puppet state of Manchoukuo meant that these exports from that region no longer figured in the Chinese returns. Other kinds of seeds and oils remained to be the most important item from this time. Eggs and egg products, hides, leather and skins, ores and metals, all made a contribution. Exports of cotton yarn and goods increased reflecting the onset of industrialisation in China, and coal exports also increased. Yet despite increased exports of cotton manufactures, overall raw materials increased as a proportion of China's exports, not exactly what one would expect from a country beginning to industrialise.[12]

Table 3.9 shows Japan to have been the major destination for China's exports pushing Hong Kong, the previous leader, into second place. Coal, raw cotton and wool were important in the Japanese trade and a whole variety of other products. The United States was also of

Table 3.9: Destination of Chinese Exports, 1919–36

	1919	1927	1931	1936[a]
	%	%	%	%
Britain	9.1	6.3	7.1	9.2
France	5.4	5.6	3.8	4.3
Germany	–	2.2	2.5	5.5
Hong Kong	20.8	18.5	16.3	15.1
Japan[b]	30.9	22.7	27.4	14.5
Russia	3.4	8.4	6.0	0.6
United States	16.0	13.3	13.2	26.4
Others	14.4	23.0	23.7	24.4
Total	100.0	100.0	100.0	100.0

Notes:

[a] Does not include Manchuria (Manchoukuo).

[b] Including Formosa in 1919 and 1927.

Source: Cheng, *Foreign Trade and Industrial Development of China*, p. 49.

great importance, taking oils, ores, silk and various animal products. As for 'others' this mainly meant exports to neighbouring countries where the overseas Chinese lived, including Siam, French Indo-China, the Philippines, Dutch East Indies and Malaya. Their share of China's exports increased markedly.[13]

Chinese imports are given in Table 3.10. Opium had been very

Table 3.10: Chinese Imports, 1913–36

	1913	1916	1920	1925	1928	1931	1936
	%	%	%	%	%	%	%
Cotton: goods	19.3	14.1	21.8	16.3	14.2	7.6	1.5
Cotton: yarn	12.7	12.4	10.6	4.4	1.6	0.3	0.2
Cotton: raw	0.5	1.6	2.4	7.4	5.7	12.6	3.8
Rice and wheat	3.3	6.6	0.8	6.8	5.7	10.6	4.1
Wheat flour	1.8	0.2	0.3	1.6	2.6	2.0	0.5
Sugar	6.4	7.1	5.2	9.5	8.3	6.0	2.2
Tobacco	2.9	5.8	4.7	4.1	5.1	4.4	1.8
Paper	1.3	1.8	1.9	2.0	2.4	3.2	4.1
Kerosene oil	4.5	6.2	7.1	7.0	5.2	4.5	4.2
Liquid fuel	–	0.2	0.4	0.9	1.4	1.8	4.1
Transportation materials	0.8	4.0	2.6	1.9	2.3	2.3	5.6
Chemical dyes	5.6	4.1	6.4	5.6	7.5	8.0	10.8
Iron, steel and metals	5.3	5.1	8.3	4.7	5.4	6.2	13.2
Machinery	1.4	1.3	3.2	1.8	1.8	3.1	6.4
Others	34.2	29.5	24.3	26.0	30.8	27.4	37.5
Total	100.0	100.0	100.0	100.0	100.0	100.0	100.0

Source: Cheng, *Foreign Trade and Industrial Development of China*, p. 32.

important in the previous century, but had been banned in 1917. So cotton goods led, their proportion declining over the years as industrialisation got under way in China itself. Yarn imports decreased for the same reason. Sugar, tobacco, mineral oils and paper were important too, as were chemical dyes, iron, steel, metals and machinery. Rice, wheat and flour imports varied according to the harvest in China.[14] Japan was the main supplier of Chinese imports in the 1920s, principally cotton piece goods, paper, coal, machinery, lumber and flour. Although Table 3.11 shows there to have been an apparently dramatic change in Hong Kong's position, this is largely illusory. After 1932 an improvement in the method of collection of the records meant that it was possible to identify the true origin of most of the imports coming into China by way of Hong Kong, the great transhipment and redistribution centre of the Orient. Imports previously recorded under Hong Kong were attributed to their true country of origin from that time. The United States was a much more important source of imports than before the war and by 1931 dominated, with petroleum, vehicles, machinery, metals, raw cotton and tobacco. Britain's share was much

Table 3.11: Origin of Chinese Imports, 1919-36

	1919	1927	1931	1936[a]
	%	%	%	%
Britain	9.5	7.3	8.3	11.7
France	0.5	1.4	1.5	2.0
Germany	–	3.8	5.8	15.9
Hong Kong	22.6	20.6	15.3	1.9
Japan[b]	36.3	28.4	20.0	16.3
Russia	2.1	2.2	1.7	0.1
United States	16.2	16.1	22.2	19.6
Others	12.8	20.2	25.2	32.5
Total	100.0	100.0	100.0	100.0

Notes:

[a] Does not include Manchuria (Manchoukuo).

[b] Including Formosa in 1919 and 1927.

Source: Cheng, *Foreign Trade and Industrial Development of China*, p. 48.

less than previously, largely because of the fall in her sales of cotton
manufactures taken by China. She still supplied metal manufactures
and machinery, particularly textile machinery. The share of China's
imports coming from her Asiatic neighbours with a large Chinese
population increased considerably, accounting for much of 'Others'.[15]
Probably the most crucial part of the story of China's trade between
the wars was the virtual demise of imports from Britain. Unlike the
case of India, total imports of cottons continued at a high level until
1929, whilst imports from Britain declined consistently, as shown on
Graph 3.8. Japan was ousting British cottons from the China market.
At the same time domestic production was growing rapidly with the
assistance only of the 5 per cent *ad valorem* tariff to which she was
limited by treaty. When China did achieve tariff autonomy in 1929
tariffs were raised very substantially, and were raised again in 1932
and yet again in 1934. In consequence imports were curtailed and
factory production continued to rise. Yet as in the case of India, it
appears that the overall domestic market for manufactured cottons
ceased to grow, judging by aggregate sales of imports and domestic
production. Even if the picture is less accurate than might be preferred
because of the complications of the loss of Manchuria, it is evident
that domestic production was the chief British rival, not Japan. Japan
was the main target for tariffs, however, as British textiles had already
ceased to be important.[16]

Graph 3.8: Chinese Factory Production and Imports of Cotton Cloth, 1919–36

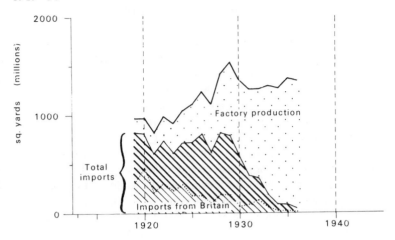

Source: Lars G. Sandberg, *Lancashire in Decline: A Study in Entrepreneurship, Technology, and International Trade* (Columbus: Ohio State University Press, 1974), pp. 192–3; see Appendix 10.

To turn now to the trade of other Asian countries, Ceylon's exports in the inter-war years centred on tea, rubber and coconut products. During the war shipping difficulties and the disincentive of fixed-price, bulk-purchase schemes by the British Government left tea planters with large stocks. The planters' associations in India and Ceylon tried to restrict their output after the war, but the emergence of the Dutch East Indies as a major producer during the 1920s led to overproduction and prices falling. By specialising in high quality Ceylon weathered the depression of the 1930s better than other tea producers. In 1933 the International Tea Regulation Scheme was signed by Ceylon, India and the Dutch East Indies, and effectively controlled production and helped sustain prices up to the war. Weak tea prices in the early years of the century encouraged planters to try rubber, and already by 1913 rubber was earning three quarters the export earnings of tea. By 1919 extensive plantings were coming to maturity, but the end of the war saw prices collapse. In 1922 the Stevenson Restriction Scheme was set up to control rubber production in Ceylon and Malaya, but it failed because the Dutch East Indies, which was emerging as a major producer, would not join. The scheme was abandoned in 1928 against a background of falling prices, which continued down into the pit of the depression. By 1932 much of the tappable area was left untapped and half the Indian labourers employed in 1929 had been laid off. Prices that year were a quarter of their 1929 level. In 1934 a new restriction scheme was introduced, this time including the Dutch East Indies, and as the international economy slowly began to revive so did the demand for rubber. Rubber was naturally more of a smallholder's industry than tea, and in 1936 smallholders held just over a fifth of the rubber acreage, not including estates under ten acres. They regarded the crop as a supplementary sideline and left it untapped when prices were too low to make it worth hiring casual workers from the village. It had been poor prices for coconut products during the war which had induced many smallholders to turn to rubber. But the coconut continued to be a major peasant crop, providing copra, oil, cake, coir, dessicated and fresh coconuts. Ceylon was the world's third largest producer of coconut exports in these years. Of the three major exports, tea was most important, rubber second and coconut products third. Tea went mainly to Britain, rubber to the United States and to Britain to a lesser extent; and coconut products went to Britain, Germany and Italy, with India becoming a purchaser in the 1930s. Rice was the most important import item to Ceylon, coming from Bengal and Burma to feed the Indian plantation workers. Cotton goods came next, with Britain increasingly being challenged by both Japan and India. By 1934 Britain was in third place, but the impact of Imperial Preference boosted Britain's share at Japan's expense after this. Coal was an important import, and so was sugar from Java. Ceylon enjoyed a trade surplus in most years from 1907 through to 1940. Her surplus with Britain for tea and rubber more than offset her deficit with India for rice. The growth of rubber exports to the United States improved Ceylon's already favourable position.[17]

Burma separated from India only on 1 April 1937, and so up to this time the development and trade of the area is subsumed into India. The development of Burma as the world's leading rice-exporting region is well known as the major triumph of peasant capitalism in the developing world. In the three years before the Second World War about 40 per cent of Burma's exports were rice, of which India was the chief purchaser, followed by Ceylon and Malaya. Another 30 per cent of her exports was petroleum, a recent development. Lead and teak were also exported. Cotton piece goods were her most important import, two-thirds of which came from India, with Japan next and Britain third. Food of various kinds and machines, including motor vehicles, were major imports.[18]

Malayan trade had been based on tin mining in the late nineteenth century and tin continued to be a major export. Primitive Chinese mining techniques gave way to gravel-pump mining, introduced by the British but soon adopted by the Chinese. Further labour saving was made possible when British and Australian companies introduced dredges, but the Chinese went on using gravel pumps successfully. By 1929 most of Malayan tin was produced by pump or dredge and the number of men employed had fallen despite increased output. Employment in the open-cast sector was negligible. Despite the new techniques, good prices and strong international demand, Malayan tin production did not expand very rapidly in the 1920s because tin reserves were becoming exhausted. In the 1930s tin output was held at the level of the 1920s because of the depression and the International Tin Control Schemes which were introduced from 1931. As in Ceylon the early years of this century saw a big expansion of rubber planting in Malaya, these two countries being the pioneer plantation-rubber areas. Also like Ceylon, the collapse of rubber prices after the war led to acceptance of the Stevenson Scheme to control production. There was particular fear that the Chinese rubber planters would be bankrupted and the Chettiar moneylenders forced to foreclose on their property, leading to a collapse of shopkeepers, traders, etc. British planters too feared the worst. As already noted, the Scheme lasted until 1928 and failed because the Dutch East Indies, who were not party to the agreement, emerged as a major producer in this period. Indeed, the Dutch East Indies benefited from the better prices resulting from the voluntary control operating in Ceylon and Malaya. The collapse of rubber prices as demand fell in the United States between 1929 and 1932 brought the industry into crisis. Thousands of workers returned to India and China from Malaya. So Malaya joined the International Rubber Regulation Scheme of 1934 along with all other major growers, including this time the Dutch East Indies. This coincided with international and American economic recovery and the rubber industry revived up until the war. Smallholders were important producers as in Ceylon and in 1933 nearly half of Malaya's rubber exports came from such peasant smallholders. They survived the depression well because they could go on producing at prices which the estates could not, rubber being a peripheral activity to most of them. So successful were the peasant smallholders that some observers have seen the Rubber Regulation Scheme as a mechanism by which the large plantations could protect their capital by preventing the small-holders from undercutting them. The banning of new planting in particular affected the smallholders. Apart from Europeans, both the Chinese and Indians were estate owners, whilst the Malayans dominated the smallholding sector. Coconut products, especially copra and oil, were produced extensively by peasant smallholders and were a significant export, although much less important than tin and rubber. Malaya was the fifth largest world exporter of coconut products and unlike rubber or tin was not subjected to controls. Production increased rapidly in the 1920s, but in 1937 the value of her exports had not quite recovered to their 1929 peak. In the 1930s Malaya added palm oil to her exports, demonstrating that despite the depression, development was still taking place in Asia. The Dutch East Indies became the world's greatest producer of palm oil during these years. Bulk shipment replaced casks, making it profitable to produce despite the low prices. It was entirely a plantation crop in both countries, unlike West Africa where it originated and was a peasant crop. But even by the end of the 1930s oil was still much less important than coconut products in Malaya. So Malayan exports consisted of rubber, which was the most important item, followed by tin, coconut products and palm oil, the latter only becoming important towards the end of the period. The United States was the leading buyer of both rubber and tin, with Britain second. Copra went to Germany and the Netherlands, palm oil to Britain and the United States; and there were rice exports, presumably re-exports, to the Dutch East Indies and Sarawak. Overall the United States was the chief buyer of Malayan exports, followed by Britain and the Dutch East Indies. As for imports, rubber from the Dutch East Indies was very important, reflecting Singapore's function as an entrepôt. Rice also featured, some for redistribution on to the Dutch East Indies, but more for domestic consumption by the Chinese and Indian immigrants. The rice came from Burma, Siam and French Indo-China. Of manufactured goods cotton textiles led, Britain being the main supplier in the 1920s but being overtaken by Japan in the 1930s, until Imperial Preference again gave Britain the advantage. So the main source of imports was the Dutch East Indies, reflecting Singapore's role as a redistribution centre, followed by Britain and Siam, with India next due to Burma's rice. As for the balance of trade, this was normally in surplus although there were deficits in 1920, 1921, 1928, 1930, 1931 and 1932.[19]

Sugar was the traditional export of the Dutch East Indies, and during the 1920s was still the leading export. A joint selling organisation had been set up during the war to co-operate over the difficulties of shipping and it continued to control nine-tenths of Javanese output.

There were many technical improvements in these years and in 1924 a new variety of cane brought a steep rise in yield. By 1929 about 180 factories were in operation and they produced nearly all the cane they milled. Peasant production was not encouraged. When the depression came importing countries protected their best sugar growers, or colonial producers. Because Holland took so little of her sugar, Java was in a very vulnerable position when trying to sell to a now restricted international market. When India, China and Japan, all big buyers, cut their imports by regulation, the industry found itself without alternative markets. So Java welcomed the Chadbourne Plan of 1931, which was an agreement between producers to have export quotas and reduce the acreage under sugar. The government supported this and the number of factories fell from 179 to 45, accompanied by a drastic reduction in acreage. As the Chadbourne Plan did not include British Empire Countries, the United States, Japan or the Soviet Union, it not surprisingly failed to achieve all that was hoped for. The advantage which the Dutch East Indies had gained by staying out of the Stevenson Scheme for rubber in the 1920s was offset by the British Empire's non-participation in the Chadbourne Plan in the 1930s. So in 1937 the International Sugar Council was set up, representing nearly all sugar producing countries, to allocate quotas. Now the industry began to revive, but this was as much due to international recovery in general and stockpiling for fear of war, as it was to the new measures. Rubber was the next most important export crop from the Dutch East Indies. Much of the early rubber had been planted on land previously under coffee, which had been attacked by disease early in the century. From 1906 the east coast of Sumatra saw a rapid development of rubber growing with Britain, France, Belgium, Holland and the United States all participating. As in other rubber areas the local peasantry soon saw the advantages of growing rubber and many Chinese started up as nurserymen to grow seedlings to sell to the smallholders. The peasants interspersed the trees with their normal crops, much as they grew coconuts. Tapping took place whenever prices made it attractive to do so. It was not until after the war that all these new plantings matured and the Dutch East Indies became a major rubber exporter. As explained previously, because the Dutch East Indies did not join the Stevenson Scheme they were able to enjoy the higher prices which resulted from it and to go on expanding production during the 1920s. But they were badly hit by the collapse of prices in 1929 and so were happy to join the International Rubber Regulation Scheme of 1934. So successful were peasant growers by this time that a special export tax was introduced in the Dutch East Indies to regulate their exports. Smallholding production was greatly underassessed, and as in the case of Malaya, there is suspicion that the whole purpose of the scheme was to protect the large estates from the smallholders. The ban on new planting hit them particularly badly. The recovery in the international demand for rubber in the late 1930s, together with the effect of restriction, made for general recovery in the industry, although peasant smallholders continued to be discriminated against. Copra and other coconut products were probably the third most important agricultural export and the coconut was essentially a peasant crop. The Dutch East Indies were the world's largest producer of coconut products between the wars, although the Philippines vied closely. Exports had begun late in the previous century and grew rapidly, so that by 1937 the value of copra was surpassed only by rubber, petroleum and tin. Coconut produce was a traditional staple of the people and cultivating and preparing it for sale required little capital. Chinese middlemen operated primitive kilns to dry the copra. Like other agricultural products the industry suffered the price swings of the depression, but on the whole fared reasonably well, without the assistance of restriction schemes. Tobacco exports dated back to before the war and there was considerable expansion during the 1920s as foreign firms established factories in Java and sought increased supplies from both peasants and estates. Seed, fertiliser and credit were often provided for the smallholders, who also grew much of the coffee which was exported. An estate crop in the previous century, the estates had switched from coffee to rubber and tea when disease struck. Dispersed smallholdings were less susceptible and by 1929 more than half the total output and nearly three-quarters of the exports were peasant grown. When prices fell subsequently the peasants began to lose interest, but after 1936 recovery took place. Tea production expanded considerably in the thirty years before the depression hit it. The introduction of British Imperial Preference in 1932 dealt the industry another severe blow and prices fell to a quarter of their 1926 level. So in 1933 the Dutch East Indies' planters joined the International Tea Regulation Scheme with Ceylon and India, limiting exports by licence and banning new planting. In 1938 the planters were replaced by government representatives on the International Tea Committee. The level of exports kept up fairly well in the 1930s but the restriction schemes only had moderate success in raising prices. Most of the output came from Western-owned estates, and only about a fifth from peasant smallholders, who lacked the facilities for preparing tea and the knowledge of the tastes of foreign consumers. Normally they sold undried leaf to be processed by plantation or independent factories. As in the case of Malaya, the oil palm only came to be cultivated extensively in the inter-war years. Bulk shipment of oil began in 1925/6, freeing the industry from the expensive chore of casking. The industry survived the depression better than many other plantation industries as like Malaya the area was a cheap producer in world terms. There were no restriction schemes and in the 1930s the acreage expanded considerably, many rubber planta- tions shifting to palm oil as a means of diversifying and risk-spreading. Sumatra was the major production area and the United States the main market. By the outbreak of war the Dutch East Indies were the world's greatest palm-oil producers, the crop being entirely estate grown. Cinchona, whose bark was used for quinine production, was a less important plantation crop. Production for export increased rapidly after 1933 and many peasants took up the crop at this time. Restric- tions by producers prevented the fall in prices experienced by other crops in the depression, but stocks piled up in consequence. From 1934 the industry was put under government supervision at the planters' request, but peasants, who produced only a tiny percentage of the crop, were largely exempt. Before leaving agricultural exports of the Dutch East Indies it can be commented that most of the estate crops were introduced by Europeans. Yet peasants took them up when it was obvious that they could be grown profitably. So it is hard to distinguish clearly between peasant and estate production. Just before the Second World War the estates grew all the latex and palm oil, most of the sugar, cinchona and cocoa, the larger share of tea and tobacco and over half the dry rubber. Peasant smallholders produced most of the coconut products, coffee and minor crops like pepper, kapok, tapioca, other oils, nutmegs and mace, substantial quantities of dry rubber, tobacco and tea and all the rice, maize, areca nuts, peanuts and peanut oil. Probably half the exports were produced by smallholders.

Petroleum was the leading mineral export, ranking third after sugar and rubber in the list of exports. Early trials dated back into the previous century, but the big step forward came with the combination of Royal Dutch and Shell in 1907. By 1913 exports were already substantial and other companies entered the field in the 1920s and 1930s. Total output of crude oil rose from 1,500 thousand metric tons in 1913 to 7,400 thousand metric tons in 1938, when there were seven refineries in operation, three in Sumatra, three in Java and one in East Borneo. The industry was not seriously affected by the depression, although the value of exports in 1937 was only slightly more than in

1929. Tin was the other mineral export of significance, the exploitation of the tin deposits going back into the previous century. Then primitive Chinese methods were employed, and there was considerable Chinese immigration. After the turn of the century production grew, particularly during the war, and expansion went on until 1929. Gravel pumping was introduced in the early years of the century and from 1920 dredging became the principal method of extraction. Dredging favoured large-scale European organisations, but the Chinese carried on working land unsuited to these methods which they leased. Much of the tin ore was exported to Singapore for smelting, but after 1933 the ore went to a new smelter in Arnhem. When international restriction schemes came in at the height of the depression the Dutch East Indies were reluctant to join as they were low-cost producers who could undercut their international competitors. But the persistence of low prices forced them to join the International Tin Committee in 1931 which controlled 95 per cent of world output. By the end of the decade the recovery of prices meant that her exports were valued at their all-time high.

To summarise the Dutch East Indies exports, sugar was the leader in the 1920s with over 20 per cent of the total, but this was considerably reduced in the 1930s when India in particular, but also China and Japan, restricted imports. Rubber was next most important and replaced sugar as the leader in the 1930s. Petroleum followed and even exceeded sugar in the last decade before the war. Tobacco, copra, tin, tea and coffee all figured, as did palm oil towards the end of the period. Exports went to the Netherlands principally, and to Singapore for processing and redistribution. British India was a major purchaser of sugar in the 1920s, but then restricted imports. The United States bought quantities of rubber and tin, but Japan's purchases were of no significance. As for imports, cottons were pre-eminent, followed by rice, although rice imports declined in the 1930s. There was a miscellany of other imports including foodstuffs and assorted manufactured goods such as metal and engineering products. Imports came mainly from the Netherlands, but Singapore was important because of her redistribution role. Japan was also a major supplier, increasing her share of the market in the 1930s. Britain was a fairly important supplier and purchaser, although her share declined after Imperial Preference came in. Generally the Dutch East Indies enjoyed a trade surplus, although 1921 was an exception.[20]

Apart from the Dutch East Indies, the Philippines were the other great sugar producer in Asia. Sugar exports dated back to the Spanish period of the previous century, but with the advantage from 1909 of duty-free access to the colonial power, the United States, the industry expanded quickly. Modern methods and processing equipment helped and the industry prospered in the 1920s. Her dependence on the United States protected her from the fall in commodity prices which began in the mid-1920s, and it was not until the American economy collapsed in 1929 that difficulties arose. In the early 1930s restrictions were introduced on the amount of sugar which could be imported into the United States duty-free, because of pressure from American interests in Cuba and the United States itself. Exports were now checked, but the Philippines continued to fare better than other exporting nations in Asia. Coconut products followed sugar in importance, and the Philippines were second only to the Dutch East Indies in exports of these commodities. Peasant smallholders were responsible for the coconut products and production trebled between 1910 and 1930. Hemp came next in importance, then tobacco, which was of much less significance. In the mid-1920s sugar provided 30 per cent of exports, coconut products 25 per cent, hemp 20 per cent and tobacco 5 per cent. This pattern was maintained during the next decade for the most part, except that hemp declined quite considerably. There was also some gold production. Imports resembled the pattern for other Asian countries, with cotton goods leading followed by a multitude of manufactured items. The United States was the major trading partner for exports and imports as one might expect of the colonial power, with Japan the only other trading partner of much size. Generally the Philippines enjoyed a trade surplus, with 1913, 1919, 1921 and 1938 being deficit years.[21]

The development of Siam as a rice exporter parallels the development of Burma and was one of the great triumphs of peasant enterprise from the middle of the nineteenth century. After 1914 this dynamic growth continued, carried out by the Siamese peasantry themselves. Chinese immigrants confined themselves to trade and commerce and did not become rice farmers. Individual peasants acted on their own initiative and there was very little government participation. As they saw the possibility of earning new cash incomés by growing rice, they cleared and planted new land. Railways constructed to the north and north-east of Bangkok to export rice in the inter-war years encouraged expansion in ever more distant regions. Tin exports also date back into the nineteenth century and with rubber and teak accounted for the rest of Siam's exports. Tin came mainly from the peninsular south, particularly the island of Phuket. The first tin dredge was introduced in 1907 and soon there were more, representing the influx of Western firms in a business previously dominated by Chinese using elementary methods. Although the number of dredges went on increasing, the Chinese still produced tin by the old methods and in 1936/7 were still producing about two-fifths of the total output. By this time the simple traditional Chinese smelters had been eliminated by competition from modern smelters in Malaya, to which the ore was sent. Teak exports also go back to before 1900, the forests being in the north and the logs floated down-river to Bangkok or into Burma. Because teak was widely used domestically for furniture, shipbuilding and houses, the proportion exported was low. British, Danish and French companies operated in the teak trade, but exports declined throughout the period. Rubber was a late arrival in Siam and only became a significant export in the late 1930s. Like tin, it was a product of the peninsula south and most of it was shipped to Malaya for treatment and transhipment. This expansion was brought about by Siamese, Malayan and Chinese smallholders, and there were few plantations of any size. So a brief examination of Siam's exports shows that rice dominated with about 70 per cent, with tin about 10 per cent. In the 1930s rice declined proportionately and tin increased, and rubber became noticeable. Imports followed the standard pattern with cottons dominating, followed by the usual array of miscellaneous items. Mineral oils were growing in importance, reflecting the rise of motor transport. Malaya was the leading destination for Siam's exports, due to rice, tin and rubber, most of which went through Singapore or Penang. Hong Kong and China took much rice. Britain was an important supplier of imports, but by the 1930s had been overtaken by Japan. The years 1920, 1934 and 1938 appear to have been deficit years for Siam's trade, otherwise she seems to have enjoyed a surplus.[22]

French Indo-China was another rice-exporting nation. Up to 1931 rice accounted for about two-thirds of total export value. Rice exports increased as canals were cut across central and western Cochin China, much as the building of railways in Siam expanded rice production. The amount exported each year fluctuated according to harvest conditions both at home and abroad. Indo-China's rice was of inferior quality to that of Burma or Siam because of the mixed grains it consisted of. The numerous rice varieties cultivated there reflect different soil, climate and irrigation conditions and they were all mixed together by the Chinese merchants who handled the trade. After 1931 rice began to decline as an export in relation to other products, particularly maize and rubber. From 1932 to 1937 corn was Indo-China's second export product. Long cultivated by the peasantry as a second food crop, the increase in exports was due to rising demand in France, helped by preference accorded there to colonial products. Rubber differed from rice and corn by being a plantation crop developed by Europeans. It was not until 1912 that the first rubber plantings began to bear, but considerable expansion followed. Government help was provided for the industry when prices fell in the early 1920s, and further help in the form of loans was made available when the International Rubber Regulation Scheme came in in 1934. In 1937 rice, corn and rubber accounted for about four-fifths of Indo-China's exports, and coal was the only other export of any significance. Small quantities of copra, cassava, tea, coffee and pepper were also exported, pepper being a Chinese speciality. As for imports, Indo-China purchased the same sorts of articles as other tropical regions, with manufactured articles, particularly cottons, predominating. By the end of the period rayon was competing with cotton. Cotton yarn imports declined in the 1930s due to the establishment of mills in Tonkin. Metal products, including machines, and machinery followed textiles in importance. In particular there was equipment for development purposes such as bar steel and iron, forged and rolled zinc and copper, rails and construction parts, locomotives, parts, tools, etc. As the period passed by there were increased imports of motor cars and motor cycles, and petroleum products.

At the beginning of the period Asia was more important than France in Indo-China's trade, because of her rice sales, but in the last decade before the war France became the leading trading area. Asian purchases declined because of the depression at a time when colonial preference stimulated French buying. France was always the most important source of imports and purchaser of exports, but her best Asian customer was Hong Kong, through which much of Indo-China's trade with Japan, the Philippines, the Netherlands Indies, Australia, and even Europe and the United States was channelled. China and France were the main markets for rice. Japan was not a large buyer of rice as she followed a policy of self-sufficiency, and even after the signing of a reciprocity treaty in 1932 imports from Japan declined. Rice exports to the Dutch East Indies also fell in the 1930s as the government there encouraged a return to rice growing from producing export crops. Singapore was an important export destination, rice being consumed there by Chinese immigrants, and rice and other goods being transhipped to other places. Imports from Singapore consisted largely of jute sacks from India.

Overall, Indo-China enjoyed a trade surplus in most years, with 1923 and 1931 being exceptions.[23]

It has already been established that Africa was much less important then Asia in world trade, even though both regions were increasing their share. Frankel's analysis of Africa's trade is given in Table 3.12 and gives a detailed picture of the trade of the various African countries south of the Sahara. South Africa dominated Africa's trade, providing more than half of Africa's exports and taking about half of her imports. Nigeria followed, a long way behind, with up to a tenth of her exports and a twentieth of her imports. By 1935 the Rhodesias were ahead of Nigeria. British Africa was overwhelmingly more important than all the other African territories added together, providing over four-fifths of the exports and taking about four-fifths of imports.

The development of South Africa was based on diamonds and gold, although diamonds declined in favour of gold during the inter-war years. Gold provided over 50 per cent of her exports in the early 1920s and over 70 per cent by 1935, whilst diamonds fell from 10 per cent to just over 2 per cent, being surpassed by wool, the third export item in rank. The diamond market had proved very sensitive to the depression. Gold was the powerhouse of South African development and the motivating force behind infrastructural construction, particularly the railways and other supporting services to the mines. Imports were made up of many items of which foodstuffs led, and cottons and apparel featured strongly. Even before the First World War motor vehicles were being imported and they increased their share throughout, in 1935 comprising a tenth of imports. Petroleum imports rose accordingly. Machinery and metal manufacture of all kinds came in quantities. Britain was South Africa's main trading partner taking nearly 90 per cent of her exports in 1913 and providing well over 50 per cent of her imports. This domination decreased a little in the 1920s when India became an increasing destination for exports, but Britain's position recovered in the 1930s when the price of gold, of which Britain was the top recipient, increased. The United States was a big supplier of imports throughout, especially motor vehicles and petroleum. South Africa was usually in surplus with Britain and had minor deficits with other countries, but still had an overall surplus. Because of the importance of gold in her exports, her trade suffered less than any other Asian or African country in these years.[24]

Nigeria, the second biggest African international trader, saw considerable diversification in its exports in the inter-war years, reflecting the enterprise of her people. Palm products had been the

Table 3.12: African Trade, 1913, 1924, 1929 and 1935

	1913					1924					1929					1935				
	Exports		Imports		Balance	Exports		Imports		Balance	Exports		Imports		Balance	Exports		Imports		Balance
	£000	%	£000	%	£000	£000	%	£000	%	£000	£000	%	£000	%	£000	£000	%	£000	%	£000
Gambia	655	0.64	611	0.76	44	856	0.58	533	0.44	323	783	0.45	539	0.32	244	376	0.21	466	0.36	-90
Sierra Leone	1,376	1.34	1,324	1.66	52	1,510	1.03	1,649	1.36	-139	1,319	0.76	1,558	0.94	-239	1,556	0.89	1,113	0.86	443
Gold Coast	5,014	4.90	3,500	4.39	1,514	9,590	6.60	7,116	5.87	2,474	12,401	7.21	9,530	5.75	2,871	9,241	5.32	7,274	5.63	1,967
Nigeria	6,779	6.62	6,006	7.54	773	14,384	9.90	10,805	8.92	3,579	17,581	10.23	13,040	7.86	4,541	11,197	6.44	7,662	5.93	3,535
British West Africa total	13,824	13.51	11,441	14.37	2,383	26,340	18.13	20,103	16.60	6,237	32,084	18.67	24,667	14.88	7,417	22,370	12.88	16,515	12.79	5,855
Kenya	444	0.43				2,240	1.54				2,746	1.59				2,978	1.71			
Uganda	564	0.55				3,897	2.68				4,275	2.48				3,631	2.09			
(Kenya & Uganda)	(1,008)	(0.98)	2,742	3.44	-1,734	(6,137)	(4.22)	6,255	5.16	-118	(7,021)	(4.08)	8,208	4.95	-1,187	(6,609)	(3.80)	4,577	3.54	-2,032
Nyasaland	201	0.19	192	0.24	9	564	0.38	543	0.44	21	589	0.34	735	0.44	-146	736	0.42	609	0.47	127
Tanganyika	1,778	1.73[a]	2,668	3.35	-890	2,611	1.79	1,974	1.63	637	3,722	2.16	4,021	2.42	-299	3,445	1.98	2,711	2.10	734
Zanzibar	604	0.59	717	0.90	-113	1,406	0.96	1,164	0.96	242	1,269	0.73	1,138	0.68	131	655	0.37	721	0.55	-66
British East Africa total	3,591	3.51	6,319	7.94	-2,728	10,718	7.37	9,936	8.20	782	12,601	7.33	14,102	8.50	-1,501	11,445	6.58	8,618	6.67	2,827
N. Rhodesia	195	0.19	247	0.31	-52	406	0.27	622	0.51	-216	819	0.47	3,551	2.14	-2,732	4,668	2.68	2,854	2.21	1,814
S. Rhodesia	3,297	3.22	2,782	3.49	515	5,120	3.52	3,521	2.90	1,599	6,609	3.84	6,783	4.09	-174	8,077	4.65	5,482	4.24	2,595
Rhodesia total	3,492	3.41	3,029	3.80	463	5,526	3.80	4,143	3.42	1,383	7,428	4.32	10,334	6.23	-2,906	12,745	7.33	8,336	6.46	4,409
British Africa total (except S. Africa)	20,907	20.44	20,789	26.12	118	42,584	29.31	34,182	28.23	8,402	52,113	30.33	49,103	29.63	3,010	46,560	26.80	33,469	25.93	13,091
South Africa	64,565	63.13	40,374	50.74	24,191	80,699	55.55	63,627	52.55	17,072	89,031	51.81	79,042	47.69	9,989	97,931	56.38	73,173	56.70	24,758
South West Africa	3,515	3.43[a]	2,171	2.72	1,344	2,851	1.96	1,746	1.44	1,105	3,524	2.05	2,993	1.80	531	2,474	1.42	1,428	1.10	1,045
Southern Africa total	68,080	66.57	42,545	53.46	25,535	83,550	57.51	65,373	53.99	18,177	92,555	53.86	82,035	49.50	10,520	100,404	57.81	74,601	57.81	25,803
British Africa total	88,987	87.01	63,334	79.59	25,653	126,134	86.82	99,555	82.22	26,579	144,668	84.19	131,138	79.13	13,530	146,964	84.61	108,070	83.70	38,894
French W. Africa	5,000	4.88	6,030	7.57	-1,030	7,649	5.26	8,935	7.37	-1,286	9,396	5.46	10,676	6.44	-1,280	9,432	5.43	8,946	6.93	486
French Equ. Africa	1,468	1.43	834	1.04	634	513	0.35	549	0.45	-36	1,223	0.71	2,238	1.35	-1,015	2,351	1.35	2,271	1.76	80
Togo	457	0.44[b]	532	0.66	-75	513	0.35	640	0.53	-70	678	0.39	822	0.49	-144	487	0.28	418	0.32	69
Cameroons	1,103	1.07[b]	1,629	2.04	-526	783	0.53	854	0.70	-71	1,370	0.79	1,565	0.94	-195	1,338	0.77	864	0.66	474
French Africa total	8,028	7.85	9,025	11.34	-997	9,659	6.64	10,982	9.07	-1,323	12,667	7.37	15,301	9.23	-2,634	13,608	7.83	12,499	9.68	1,109
Angola	1,068	1.04	1,697	2.13	-629	1,471	1.01	1,776	1.46	-305	2,610	1.51	2,909	1.75	-299	2,018	1.16	1,495	1.15	523
Mozambique	1,678	1.64	2,341	2.94	-663	2,617	1.80	3,146	2.59	-529	3,089	1.79	4,537	2.73	-1,448	1,753	1.00	2,763	2.14	-1,010
Guinea	310	0.30	323	0.40	-13	416	0.28	513	0.42	-97	458	0.26	401	0.24	57					
Portuguese Africa total	3,056	2.98	4,361	5.48	-1,305	4,504	3.10	5,435	4.48	-931	6,157	3.58	7,847	4.73	-1,690	3,771	2.17	4,258	3.29	-487
Belgian Congo	2,190	2.14	2,850	3.58	-660	4,970	3.42	5,103	4.21	-133	8,326	4.84	11,428	6.89	-3,102	9,336	5.37	4,204	3.25	5,132
Non-British Africa total	13,274	12.98	16,236	20.40	-2,962	19,133	13.17	21,520	17.77	-2,387	27,150	15.80	34,576	20.86	-7,426	26,715	15.38	20,961	16.24	5,754
Total	102,261	100.00	79,570	100.00	22,691	145,267	100.00	121,075	100.00	24,192	171,818	100.00	165,714	100.00	6,104	173,679	100.00	129,031	100.00	44,648

Notes: [a] Transferred to Britain after First World War. [b] Transferred to France after First World War.

Source: S. H. Frankel, *Capital Investment in Africa: Its Course and Effects* (London: Oxford University Press, 1938), pp. 194–5, 196–7.

basis of her development in the previous century, with a little tin after the turn of the century. But from 1913 groundnuts and cocoa, both peasant crops, expanded quickly, groundnuts being helped by the extension of railway building to the north. By 1935 palm products were contributing only 37 per cent of exports, with groundnuts nearly 20 per cent, cocoa over 10 per cent and tin 11 per cent, only tin being a product of foreign enterprise. Nigeria's experience amply demonstrates the responsiveness of African peasants to increasing opportunities. Imports to Nigeria were cottons and foodstuffs of which stockfish was a notable item, fulfilling a need for high protein. Motor vehicles and petroleum imports increased and so did iron and steel manufactures. Britain was the main purchaser of exports and supplier of imports, but, except for the war years, Germany was a prominent buyer of palm kernels. Nigeria was usually in trade surplus, except for 1920–3. Her deficit with Britain was more than covered by her surpluses with Germany, the United States and France.[25]

After Nigeria came the Gold Coast, her exports also being based on the produce of her peasant farmers, principally cocoa, and there was some gold. Negligible at the turn of the century, cocoa exports grew speedily and by the 1920s accounted for three-quarters of her trade. They fell back a little in the 1930s because of the fall in prices and the rise in price of her gold exports. By this time nearly half the world's production of cocoa came from the Gold Coast. Her imports were the usual cottons-dominated miscellany, with motor vehicles and petroleum ever more important. Britain was the leading trading partner, but Germany bought large quantities of cocoa. Usually in deficit with Britain, her surplus with other countries like Germany, the Netherlands, France and the United States tended to give her an overall surplus.[26]

Sierra Leone and the Gambia, the other two British possessions in West Africa, were of minor importance. Sierra Leone supplied only about one per cent of Sub-Saharan Africa's exports, and the Gambia less than that. Palm kernels were the main export from Sierra Leone, and kola nuts, an African stimulant, bought by Nigeria. The Gambia exported groundnuts. These two countries were usually in deficit with Britain, but in surplus overall by way of their sales to Germany and other European buyers. Their imports followed the typical pattern.[27]

Unlike West Africa, East Africa was a region where economic activity, both European and African, was heavily dependent on government activity, particularly the building of roads and railways. This was especially so of Kenya and Uganda, who between them provided about 4 per cent of Africa's exports. The building of the Kenya and Uganda railway opened up the region to agricultural exports and the Africans responded quickly to the new commercial opportunities. The development of Uganda remained largely in African hands, but there was European settlement in Kenya. The accounts do not separate the trade of Kenya and Uganda and for much of the period half the exports were cotton, with smaller percentages of coffee, sisal and maize. Of these cotton was produced by peasants in Uganda, the whole development of cotton production there dating only from 1905. Coffee and sisal were grown on European plantations in Kenya and maize was a peasant crop in Kenya. Hides and skins were also a peasant product, so that it can be said that the Africans produced a bigger proportion of exports than the Europeans. India emerged as the leading purchaser of Ugandan cotton in the 1920s and 1930s, coffee and maize went to Britain and sisal to Britain and Belgo-Luxemburg. Cottons dominated Kenyan and Ugandan imports, of which Japan was the leading supplier, followed by Britain and India. There were also substantial imports of iron and steel building sections and parts, galvanised sheets, rails, sleepers, fishplates, tubes, pipes and fittings, and various machines and vehicles of which motor vehicles from Canada and the United States stand out. Petroleum also featured. This reflected the development which was taking place, as does the fact that the colony usually had a trade deficit as it bought more abroad than it sold, particularly for development purposes.[28]

Zanzibar's exports were cloves and copra, the cloves going to India and the Dutch East Indies, the copra going to France and Italy, with India overall the leading export market. Rice and cottons were her major imports, with India the chief supplier. She enjoyed a trade surplus in the 1920s but ran into heavy deficits in the 1930s.[29]

Nyasaland was of minor significance, but counted more than Zanzibar. Its exports were peasant-grown cotton and tobacco, of which tobacco led. She also exported labour to Southern Rhodesia and South Africa. European-grown tea began to be exported in the 1930s. The region's development was held back by the fact that it was not until 1935 that the Protectorate first had direct railway connection with the sea.[30]

Tanganyika's exports featured sisal strongly, a crop introduced by the Germans before 1914. Exports increased during the 1920s for this plantation crop and accounted for half the total in 1931. Then there was a catastrophic fall in prices which reduced the share of the crop, even though the quantity exported continued to rise, a phenomenon seen in most tropical agricultural exporters at this time. Peasant-grown coffee and cotton were the other exports and gold became important in the 1930s. If sisal, cotton, coffee and gold accounted for three-quarters of exports in 1936, the remaining quarter was made up of groundnuts, sesame, cocoa, beeswax, ghee, tobacco and grain, mainly of peasant production. Peasant production can be said to have predominated there.[31]

In 1938 Southern Rhodesia was second only to South Africa as a mineral producer in Africa. At least 27 minerals were mined, of which asbestos, coal, chrome and copper ranked highly, but gold over-shadowed all. Most of the gold was produced in small mines, rather than large operations whose share of total output actually fell. The only non-mineral exports worth mentioning were maize and tobacco, some of the maize being peasant produce. Britain bought most of Rhodesian exports of gold, tobacco and maize, and supplied many of her imports which included a high proportion of machinery, iron and steel goods and motor vehicles. She was usually in surplus because of her gold exports.[32]

In the space of about ten years Northern Rhodesia developed from almost nothing to being one of the pre-eminent mineral territories in the continent. This was due to the exploitation of the copper field, which transformed the economic structure of the territory. In 1924 there was only one copper mine and that worked intermittently. But a revival of interest in copper production and new discoveries led to the recognition of a giant field well suited to rapid development. Railways were built to link with the mines, so that by 1938 there was railway connection with Biera on the east, South Africa on the south and with Lobito Bay via the Rhodesia and Benguella Railways on the west. The depression led to a cessation of development after 1932, but as the international economy recovered expansion began again. Thus copper was the principal export of Northern Rhodesia and tobacco the only agricultural export worth mentioning. Britain bought most of the copper, but Germany and the United States were also purchasers. Her imports reflect the fact that considerable economic progress was taking place, with large quantities of metal and engineering products and cottons much less prominent than in many Asian and African countries.[33]

The characteristics of South West Africa were its size, poverty and the importance of diamonds in its economic development. Even during the German period much capital had come from British investors and during the war the railway system was linked to the South African network. The exports of the colony were hit by the depression which affected the diamond trade, but there was recovery when the diamond trade revived as the world economy pulled out of the slump. Her copper trade, second in importance after diamonds, was also badly hit, and South West Africa was probably the worst-affected country in Africa. But she generally had a trade surplus.[34]

Peasant enterprise was the mainspring of development in French West Africa. Senegal specialised in groundnuts, Guinea in cocoa, the Ivory Coast in timber, Dahomey and Togo in palm produce. Of these Senegal's groundnuts were most important, and date back as an export far into the previous century. The extension of the railways encouraged the spread of the crop, and although exports were hit by the depression they had recovered by 1936. Coffee exports from Ivory Coast began in this period and in the 1930s, bananas from Guinea.[35]

The exports of French Equatorial Africa were worth less than a quarter those of French West Africa in 1935 and even less than South West Africa. Yet the trade of the area grew quickly in the 1920s and 1930s as timber stands there were put to the axe. Palm products also featured. Expansion was assisted by the building of the Congo-Point Noire Railway after 1924. The French Cameroons exported palm produce, with some cocoa, timber and groundnuts. Like other palm producers she was badly hit by the depression.[36]

The importance of Portuguese East Africa lay in the fact that the two main railways, built with British capital, to Rhodesia and Nyasaland traversed the territory. Peasant-grown groundnuts were the colony's main export crop and there was some maize. Sugar and sisal, both plantation crops, developed over the period.[37]

Angola's main export was diamonds, followed by maize, coffee and sugar. Dried fish was a notable export to begin with, but its value dropped in the later years.[38]

Mining was the main feature of the development of the Belgian Congo. In 1932 there were approximately 200 companies operating there. The Société Generale was the key group, controlling nearly all the production of copper, diamonds, radium, cement and much of the gold. Palm-oil exports grew over this period, particularly because of the activities of Lever Brothers and its subsidiary Société des Huileries du Congo Belge. By 1935 the Congo was the world's third largest palm-oil exporter and a major exporter of kernels. Cotton exports increased in the 1930s.[39]

In concluding this chapter on trade, it is possible to draw together the features of the experience of the developing countries of Africa and

Graph 3.9: Exports from Selected Developing Countries, 1913–38

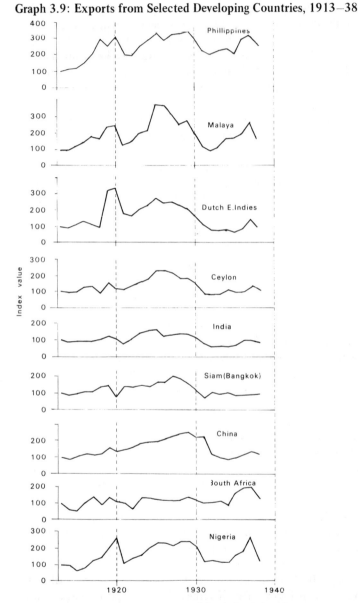

Source: League of Nations, *International Trade Statistics* (Geneva: League of Nations, 1932, etc.); League of Nations, *Memorandum on International Trade and Balance of Payments: Trade Statistics of Sixty-Four Countries* (Geneva: League of Nations, 1928, etc.); see Appendix 11.

Graph 3.10: Imports to Selected Developing Countries, 1913–38

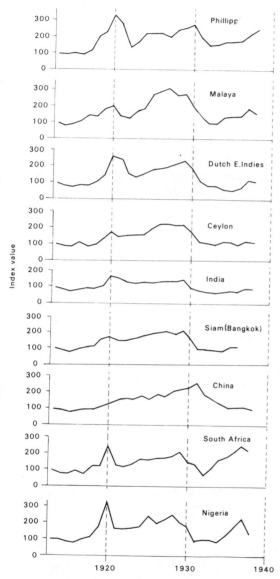

Source: League of Nations, *International Trade Statistics* (Geneva: League of Nations, 1932, etc.); League of Nations, *Memorandum on International Trade and Balance of Payments: Trade Statistics of Sixty-Four Countries* (Geneva: League of Nations, 1929, etc.); see Appendix 11.

Asia in this period, by representing their exports on Graph 3.9. This shows how exports from India, Ceylon, Malaya, Dutch East Indies, Siam, the Philippines, South Africa and Nigeria fluctuated. The boom years of the 1920s stand out, and the depression years of the early 1930s. What is particularly significant is that for many countries the fall in export earnings comes before 1929, the year traditionally associated with the onset of the depression. For India, Ceylon, the Dutch East Indies and Malaya, the downturn came in 1925 or 1926, and for Siam it was 1927. Only for the Philippines, which was heavily dependent on the United States, and for China, Nigeria and South Africa was 1929 the year of the downturn. So for much of the developing world the slide down into the depression was already taking place three or four years before the Wall Street crash. This was because of the fall in prices which agricultural products were experiencing at this time the world over. A look at the imports of these same countries (Graph 3.10) shows 1929 to be a much more crucial year, and only Malaya and Nigeria show a decline in imports before 1929. In China's case imports go on rising until 1931. Presumably imports were being propped up in many countries by capital inflows for development, despite the falling level of their exports. As for trade balances, Appendix 11 shows that nearly all the countries had trade surpluses throughout the period since 1913, although several had temporary deficits about 1920 or 1921, notably South Africa, Dutch East Indies, Siam, India, Ceylon, Malaya and Nigeria, with China being in deficit throughout the period. Even at the height of the depression most countries remained in surplus, except for Siam in one year, Ceylon in one year, and Malaya in four years.

Notes

1. League of Nations, *The Network of World Trade* (Geneva: League of Nations, 1942), p. 78.
2. S. B. Saul, *Studies in British Overseas Trade, 1870–1914* (Liverpool: Liverpool University Press, 1960), p. 58.
3. Latham, *International Economy*, p. 71.
4. P. J. Thomas, 'India in the World Depression', *Economic Journal*, 45 (1935), p. 475; A. J. H. Latham, 'Multilateral Merchandise Trade Imbalances and Uneven Economic Development in India and China', *Journal of European Economic History*, 7 (1978), pp. 33–60; B. R. Tomlinson, 'Britain and the Indian Currency Crisis, 1930–2', *Economic History Review*, 32 (1979), pp. 96–8.
5. H. Venkatasubbiah, *Foreign Trade of India: 1900–1940, A Statistical Analysis* (Bombay: Oxford University Press, 1946), pp. 31–69; J. Adams III, 'Economic Change, Exports and Imports: The Case of India, 1870–1960'. PhD

dissertation, University of Texas, 1966, pp. 132–51; Vera Anstey, *The Economic Development of India* (London: Longmans, Green & Co., 3rd edition, 1949), p. 338; Latham, *Multilateral Merchandise Trade Imbalances*, pp. 33–60.

6. Venkatasubbiah, *Trade of India*, pp. 31–69; *Statistical Abstracts for British India.*

7. Adams, *Economic Change*, pp. 390–5; Clive Dewey, 'The End of the Imperialism of Free Trade: The Eclipse of the Lancashire Lobby and the Concession of Fiscal Autonomy to India', in *The Imperial Impact: Studies in the Economic History of Africa and India* (London: Athlone Press, 1978), pp. 35–67.

8. Venkatasubbiah, *Trade of India*, pp. 31–69; Adams, *Economic Change*, pp. 186–99.

9. Venkatasubbiah, *Trade of India*, pp. 31–69.

10. Lars G. Sandberg, *Lancashire in Decline: A Study in Entrepreneurship, Technology, and International Trade* (Columbus: Ohio State University Press, 1974), pp. 182–91.

11. Hsiao Liang-lin, *China's Foreign Trade Statistics, 1864–1949* (Cambridge, Mass.: Harvard University Press, 1974), p. 9.

12. Yu-Kwei Cheng, *Foreign Trade and Industrial Development of China. An Historical and Integrated Analysis through 1948* (Washington D.C.: University Press, 1956), pp. 32–6.

13. Ping-Yin Ho, *The Foreign Trade of China* (Shanghai: Commercial Press, 1935), pp. 83, 113, 168, 235–42, 270, 348.

14. Cheng, *Foreign Trade*, pp. 30–1.

15. Cheng, *Foreign Trade*, pp. 43–7; Ho, *Foreign Trade of China*, pp. 114–27, 160, 226–35, 257–8, 350.

16. Sandberg, *Lancashire in Decline*, pp. 191–5.

17. Donald R. Snodgrass, *Ceylon: An Export Economy in Transition* (Homewood, Illinois: Richard D. Irwin, 1966), pp. 19–20, 34–5, 38–40, 42–4, 370–1, Table A-52; S. Rajaratnam, 'The Growth of Plantation Agriculture in Ceylon, 1886–1931', *Ceylon Journal of Historical Studies*, Jan–June (1961), pp. 1–20; S. Rajaratnam, 'The Ceylon Tea Industry, 1886–1931', *Ceylon Journal of Historical and Social Studies*, July–Dec (1961), pp. 169–202; Empire Marketing Board, *Survey of Oil Seeds and Vegetable Oils*, Vol 2, *Coconut Palm Products. A Summary of Production and Trade in the Empire and Foreign Countries* (London: HMSO, 1932), pp. 27–37, 182–3; *Statistical Abstracts for the British Empire*; League of Nations, *Memorandum on International Trade and Balances of Payments* (Geneva: League of Nations); League of Nations, *International Trade Statistics* (Geneva: League of Nations).

18. Siok-Hwa Cheng, *The Rice Industry of Burma, 1852–1940* (Kuala Lumpur: University of Malaya Press, 1968); Michael Adas, *The Burma Delta. Economic Development and Social Change on an Asian Rice Frontier, 1852–1941* (Madison, Wisconsin: University of Wisconsin Press, 1974); League of Nations, *International Trade Statistics*; League of Nations, *International Trade and Balances of Payments; Statistical Abstracts for the British Empire*. J. S. Furnivall, *Colonial Policy and Practice. A Comparative Study of Burma and Netherlands India* (Cambridge: University Press, 1948).

19. Lim Chong-Yah, *Economic Development of Modern Malaya* (Kuala Lumpur: Oxford University Press, 1967), pp. 49–51, 55–9, 73–83, 95, 112–14, 128–41; G. C. Allen and Audrey G. Donnithorne, *Western Enterprise in Indonesia and Malaya. A Study in Economic Development* (London: George Allen & Unwin, 1957), pp. 106–27, 151–62, 293; P. T. Bauer, *The Rubber Industry. A Study in Competition and Monopoly* (London: Longmans, Green & Co., 1948), pp. 4, 34–7, 56–9, 81, 99–100, 210–13; Empire Marketing Board, *Survey of Vegetable Oilseeds and Oils*, Vol 1, *Oil Palm Products* (London: HMSO,

1932), pp. 18–21, 75–7; *Statistical Abstracts for the British Empire*; League of Nations, *International Trade and Balances of Payments;* League of Nations, *International Trade Statistics.*

20. Allen and Donnithorne, *Indonesia and Malaya*, pp. 71–2, 84–5, 90–1, 93–4, 99–100, 103–5, 117–24, 139–42, 175–9, 291; J. S. Furnivall, *Netherlands India. A Study of Plural Economy* (Cambridge: University Press, 1944), pp. 435–8; Chong-Yah, *Modern Malaya*, pp. 80–3, 134–5; Bauer, *Rubber Industry*, pp. 4, 6, 38–9, 65–9, 81–4, 208–9; Empire Marketing Board, *Coconut Palm Products*, pp. 80–90, 182; Empire Marketing Board, *Oil Palm Products*, pp. 32–4, 78–81; League of Nations, *International Trade and Balances of Payments*; League of Nations, *International Trade Statistics.*

21. Department of Overseas Trade, *Economic Conditions in the Philippine Islands, 1933–34* (London: HMSO, 1935), pp. 12–16, 19; Empire Marketing Board, *Coconut Palm Products*, pp. 69–80, 182; League of Nations, *International Trade and Balances of Payments*; League of Nations, *International Trade Statistics.*

22. James C. Ingram, *Economic Change in Thailand, 1850–1970* (Stanford: Stanford University Press, 1971), pp. 43–8, 52, 66, 93–107; James C. Ingram, 'Thailand's Rice Trade and the Allocation of Resources', in *The Economic Development of South East Asia. Studies in Economic History and Political Economy*, C. D. Cowan (ed.) (London: George Allen and Unwin, 1964), pp. 120–2; League of Nations, *International Trade Statistics*; League of Nations, *International Trade and Balances of Payments.*

23. Charles Robequain, *The Economic Development of French Indo-China* (London: Oxford University Press, 1944), pp. 305–40.

24. S. H. Frankel, *Capital Investment in Africa: Its Course and Effects* (London: Oxford University Press, 1938), pp. 72–3, 107–8, 121; D. H. Houghton, 'Economic Development, 1865–1965', in *The Oxford History of South Africa*, Monica Wilson and Leonard Thompson (eds) (Oxford: Clarendon Press, 1971), Vol 2, pp. 1–48; League of Nations, *International Trade Statistics*; League of Nations, *International Trade and Balances of Payments*; *Statistical Abstracts for the British Empire.*

25. Frankel, *Capital Investment in Africa*, pp. 307–16; R. O. Ekundare, *An Economic History of Nigeria, 1860–1960* (London: Methuen, 1973), pp. 197–222; A. G. Hopkins, 'Innovation in a Colonial Context: African Origins of the Nigerian Cocoa Farming Industry, 1880–1920', in *The Imperial Impact*, pp. 83–96; League of Nations, *International Trade Statistics*; League of Nations, *International Trade and Balances of Payments; Statistical Abstracts for the British Empire*; A. G. Hopkins, *An Economic History of West Africa* (London: Longmans, 1973), pp. 219–20.

26. Frankel, *Capital Investment in Africa*, pp. 316–25; Polly Hill, *The Migrant Cocoa Farmers of Southern Ghana, A Study in Rural Capitalism* (Cambridge: Cambridge University Press, 1963); *Statistical Abstracts for the British Empire.*

27. Frankel, *Capital Investment in Africa*, pp. 325–31; *Statistical Abstracts for the British Empire.*

28. Frankel, *Capital Investment in Africa*, pp. 260–75; *Statistical Abstracts for the British Empire.*

29. *Statistical Abstracts for the British Empire.*

30. Frankel, *Capital Investment in Africa*, pp. 282–9.

31. Ibid., pp. 276–82; J. Forbes Munro, *Africa and the International Economy, 1800–1960* (London: Dent & Sons, 1976), pp. 124, 126, 138–9, 157, 161, 162, 165–6.

32. Frankel, *Capital Investment in Africa*, pp. 232–47; *Statistical Abstracts for the British Empire.*

33. Frankel, *Capital Investment in Africa*, pp. 247–53; *Statistical Abstracts for the British Empire.*

34. Frankel, *Capital Investment in Africa*, pp. 247–53; *Statistical Abstracts for the British Empire.*

35. Frankel, *Capital Investment in Africa*, pp. 331–47; Hopkins, *West Africa*, pp. 218–21.

36. Frankel, *Capital Investment in Africa*, pp. 352–4.

37. Ibid., pp. 367–71.

38. Ibid., pp. 371–3.

39. Ibid., pp. 289–301.

4   POPULATION AND MIGRATION

The population explosion which was to shake the developing world in the twentieth century began during the 1920s. Until then population growth in Asia and Africa was below that in Europe and North America. In that decade the Asian and African rate of population increase surged above the European rate and in the 1930s rose again, whilst the North American rate actually fell back. Whilst all population estimates for the developing world in this period are little more than guesswork, it does seem that the annual rate of population growth in Asia and Africa rose above 10 per thousand for the first time in the 1920s, and was even higher in the 1930s, as shown in Table 4.1. On these estimates the population of Asia rose from 966 million in 1920 to 1,212 million in 1940, and of Africa from 140 million to 172 million. The population of Africa was only a seventh that of Asia. In proportion to the rest of the world there was little change, Asia having more than half the world's population throughout, 53.4 per cent in 1920 and 54 per cent in 1940, and Africa having 7.7 per cent in both years.

India is the best-documented country. Here may be sought an explanation of the population explosion which may have application to Asia and the rest of the developing world. Table 4.2 gives the path of population growth in India from 1901 to 1941. From 1871 to 1921 decades of low increase alternated with decades of high increase. There were consecutive ten-year percentage increases of 0.86; 9.61; 1.11; 6.20; and 0.88. From 1921 there came another ten years of high growth in which the population grew 10.62 per cent. On the previous pattern there should now have followed ten years of low population increase, but instead growth was even higher and the population grew 15.02 per cent. What explanation is there for this? The low-growth decades previously were associated with famine and epidemic. In the 1870s there was famine 1876–8, and in the 1890s there was famine 1898–1900. The low growth from 1911 was due to the famine and the influenza epidemic of 1918. But no such catastrophes occurred during the 1920s and 1930s. This may have been due to better medical provision to combat malaria, tuberculosis, plague, smallpox and cholera. But a more convincing argument is that the good crops of these years meant that there was no famine, and because people were better fed they were more able to resist infection. These good harvests

Table 4.1: Estimated World Population, 1900–40 (millions)

	1900 (a)	1900 (b)	1920 (c)	1930 (c)	1940 (c)
Africa	120	141	140	155	172
North America	81	81	117	135	146
Latin America	63	63	91	109	131
Asia	915	857	966	1,072	1,212
Europe & USSR	423	423	487	532	573
Oceania	6	6	9	10	11
Total	1,608	1,571	1,810	2,013	2,246

Distribution of World Population, 1900–40 (%)

	1900 (a)	1900 (b)	1920 (c)	1930 (c)	1940 (c)
Africa	7.5	9.0	7.7	7.7	7.7
North America	5.0	5.2	6.5	6.7	6.5
Latin America	3.9	4.0	5.0	5.4	5.8
Asia	56.9	54.6	53.4	53.3	54.0
Europe & USSR	26.3	26.9	26.9	26.4	25.5
Oceania	0.4	0.4	0.5	0.5	0.5
Total	100.0	100.0	100.0	100.0	100.0

Annual Rate of Increase of World Population, 1900–40 (per 1000)

	1900–20 (a)	1900–20 (b)	1920–30 (c)	1930–40 (c)
Africa	7.7	−0.4	10.2	10.4
North America	18.6	18.6	14.4	7.9
Latin America	18.6	18.6	18.2	18.6
Asia	2.8	6.1	10.5	12.3
Europe & USSR	7.0	7.0	8.9	7.5
Oceania	—	—	16.8	8.3
Total	5.9	7.1	10.7	11.0

Notes:
(a) A. M. Carr-Saunders, *World Population* (London: Royal Institute of International Affairs, 1936), pp. 30–45.
(b) W. F. Wilcox, 'Population of the World and its Modern Increase', in *Studies in American Demography* (Ithaca: Cornell University Press, 1940), pp. 22–51, 511–40.
(c) *U.N. Demographic Yearbook* (New York, 1956), p. 151.

Source: D. V. Glass and E. Grebenik, 'World Population, 1800–1950', in *The Cambridge Economic History of Europe*, H. J. Habakkuk and M. Postan (eds) (Cambridge: Cambridge University Press, 1965), Vol. 6, p. 58.

Table 4.2: Population of India, 1901–41[a] (000)

	Census population	% growth over 10 years	Estimated population	% growth over 10 years
1901	283,870		285,288	
1911	303,041	6.75	302,985	6.20
1921	305,730	0.88	305,679	0.88
1931	338,171	10.61	338,171	10.62
1941	388,998	15.02	388,998	15.02

Note:

[a] Burma not included.

Source: Kingsley Davis, *The Population of India and Pakistan* (Princeton, New Jersey: Princeton University Press, 1951), p. 27.

explain much of the experience of the developing world between the wars. Certainly the fall in the death rate was the crucial factor as Table 4.3 shows. There was no sudden increase in the birth rate to explain the growth of population, for in fact the birth rate was declining.[1]

There was much internal migration in India in these years. In the north there was migration to the urban and industrial regions of Bengal, and to the tea estates and farm districts of Assam. Further south there was migration to Bombay and the agricultural estates of the Western Ghats. In 1931 the estates in the uplands of the Western Ghats were employing 14 per cent of all labourers in India growing tea, coffee and rubber, whilst the estates in Assam had 82 per cent. Labourers were recruited to Assam from Bihar and Orissa and more distant provinces because the local people were unwilling to leave their farms to work on the estates. Although many of the migrants subsequently returned to their home districts, others bought land in Assam and became rice farmers. In 1931 there were 900,000 of the coolie class employed in the

Table 4.3: Birth and Death Rates in India, 1901–11 to 1931–41

	Average annual rate per 1000		
	Birth	Death	Natural increase
1901–11	49.2	42.6	6.6
1911–21	48.1	47.2	0.9
1921–31	46.4	36.3	10.1
1931–41	45.2	31.2	14.0

Source: Kingsley Davis, *The Population of India*, p. 85.

estates and 500,000 outside. Assam also saw a mass migration of
Bengalese peasant farmers from Mymensingh who came to grow rice.
This movement did not begin much before 1914, but by 1921 there
were nearly 348,000 of them, and 575,000 by 1931. They came of
their own initiative without any government encouragement, a fine
example of peasant capitalism. Peasants also took up newly irrigated
land in the canal colonies of the Punjab, encouraged by the government.
Some 240,000 took up land there between 1921 and 1931 alone, and
in the 1930s there was migration to Sind, where massive new irrigation
schemes had begun.[2]

Besides internal migration there was also external migration although
the outflow was negligible in relation to the total population. As was
true in the nineteenth century many of the migrants returned to India,
and of the 30 million who left between 1834 and 1936 nearly 24
million returned, just over 6 million leaving for good. Table 4.4 gives
estimates of migration from India between 1901 and 1937.

Table 4.4: Estimated Migration from India, 1901–37 (000)

	Emigrants	Returned migrants	Net
1901–5	1,428	957	471
1906–10	1,864	1,482	383
1911–15	2,483	1,868	615
1916–20	2,087	1,867	220
1921–5	2,762	2,216	547
1926–30	3,298	2,857	441
1931–5	1,940	2,093	–162
1936–7	815	755	59

Source: Kingsley Davis, *The Population of India*, p. 99.

The migration figures show how migrants responded to the international economic climate. In the boom years of 1911–15 net migrants
reached 615,000 then declined during the difficult years of the war.
Between 1921 and 1925 there was another large outflow of 547,000,
followed by a smaller exodus of 441,000 between 1926 and 1930,
foreshadowing the coming depression. Between 1931 and 1935 more
Indians returned to India than left, there being a net influx of 162,000.
Burma, Ceylon and Malaya were the main destinations for the migrants,
most of whom were Tamils from Madras Province, although some were
from the Central Provinces and Bengal. Early migrants had been

indentured, their contract usually leading to the status of free labourer after five years. Then they could re-indenture or return home. But abuses of the system led to its regulation and eventually abolition in 1920. Meanwhile workers were being recruited under the *kangani* system which had begun in Ceylon in the late nineteenth century. The kangani, like the *maistry* in Burma, recruited the workers for a short period by verbal contract and as ganger supervised them in their work. By 1920 nearly 90 per cent of the Indian coolies in Malaya were recruited in this way. But during the 1920s the kangani system too declined, partly because of government regulations, and partly because workers more and more preferred to travel in voluntary groups organised by themselves. By the middle of the 1930s only a small percentage of Indian workers abroad had been recruited. Following the coolies came moneylenders, merchants, shopkeepers and pedlars, particularly Chettiars from Madras.[3]

Burma was a major destination for Indian emigrants until she separated from British India in 1937. The growth of her population is shown in Table 4.5. In the decade 1901 to 1911 the population of

Table 4.5: Population of Burma, 1901–41

	Estimated population	% growth over 10 years
1901	10,866	
1911	12,288	13.08
1921	13,295	8.19
1931	14,667	10.31
1941	16,824	14.70

Source: Davis, *Population of India*, p. 236.

Burma grew 13 per cent, whilst that of India rose by just over 6 per cent. Between 1911 and 1921 Burma's population increased more than 8 per cent whilst India's grew hardly at all. In the 1920s and 1930s when Burma's population grew at 10.31 per cent and 14.70 per cent in consecutive decades, India's population rose even faster. Immigration contributed to Burma's higher population growth before 1921, but more important was Burma's happy avoidance of major crises of famine or disease. Whilst she did not miss the influenza epidemic of 1918, it did not cause the number of deaths it did in India as it was not exaggerated by famine. Graph 4.1 shows that the inflow of Indians was high in 1913 and 1914 due to food shortages and bad weather in India,

Graph 4.1: Migration to Burma, Ceylon and Malaya

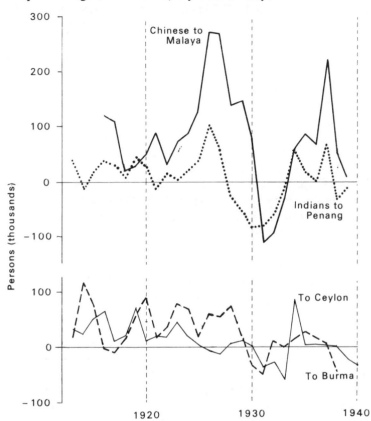

Source: D. R. Snodgrass, *Ceylon: An Export Economy in Transition* (Homewood, Illinois: Richard D. Irwin, 1966), p. 308; J. N. Parmer, *Colonial Labor Policy and Administration: A History of Labor in the Rubber Plantation Industry in Malaya, c. 1910–1941* (New York: J. J. Augustin, 1960), pp. 270–1; Siok-Hwa Cheng, *The Rice Industry of Burma, 1852–1940* (Kuala Lumpur: University of Malaya Press, 1968), p. 262; see Appendix 13.

but numbers dropped during the war because of shipping difficulties. After the war there was another great influx as shipping returned to normal and as general famine hit India in 1918/19. Another peak in 1923 followed severe weather in India, and the high inflow of 1926–8 came after bad harvests in the United Provinces. But as the depression struck the inflow of migrants fell and in 1930 there was an outflow of

30,700, followed in 1931 by an even bigger exodus of 57,700. As the rice market collapsed in 1929/30 Burmese labourers became jealous of the jobs held by Indians on the wharves of Rangoon. In May 1930 they attacked them in bloody riots. Immediately Indians flocked from the country fearing further violence. Although immigration from India did resume it was at a lower level than before the depression and there was a small outflow in 1933. In 1938 further riots took place, prompting a further mass exodus which continued as the invading Japanese approached.

Burma was not a plantation economy like Ceylon and Malaya, so the Indian coolies did not become estate workers. Nor did they normally grow rice, which for the most part remained in Burmese hands. Instead they worked as labourers in the docks and in the rice mills. As rice cultivation moved further inland in the 1920s the Indians followed, working in the small upcountry rice mills and in transport. In 1934 74 per cent of the skilled rice-mill workers in Burma were Indians and 81 per cent of the unskilled. Indian Chettiars were active as moneylenders to the Burmese, and through foreclosures gradually an Indian landlord class grew up. They accepted Indian tenants, who in turn employed Indian labourers in the fields. By 1931 8 per cent of tenant farmers in Burma were Indians. Even the Burmese eventually came to employ some Indian labourers in the fields, to which they migrated seasonally from the rice mills. The Indians were originally recruited in maistry gangs, but voluntary groups became increasingly common as the coolies gained experience of Burma. There were also Chinese in Burma, some 193,594 being enumerated in the 1931 census. From Fukien and Canton, they were traders, merchants and craftsmen, and they were to be found along the railway and steamer routes, wherever business concentrated.[4]

In Ceylon, another immigrant area, the population grew even faster than in Burma as Table 4.6 shows. Although the census population and the estimated population differ substantially, both confirm that there was high population growth. Like Burma, Ceylon did not suffer as badly from the influenza epidemic of 1918 as India did, and the decennial growth in the thirty years from 1901 to 1931 was the highest of all three countries. Because there is no figure for 1941 direct comparison for the crucial years of the 1930s cannot be made, but the implication is that Ceylon, like her neighbours, experienced continuing high rates of population growth. As with India, the growth of population is explained by the death rate falling faster than the birth rate. Immigration helped, and Tamil coolies continued to come from Madras. In the past they had come to work on the coffee and tea estates, and

Table 4.6: Population of Ceylon, 1901–46 (000)

	Census population	% growth over 10 years	Estimated population	% growth over 10 years
1901	3,566		4,031	
1911	4,106	15.14	4,702	16.64
1921	4,499	9.57	5,304	12.80
1931	5,307	17.95	6,053	14.12
1946	6,657	25.43[a]	7,122	17.66[a]

Note:

[a] % growth over 15 years.

Source: N. K. Sarkar, *The Demography of Ceylon* (Colombo: Ceylon Government Press, 1957), p. 22.

now the development of rubber plantations created a new demand for them. Graph 4.1 shows that net migrants reached a peak in 1916 when 68,100 came, and there was another high in 1919 when 78,100 entered. After yet another peak of 41,700 in 1923 there was a protracted decline associated with the difficulties of the rubber industry, and in 1926 and 1927 there was in sum an outflow. In 1929 there was a sharp recovery in immigration with an inflow of 18,500 and more the following year. Then came the full impact of the depression and the losses in 1931, 1932 and 1933 were 31,900, 28,800 and 60,100 respectively. There was a recovery in 1934 with 97,600 net incomers, but with the exception of 1937 the following years saw the drain continue. Whilst the fortunes of the rubber industry were an important force in the migrant flows, more migrants were actually employed in the tea gardens and in 1929 it is estimated that of 540,000 Indian estate workers, only 100,000 were in the rubber industry.[5]

Malaya also drew Indian immigrants into her rubber plantations and her rate of population growth was even higher than Ceylon's, as Table 4.7 shows. With nearly 25 per cent increase between 1911 and 1921 and 30 per cent in the 1920s, exceptional growth was experienced. Immigration from both India and China contributed to this great expansion. The ethnic structure of the population is given in Table 4.8. This shows how the immigrant community came by 1931 to account for half the total population. Of the immigrants, Chinese outnumbered Indians by more than two to one. Some indication of the inflow of Indians and Chinese is shown in Graph 4.1. The Chinese provided the biggest flow of net immigrants. In the peak year of 1926 the inflow from China was 228,285, whilst the comparable number of Indians was

Table 4.7: Population of Malaya, 1911–47 (000)

	Population	% growth over 10 years
1911	2,340	
1921	2,910	24.35
1931	3,790	30.24
1947	4,910	29.55[a]

Note:

[a] % growth over 16 years.

Source: Lim Chong-Yah, *Economic Development of Modern Malaya* (Kuala Lumpur: Oxford University Press, 1967), p. 181.

Table 4.8: Ethnic Structure of Malayan Population, 1911–47

	1911	1921	1931	1947
Malays[a]	59	54	49	50
Chinese	30	29	34	38
Indians	10	15	15	11
Total	99	98	98	99

Note:

[a] Including Javanese.

Source: Chong-Yah, *Modern Malaya*, p. 192.

only 109,009. Between 1911 and 1931 there was unrestricted immigration to Malaya because labourers were needed in the rubber industry, and to a lesser extent in the tin industry. That the Indians and Chinese were responding to this demand for labour is confirmed by the fact that the immigration flows from both countries show a similar pattern, both reaching a peak in 1925, leading to a decline and then a net outflow in the early 1930s up to 1934. The year 1937 saw a new peak of immigration but it fell away in the last years before the war. There was also immigration from Java, but the numbers were smaller and there are no reliable estimates. Whilst the Indians were mainly employed on the large European-owned rubber estates and the Chinese in Chinese-run mines and rubber plantations, the Javanese developed rubber smallholdings, much as the Malays converted their rice fields and orchards to rubber. As the depression bit, immigration restrictions were imposed against alien males, which hit the Chinese but not the Indians, who were British subjects. But Chinese females were free to come and did so in large numbers, working in building, domestic service and entertainment. The 1930s also saw a change in the kind of Indians who came to Malaya. Whilst coolies from the south were in less demand, tradesmen, shopkeepers, pedlars and moneylenders from the north came in looking for business opportunities. So Malaya was the meeting place of the two great migrant flows of Asia, of Indians moving east and of Chinese moving west. Graph 4.1 shows that these migrant flows responded to the same economic forces, with the migrants to Burma, Ceylon and Malaya all returning to their respective homelands in India and China as the depression struck. If the main body of migrants was of coolies, there were also petty capitalists of all kinds, craftsmen, traders, bankers and moneylenders. In Malaya Chinese entrepreneurs operated tin mines and rubber plantations, and Indian Chettiar moneylenders were vital providers of capital, even to the Chinese.

The Chinese labourers were recruited to Malaya in a manner which resembled the kangani system by which so many Indians were recruited. European employers obtained workers through a headman known as a *kheh thau* or *kepala* who contracted the workers from China or from lodging houses in Malaya, supervised their work and paid them. The lodging houses themselves also obtained coolies from China using professional recruiters. But when the depression struck and immigration was restricted, the lodging houses became unofficial labour exchanges for men who were out of work. Of the main Chinese tribes in Malaya there were Hokkiens from Fukien, and Kwong-Fu, Hakkas, and Teochius from Kwantung. There were also Hailams from Hainan. Members of these tribes were found all over South East Asia.[6]

Chinese migrants also went to the Dutch East Indies. Population figures for this area relate mainly to Java, and for other regions are little better than guesses, as is only too clear from Table 4.9.

Table 4.9: **Population of the Dutch East Indies, 1905–30 (000)**

	Java	% increase between censuses	Outer provinces	% increase between censuses	Total	% increase between censuses
1905	30,098		7,619		37,717	
		16.23		88.55		30.84
1920	34,984		14,366		49,350	
		19.24		32.33		23.05
1930	41,717		19,011		60,728	

Source: J. S. Furnivall, *Netherlands India: A Study of Plural Economy* (Cambridge: Cambridge University Press, 1944), p. 347.

Obviously the 88 per cent increase for the Outer Provinces between
1905 and 1920 is unbelievable in comparison with the 16 per cent
increase in Java, and even the 32 per cent increase between 1920 and
1930 is hard to credit when set against the 19 per cent increase in Java.
It follows that the increases for the Dutch East Indies in total cannot
be accepted. The figures for Java itself are probably much more
accurate and suggest a genuinely high rate of population increase. The
fact that the growth between 1905 and 1920 is less than the increase
between 1920 and 1930 is partly accounted for by the influenza
epidemic of 1918 which caused such havoc in India and other parts of
the developing world. The registered number of deaths in November
1918 was 416,000 more than the same month in the previous year.
Because there are no more reliable estimates of population until the
1950s, it is difficult to say much about the 1930s, but it is clear that
many migrants from Java to the tobacco plantations of East Sumatra
returned to their home villages because of the depression. At the same
time the collapse of the sugar industry on Java itself seriously affected
the village economies with which it was interrelated, as sugar was grown
in rotation with village food crops to prevent soil exhaustion. The best
available estimates suggest that the population of Java grew from
41,718,000 in 1930 to 49,024,000 in 1940, an increase of 17.51 per
cent. A high level of population growth seems to have continued. There
were many Chinese immigrants and the Chinese population was
563,449 in 1905, 809,039 in 1920 and 1,233,214 in 1930, or about 2
per cent of the total population in the latter year. They were divided
about equally between Java and the Outer Provinces. The numbers of
Chinese probably declined somewhat in the following years, particularly
in Sumatra following the economic difficulties of the plantations there,
but immigration did continue. Although the same tribes came to the
Dutch East Indies as came to Malaya, the Hokkiens were the most
important group, followed by the Hakkas, Kwong Fu, and Teochius.
They were active in every aspect of commerce, especially as middlemen,
but some were involved in mining, agriculture and market gardening,
and of course there were those who were coolies on the tobacco estates
of Sumatra and in the mines of Bangka and Billiton.[7]

The Philippines also experienced an influx of Chinese. Population
figures for these islands are not much more than guesswork, although
the census of 1918 gave a population of 10,314,310 and the preliminary
returns for the 1939 census gave a population of 15,984,247. On these
estimates the Philippines too were experiencing rapid population
growth, 54.97 per cent in 21 years. Basically the population was Malay

and mainly Christian, but the Chinese population in 1918 was 43,802 and in 1939 117,487. This implies their numbers were growing faster than that of the general population. Nearly half of them lived in and around Manila, and as in the Dutch East Indies, Hokkiens predominated, probably three-quarters of them being of this tribe. The remainder were mostly Kwong-Fu. Up until 1932 when the Japanese became very active, the Chinese handled between 70 and 80 per cent of the retail trade and much of the internal commerce of the islands. Credit, lumber, rice mills and nearly every kind of business were in Chinese hands. They also dominated the wholesale trade, and as in Siam and Indo-China they financed the rice growing and its milling and distribution. They were important agents of development penetrating to the remotest villages with trade goods such as cottons as exchange for copra, hemp, gutta percha and other local products. Although they were not allowed to buy public land they began to get round this by marrying local women and acquiring land in their wives' names.[8]

In Siam where the Chinese were again numerous, there was also substantial population increase in these years as Table 4.10 indicates.

Table 4.10: Population of Siam, 1911–37 (000)

	Population	% growth between censuses
1911	8,266	
1919	9,207	11.38
1929	11,506	24.97
1937	14,464	25.70

Source: James C. Ingram, *Economic Change in Thailand, 1850–1970* (Stanford: Stanford University Press, 1971), p. 46.

Population growth seems to have surged forward during the 1920s, and to have continued vigorously in the 1930s, the population growing just under 25 per cent between 1919 and 1929, and just over 25 per cent between 1929 and 1937. These increases suggest one of the highest rates of population growth in the developing world. There were 260,194 Chinese in 1919, 445,274 in 1929 and 524,062 in 1937. But these were only Chinese who were not citizens of Siam. If the number of Chinese by race is sought, to be comparable with estimates of Chinese in Burma, Malaya, the Dutch East Indies and the Philippines, a much higher figure would apply. In 1919, for example, there were an additional 113,050 who were classified as Siamese, and one estimate

puts the true number of Chinese in Siam at 2.4 million in 1937.
Certainly the Chinese flooded in between 1919 and 1929, net
immigration between those years amounting to 400,000. They were
attracted by Siam's booming rice trade and driven out by the political
chaos in China. As in other Chinese immigrant areas the proportion of
women increased at this time. In the 1930s the government took steps
to curb immigration because there were so many Chinese in the country,
but there was much illegal immigration. About a quarter of the Chinese
clustered in the commercial districts around Bangkok. They were closely
involved in the rice trade, having brokers and buyers all over the rice
growing regions at focal points in the water-transport system of the
Menam delta. The rice was bought and sent to the mills, more than
four-fifths of which were owned by Chinese and manned by Chinese
coolies. There was a continuous movement of coolies backward and
forward between Bangkok and Swatow. Some Chinese were fruit and
market gardeners near Bangkok and others grew sugar and pepper, or
lived in fishing villages along the coast. In the Malay peninsula part of
the country Chinese owned rubber and tapioca plantations, and others
owned and operated tin and tungsten mines. These Chinese miners
were part of the group who operated mines in Malaya and in Billiton
and Bangka in the Dutch East Indies. The Teochius from Swatow were
the biggest group, followed by the Hailams embarking from Kiungchow
in Hainan. But the Kwong-Fu were second only to the Teochius in
commerce, and the Hokkien dominated the mining areas. There were
also Hakkas present.[9]

The population figures for French Indo-China are only approximate,
and it is said that to suggest even a 10 per cent error would be
optimistic. In 1914 the population is given at 16,990,229, with
20,700,000 in 1926 and 23,853,500 in 1940. This implies a growth of
some 40 per cent over the period. The introduction of law and order
and mass vaccination had helped this population expansion, as in other
parts of the developing world. There was considerable internal
migration, Annamites moving from the north to the plains in the south
to grow rice on the land being made available by canal drainage. Many
also went to work on the French rubber plantations in Cochin China
and Cambodia as they expanded after the First World War. Chinese
immigrants also came to Indo-China, and the numbers of Chinese in the
country rose from 293,000 in 1912 to 400,000 in 1926 and 419,000 in
1931, falling to 326,000 in 1937 when many had left because of the
depression. If people of Chinese descent are included, there were
another 141,000 in 1937, giving a total Chinese population of 467,000.

The turning point in the history of Chinese immigration came after several years of high inflow as the roads and railways were built. In 1927 the net gain was 31,000 and in 1928 and 1929 it was 30,000. In 1931 the numbers dropped to 18,000 and in 1931 there was, for the first time, an outflow of 8,000. In the following year 16,000 left and a further 8,000 in 1933. Then Chinese immigration began to recover. Cochin China had absorbed more than half the Chinese in Indo-China and as in Siam they had built up a comprehensive system of rice financing and purchasing. They channelled the crop by water to their own mills, which were operated by coolies who were their fellow countrymen. They also were involved in cotton production, sugar, condiments, silk and tea, linking great native landowners, European companies and Chettiar moneylenders into an effective web of commerce. When the Chinese withdrew during the depression this web disintegrated, and they never regained the control they had previously exercised. Annamite merchants had taken their place and trade links had shifted away from China to France, destroying their advantage. The Kwong-Fu were the most numerous group, being active in commerce, but also providing many workmen, artisans and boatmen. The Hokkien were less numerous but had great commercial influence. The Hailams had a monopoly of pepper cultivation and were domestic servants, the Teochius were agriculturalists, boatmen and coolies, and the Hakkas were similar, although some were artisans and tea merchants.[10]

China has worse population statistics than all the countries so far discussed, and although there were enumerations in 1909—11, 1912, and 1928/9, little reliance can be placed upon them. Recent estimates suggest a population of 417 million in 1851 and 518 million in 1953, the latter figure based on the census of that year. Assuming a steady growth rate of 0.21 per cent per annum between those two dates, the population can be put at 474 million in 1913 and 503.8 million in 1940. This would give an increase between 1913 and 1940 of 6.28 per cent. But what fluctuations took place, and whether the pace of population growth increased during the 1920s and 1930s cannot be known. What, however, is clear is that the exodus of Chinese migrants was high, particularly during the 1920s, to Malaya, the Dutch East Indies, the Philippines, Siam and French Indo-China. Migrants came from the Kwong-Fu, Hakka and Teochiu tribes of Kwantung Province, and Hokkiens from Fukien Province, although there were also Hailams from Hainan and people from other tribes. Economic and political disorder at home seems to have been a strong force driving these people abroad and the incentive was certainly economic opportunity. Many were coolies, and artisans, but their preferred occupation was commerce. They established an organisational structure to the rice trade in South East Asia reaching as far as Burma and they dominated the trade in Siam and Indo-China. There they provided credit to the farmers, bought the crop, transported it, milled it and shipped it. They were active in all sorts of other commerce too: tin, copra, hemp, fish, foodstuffs, spices and the retailing of imported cottons and manufactures. So the Chinese played a crucial role in the development of South East Asia as the commercial entrepreneurs of the wholesale and retail trades. Their control of the main articles of business transcended political frontiers and linked peasant capitalists to the major international markets. When the depression struck and business declined, many Chinese left their adoptive lands and returned home, severely impeding the internal and external trade of many countries. Like the good capitalists they were, they were responding to the force of the market, and home was still China however much the possibility of profit had drawn them away in the good years.[11]

African population estimates are, if anything, worse than those in Asia. British Africa probably has the best sets of figures, but even they are speculative. They are given in Table 4.11. Nigeria was by far and away the most populous of British African territories, and indeed of all African territories. Her population of 17 million in 1911 was nearly three times as large as South Africa's 6 million. But her population did not grow as fast as South Africa's, for the 1937 estimate of just over 20 million was only about double that for South Africa of almost 10 million. Some of South Africa's growth was due to immigration from Europe, but much more important was immigration by Africans from adjacent territories looking for work in the mines. Yet the proportion of the races did not change much, in 1911 21 per cent being European and 78 per cent non-European, and in 1936 20 per cent were European and 79 per cent non-European. Of the non-European population in 1936, 6,596,689 were African, 219,691 Asian and 769,661 other races. The Asian community had been established before the war, when there was Indian migration to Natal. But the Indian Government had ended indentured migration in 1911 and the final indentures were worked out during the war. Anti-Indian agitation continued and under the Cape Town Agreement of 1927 the Indian Government agreed to a voluntary repatriation scheme. But it was a failure, some 3,477 going back to India in 1928, the only year in which those returning exceeded those born. Fewer and fewer returned home in the following years. Temporary migration to the mines by Africans from Swaziland,

Table 4.11: **Population of British African Territories, 1911–37**

	Census 1911	Census 1921	Census 1931	Estimate 31 Dec 1937
West Africa				
Nigeria	17,126,983	18,631,442	19,928,171	20,476,795
Cameroons	–	660,024	797,312	830,695
Gold Coast	1,503,911	2,110,454	2,869,750	3,746,712
Togoland	–	187,959	293,714	–
Sierra Leone	1,400,097	1,540,544	1,768,480	–
Gambia	146,101	210,530	199,520	192,818
Total	20,177,092	23,340,953	25,856,947	25,247,020
Southern Africa				
Union of South Africa	5,973,394	6,928,580	8,132,600	9,887,200
Swaziland	156,715	112,951	125,055	99,959
Basutoland	404,507	498,781	650,000	562,311
Bechuanaland	125,350	152,983	–	265,756
Rhodesia:				
Southern	771,077	899,187	1,118,000	1,357,000
Northern	822,482	983,539	1,345,075	–
South West Africa	–	227,739	240,520	365,000
Total	8,253,525	9,803,760	11,611,250	12,537,226
East Africa				
Nyasaland	970,430	1,201,983	1,603,454	1,639,329
Tanganyika	–	4,123,493	5,063,660	5,182,515
Uganda	2,843,325	2,921,608	3,552,418	3,711,494
Kenya	2,402,863	2,574,006	3,040,850	3,334,191
Zanzibar	197,200	209,214	235,428	243,135
Total	6,413,818	11,030,304	13,495,810	14,110,664
Grand Total	34,844,435	44,175,017	50,964,007	51,894,910

Source: *Statistical Abstract for British Dominions and Protectorates.*

Basutoland and Bechuanaland was substantial, and there were important immigrant flows from Nyasaland and especially Portuguese East Africa or Mozambique. The latter were skilled mineworkers who were used to counteract the seasonal cycle of local mineworkers who returned home at ploughing and harvest time. Recruitment from Mozambique fell during the 1930s as depression in agriculture and other industries meant there was more labour available for the mines in South Africa itself.[12]

The adjacent territory of South West Africa had a tiny population given as 227,739 in 1921 and 365,000 in 1937. As large areas along the coast and in the north were not developed it is impossible to say how accurate these figures are. It was particularly difficult to estimate the numerous population of Bushmen in the North East.[13] But like South

Africa, Southern Rhodesia saw rapid population growth, nearly
doubling from 771,077 in 1911 to an estimated 1,357,000 in 1937 in
so far as these figures can be believed. As part of the Southern and
Central African mining belt, it attracted large numbers of migrants from
neighbouring countries, particularly Nyasaland. Immigration reached a
peak in 1929 of 23,126 before falling to a low of 10,844 in 1932 and
rising to a new peak of 28,841 in 1937. As the copper deposits of
Northern Rhodesia began to be developed after 1925 more workers
were needed. They came from Nyasaland, the Belgian Congo and
Mozambique, but the most important flow was from the Barotse
province of Angola. Thus the estimated population of Northern
Rhodesia rose from 983,538 in 1921 to 1,345,075 in 1931. Immigration continued until about 1934 when the decline in copper prices led
to homegoers exceeding incomers. Nyasaland's importance to the
Rhodesian mining belt was as a supplier of labour, much as Mozambique
was to South Africa. In 1931 there were 54,000 Nyasalanders employed
in the Rhodesias, and if migrants to South Africa, the Belgian Congo,
Mozambique and Tanganyika were added, a total of 75,000 were
employed in other territories. Numbers going away to work fell in the
next couple of years due to the depression, but then they began to rise
from 1933 to higher levels than before.[14]

The population figures for the British territories of East Africa are
all quite uncertain, so little reliance can be put on the information that
Tanganyika's population grew from 4,123,493 in 1921 to 5,182,515 in
1937. She supplied migrant workers to Uganda and received others
from Nyasaland to work on her plantations. Uganda is supposed to
have seen an increase from 2,843,325 in 1911 to 3,711,494 in 1937,
and she certainly attracted workers from surrounding areas. They did
not come only from Tanganyika, for of the 57,646 immigrant workers
in 1928 some 35,000 were from the neighbouring Belgian colonies. In
1938 there were 11,000 from Tanganyika and 90,000 from Belgian
areas. The other important immigrant movement was of Indians. There
were few Indians in Uganda before the First World War once the
coolies employed in building the railway had gone home. But in the
1920s merchants and traders came in as the country developed. By
1931 there were 13,000 and possibly 17,000 by 1938/9. Kenya's
experience was similar, with about 7,000 at the outbreak of war,
rising to 40,000 in 1921 and 45,000 in 1938/9. But Kenya did not
draw in many migrant African workers even though her population is
put at 2,402,863 in 1911 and 3,334,191 in 1937. Presumably she had
enough of her own people for the jobs available. Indians were also

present in Tanganyika, some 9,000 in 1921 rising to 23,400 in 1931, and Zanzibar had an ancient Indian population which rose from 12,900 in 1921 to 14,200 in 1931.[15]

Nigeria had the biggest population of all the African countries as has been seen, and the other British West African colonies were much less important. As far as estimates can be obtained the Gold Coast population rose from 1,503,911 in 1911 to 3,746,712 in 1937, and Sierra Leone from 1,400,097 to 1,768,480 in 1931. The remaining British territories, the Cameroons, Togoland and the Gambia had populations of under a million and were of little significance in population terms.[16]

As for the non-British territories, they were, if anything, even worse favoured with population details, and beyond the vague impression that their numbers were growing, very little can usefully be said. Estimates for French Africa show the population of Senegal rising from 1,204,113 in 1920 to 1,666,374 in 1937, and that of Guinea from 1,851,200 to 2,065,527. Similarly the population of the Ivory Coast rose from 1,407,030 to 3,981,459, and of Dahomey from 860,590 to 1,289,128. French Equatorial Africa had a population of 3,418,066 in 1936, and Togo had 780,597 in 1938, the Cameroons having 2,516,623 that year.[17] The Belgian Congo showed a population rise from 7,708,000 in 1925 to 10,370,000 in 1934, according to United Nations estimates. This would make her the second most populous African country. Angola and Mozambique had populations of 3,484,300 and 4,995,750 respectively in 1936, it is said. What is true of these last two countries is that they were important suppliers of migrant workers to the mining areas.[18]

So these were important years in terms of the population history of the developing world. The population explosion had begun, and at the same time there were important migrant flows from China and India to supply labour to important nodal points of development. If the depression saw a reversal of these migrant flows, it did not see a check to the upward surge of population growth in the developing world in general.

Notes

1. D. V. Glass and E. Grebenick, 'World Population 1800–1950', in *The Cambridge History of Europe*, H. J. Habakkuk and M. Postan (eds) (Cambridge: Cambridge University Press, 1965), Vol. 6, pp. 60, 83–5; Kingsley Davis, *The Population of India and Pakistan* (Princeton, New Jersey: Princeton University Press, 1951), pp. 27–8, 38–52.

2. Davis, *Population of India*, pp. 109–22.

3. Davis, *Population of India*, pp. 93–105; Michael Adas, *The Burma Delta. Economic Development and Social Change on an Asian Rice Frontier, 1852–1941* (Madison, Wisconsin: University of Wisconsin Press, 1974), pp. 86–7; K. S. Sandhu, 'Some Preliminary Observations of the Origins and Characteristics of Indian Migration to Malaya, 1786–1957' in *Papers on Malayan History*, K. G. Tregonning (ed.) (Singapore: Journal of South East Asian History, 1962), pp. 71–2; J. N. Parmer, *Colonial Labor Policy and Administration. A History of Labor in the Rubber Plantation Industry in Malaya, c. 1910–1941* (New York: J. J. Augustin, 1960), p. 53–7; D. R. Snodgrass, *Ceylon: An Export Economy in Transition* (Homewood, Illinois: Irwin, 1966), pp. 37–8; K. C. Zachariah, *A Historical Study of Internal Migration in the Indian Sub-Continent, 1901–1931* (Bombay: Asia Publishing House, 1964), pp. 168–242.

4. Adas, *Burma Delta*, pp. 159–208; Siok-Hwa Cheng, *The Rice Industry of Burma, 1852–1940* (Kuala Lumpur: University of Malaya Press, 1968), pp. 122–36, 262; Victor Purcell, *The Chinese in South East Asia* (London: Oxford University Press, 1951), pp. 55–61.

5. Snodgrass, *Ceylon*, pp. 37–40; N. K. Sarkar, *The Demography of Ceylon* (Colombo: Ceylon Government Press, 1957), pp. 22–4.

6. Lim Chong-Yah, *Economic Development of Modern Malaya* (Kuala Lumpur: Oxford University Press, 1967), pp. 49–55, 76–7, 112–20, 181–95, 334; Victor Purcell, *The Chinese in Malaya* (London: Oxford University Press, 1948), pp. 198–205; Purcell, *Chinese in South East Asia*, pp. 271–2, 347–53; R. N. Jackson, *Immigrant Labour and the Development of Malaya, 1786–1920* (Kuala Lumpur: Government Press, 1961), pp. 132–57; Sinnappah Arasaratnam, *Indians in Malaysia and Singapore* (Bombay and Kuala Lumpur: Oxford University Press, 1970), pp. 29–30; Parmer, *Colonial Labour Policy*, pp. 56–7, 74, 79–113, 270; Sandhu, *Indian Migration*, pp. 68–72.

7. Nitisastro Widjojo, *Population Trends in Indonesia* (Ithaca: Cornell University Press, 1970), pp. 3–8, 63–93, 112–13, 149, 158, 161; J. S. Furnivall, *Netherlands India. A Study of Plural Economy* (Cambridge: University Press, 1944), pp. 347, 408–13; Purcell, *Chinese in South East Asia*, pp. 534–44.

8. *Statesman's Year Book, 1941*, p. 665; Department of Overseas Trade, *Economic Conditions in the Philippine Islands, 1933–34* (London: HMSO, 1935), p. iv; Purcell, *Chinese in South East Asia*, pp. 572–6, 626–9.

9. James C. Ingram, *Economic Change in Thailand, 1850–1970* (Stanford: Stanford University Press, 1971), pp. 46, 70–1; Purcell, *Chinese in South East Asia*, pp. 104–8; K. P. Landon, *The Chinese in Thailand* (London: Oxford University Press, 1941), pp. 22, 200–11.

10. Purcell, *Chinese in South East Asia*, pp. 209–19, 238–49; Charles Robequain, *The Economic Development of French Indo-China* (London: Oxford University Press, 1944), pp. 34–5, 43–7, 54; *Statesman's Year Book, 1941*, p. 904–5; *Statesman's Year Book, 1921*, p. 874.

11. J. D. Durand, 'The Population Statistics of China, AD 2–1953', *Population Studies* 13 (1959–60), pp. 245–9; Ping-ti Ho, *Studies on the Population of China, 1368–1953* (Cambridge, Mass.: Harvard University Press, 1959), pp. 73–86; Purcell, *Chinese in South East Asia*, pp. 1–10 & c.

12. D. H. Houghton, *The South African Economy*, (Cape Town: Oxford University Press, 1964), p. 35; Mabel Palmer, *The History of the Indians in Natal* (Cape Town: Oxford University Press, 1957), p. 76, 90, 97, 104, 105; Sheila T. Van Der Horst, *Native Labour in South Africa* (London: Oxford University Press, 1942), pp. 215–20; *Statesman's Year Book, 1941*, pp. 434–6.

13. *Statesman's Year Book, 1941*, p. 459.

14. R. R. Kuczynski, *A Demographic Survey of the British Colonial Empire*,

Vol. 2, *East Africa* (London: Oxford University Press, 1949), pp. 424, 443–4, 549–57.

15. Kuczynski, *East Africa*, pp. 97–101, 241–2; R. M. A. van Zwanenberg with Anne King, *An Economic History of Kenya and Uganda* (London: Macmillan, 1975), pp. 7–14.

16. Kuczynski, *Demographic Survey of the British Colonial Empire*, Vol. 1, *West Africa* (London: Oxford University Press, 1948), pp. 29, 417–19, 542.

17. *Statesman's Year Book, 1921*, p. 895; *Statesman's Year Book, 1941*, p. 929, 939, 947.

18. *Statesman's Year Book, 1941*, pp. 1236–7; United Nations, *Demographic Yearbook, 1956* (United Nations, New York, 1956), p. 152.

5 DEVELOPMENT AND DEPRESSION

The economic development which had been taking place so vigorously in Asia and Africa before the First World War continued during the 1920s. But this progress partly created the situation in which the international economy was plunged into depression at the end of the decade. The success of the 1920s caused the problems of the 1930s.

Development

Any attempt to calculate the national and *per capita* incomes of the countries of the developing world in these years must be largely guesswork, but Zimmerman has suggested the estimates shown in Tables 5.1 and 5.2. Although these figures are very speculative they imply that national incomes and *per capita* incomes continued to grow in Asia as they had before 1913. The Philippines, Malaya, the Dutch East Indies, India, Burma and China were not stagnating or becoming poorer up to 1929; they were becoming wealthier. So this period can be seen as a continuation of the surge of economic growth which the developing world experienced in the previous fifty years. Of all the countries in the world, Japan seems to have experienced the most rapid growth in these years at 4.06 per cent each year, but Latin America grew quickly at 2.82 per cent, and North America at 2.75 per cent. Yet the Far East grew nearly as fast at 2.37 per cent, the Far East comprising the Philippines, Malaya, and the Dutch East Indies. Malaya had exceptional growth at 5.19 per cent as is shown in Table 5.3. This was even faster than Japan. The Philippines and the Dutch East Indies grew at 2.37 per cent and 2.03 per cent respectively. So high growth was perfectly feasible in colonial mining and plantation economies. By contrast India and Burma only grew at 0.77 per cent annually, and China at 0.58 per cent despite the industrialisation which was taking place in those countries. Clearly industrialisation was no guarantee of high growth, or even necessary for it.

Zimmerman's estimates of population growth are given in Tables 5.5 and 5.6. As these show population growth to be spread unevenly, the consequent figures for *per capita* income growth show a slightly different pattern from those for national income growth. Japan

Table 5.1: Distribution of World Income, 1913–29

	Aggregate income ($ of 1953 millions)					
	1913	%	1929	%	% increase 1913–29	Annual % increase
North America	100.3	32.90	154.9	38.25	54.43	2.75
Oceania	4.1	1.34	5.4	1.33	31.70	1.73
North West Europe	84.0	27.55	97.0	23.95	15.47	0.90
Soviet Union	22.5	7.38	26.7	6.59	18.66	1.07
South East Europe	26.0	8.53	33.9	8.37	30.38	1.67
Latin America	12.3	4.03	19.2	4.74	56.09	2.82
Japan	4.6	1.50	8.7	2.14	89.13	4.06
Near East	--	--	--	--	–	--
Far East	5.7	1.87	8.3	2.04	45.61	2.37
Central Africa	–	–	--	--	–	–
South East Asia	21.0	6.88	24.2	5.97	15.23	0.89
China	24.3	7.97	26.6	6.56	9.46	0.56
Total	304.8	100.00	404.9	100.00	32.84	1.79

Source: L. J. Zimmerman, 'The Distribution of World Income, 1860–1960' in *Essays on Unbalanced Growth*, Egbert De Vries (ed.) ('S-Gravenhage: Mouton & Co., 1962), pp. 55–6.

Table 5.2: World *Per Capita* Incomes, 1913–29 ($ of 1953)

	1913	1939	% increase	Annual % increase
North America	1,000	1,180	18.00	1.03
Oceania	580	680	17.24	0.99
North West Europe	460	510	10.86	0.64
Soviet Union	160	180	12.50	0.73
South East Europe	200	210	5.00	0.30
Latin America	160	180	12.50	0.73
Japan	90	140	55.55	2.80
Near East	--	–	–	--
Far East	93	106	13.97	0.82
Central Africa	–	--	--	–
South East Asia	65	67	3.07	0.18
China	47	49	4.25	0.26
Average[a]	200	230	15.00	0.87

Note:
[a] Rounded up to nearest 10 above.
Source: Zimmerman, *World Income*, pp. 55–6.

Table 5.3: National Incomes of Developing World, 1913–29 ($ of 1953 millions)

	1913	%	1929	%	% increase 1913–29	Annual % increase
Philippines	1,100	0.36	1,600	0.39	45.45	2.37
Malaya	400	0.13	900	0.22	125.00	5.19
Dutch East Indies	4,200	1.37	5,800	1.43	38.09	2.03
India and Burma	19,700	6.46	22,300	5.50	13.19	0.77
China	24,300	7.97	26,600	6.56	9.46	0.56
Total	49,700	16.30	57,200	14.12	15.09	0.58
World Total	304,800	100.00	404,900	100.00	32.84	1.79

Source: Zimmerman, *World Income*, pp. 50–1.

Table 5.4: *Per Capita* Incomes of Undeveloped World, 1913–29 ($ of 1953)

	1913	1929	% increase	Annual % increase
Philippines	120	130	8.33	0.50
Malaya	140	210	50.00	2.56
Dutch East Indies	85	95	11.76	0.69
India and Burma	65	67	3.07	0.18
China	47	49	4.25	0.26
World *per capita* income	200	230	15.00	0.87

Source: Zimmerman, *World Income*, pp. 52–3.

experienced the highest *per capita* income growth at 2.80 per cent annually, but North America grew rapidly at 1.03 per cent. In the Far East incomes increased at 0.82 per cent which was faster than in North West Europe where the figure was only 0.64 per cent. Of the Far East countries, Malaya led, with *per capita* incomes growing at 2.56 per cent each year, which was second in the world only to Japan. The Dutch East Indies and the Philippines had much lower levels of income growth at 0.69 per cent and 0.50 per cent respectively. In China *per capita* income growth was as low as 0.26 per cent annually, and in India, the most highly industrialised country in the developing world, it was as low as 0.18 per cent. Once again it appears that plantation and mining economies were more successful than those in which there was industrialisation. Yet even in India and China, which together held over

Table 5.5: Distribution of World Population, 1913–29 (millions)

	1913	%	1929	%	% increase 1913–29	Annual % increase
North America	99.8	6.26	131.8	7.38	32.06	1.75
Oceania	7.0	0.43	7.9	0.44	12.85	0.75
North West Europe	183.7	11.52	190.4	10.66	3.64	0.22
Soviet Union	139.0	8.72	150.0	8.40	7.91	0.47
South East Europe	130.4	8.18	159.7	8.94	22.46	1.26
Latin America	79.5	4.98	106.4	5.96	33.83	1.83
Japan	51.9	3.25	62.9	3.52	21.19	1.20
Near East	—	—	—	—	—	—
Far East	61.1	3.83	78.2	4.38	27.98	1.55
Central Africa	—	—	—	—	—	—
South East Asia	323.7	20.31	355.5	19.91	9.82	0.58
China	517.4	32.46	542.1	30.37	4.77	0.29
Total	1593.5	100.00	1784.9	100.00	12.01	0.71

Source: Zimmerman, *World Income*, pp. 55–6.

Table 5.6: Population of the Developing World, 1913–29 (millions)

	1913	%	1929	%	% increase 1913–29	Annual % increase
Philippines	9.4	0.58	13.1	0.73	39.36	2.09
Malaya	2.7	0.16	4.4	0.24	62.96	3.10
Dutch East Indies	49.0	3.07	60.7	3.40	23.87	1.34
India	303.0	19.07	330.0	18.48	8.91	0.53
Burma	12.4	0.77	14.0	0.78	12.90	0.76
Siam	8.3	0.52	11.5	0.64	38.55	2.06
China	517.4	32.46	542.1	30.37	104.77	0.29
Total	902.2	56.61	975.8	54.66	8.15	0.49
World Total	1593.5	100.00	1784.9	100.00	12.01	0.71

Source: Zimmerman, *World Income*, pp. 48–9.

half the world's population, people were getting richer, not poorer, if Zimmerman is to be believed.[1]

There are no comparable figures for the 1930s, but it is probably a fair assumption that this was a period of stagnation for most countries of the developing world. Certainly the trade of most countries was affected badly by the depression, with the exception of South Africa. To understand in more detail the development which took place before

1929 and the retrenchment which followed it is necessary to examine the experience of the individual countries. As the depression was most marked in international trade, those countries that had large parts of their economy dependent on exports felt the depression most seriously. Economies more firmly based on peasant agriculture were better able to adjust to the lower trade levels of the 1930s than those with a heavy dependence on plantation and mines.

In India *per capita* incomes grew until the late 1920s, when they levelled out. They did not resume an upward path until the late 1930s. This is shown in Mukherjee's estimate of *per capita* real income in India, given in Table 5.7.

Table 5.7: **Average *Per Capita* National Income of India**[a] **at 1948–9 Prices for Overlapping Nine Year Periods, 1905–40**

Period	Centring	*Per capita* income 1948–9 (Rupees)
1901–9	1905	203
1906–14	1910	220
1911–19	1915	241
1916–24	1920	253
1921–9	1925	261
1926–34	1930	260
1931–9	1935	260
1936–44	1940	265

Note:

[a] Excluding areas now in Pakistan, Bangladesh and Burma.

Source: M. Mukherjee, *National Income of India: Trends and Structure* (Calcutta: Statistical Publishing Society, 1969), p. 61.

These figures fit well with those for the consumption of factory-produced cotton goods in British India, discussed in Chapter 3, page 101–2. Total yardage of cotton goods supplied to the Indian market by imports and Indian factories rose until 1926/8 and then fell to 1930/1. Despite some recovery, even in 1935/6 the level of 1927/8 had not been passed.

The cotton industry led the industrialisation which India experienced in these years. Textiles from Indian factories increasingly replaced imports and the number of mills rose from 271 in 1914 to 365 in 1935. This import substitution was helped by the tariffs placed on imported cottons after 1921, which reached higher and higher levels in 1927, 1930, 1931 and 1934. Special agreements on imports were made with Britain and Japan in 1934 and later years. Cloth production expanded faster than yarn production, because yarn export markets in China and the East had been lost during the war whilst the domestic cloth market was now protected. So the yarn producing centre of Bombay was less successful than the rapidly growing new weaving centre Ahmedabad, which was better situated to supply the home market and equipped to replace high quality imports. New factories were established also in Bengal and other parts of India. Although the depression held back total consumption of factory produced cottons, Indian factory production continued to expand helped by tariffs, trade agreements and the Swadeshi movement, which for political reasons encouraged consumption of Indian cloth in preference to British cloth. Nearly all the cotton mills were owned by Indians and by the mid-1930s they also owned more than half the jute industry, India's other major factory industry. This trade centred on Calcutta. There were 76 mills in 1918 and 110 by 1939. Heavily dependent on international demand for grainsacks and sandbags, the industry boomed during the First World War. After the recession of 1921/2 there was substantial expansion. The depression checked the industry, but from 1933 there was recovery and by 1937 production was almost back to the previous height, although 1938 was a very bad year. Various agreements were made between the companies to try to restrict production in the bad years, but they were soon broken when times improved. Both the cotton industry and the jute industry had been established before the turn of the century, but the most important new development was the establishment of an Indian-owned iron and steel industry. The Tata Iron and Steel Company made its first steel at Jamshedpur in 1913, and by 1916 production was 147,497 tons of pig iron, 139,433 tons of steel ingots and 98,726 tons of finished steel, mainly rails and girders. The war favoured production of steel and other companies entered the industry. The Bengal Iron Company, which pre-dated Tata, continued to produce the cheapest pig iron in the world, at a rate of 200,000 tons a year, most of which was used by other Indian foundries. But there was a slump in 1919, a boom in 1921 and a further slump in 1921, and in 1924 the industry was given protection. This was extended in 1927 for a further period of seven years. It was the first industry to be deliberately protected, apart from simply benefiting from tariffs imposed to raise revenue, like the cotton industry. Exports of pig iron and internal demand for iron and steel fell

after 1929/30 due to the depression but protection meant that
domestic production was sustained. Recovery of both internal and
external demand took place from 1933. Tariffs were actually lowered
then as high levels of protection were no longer needed. From 1936 the
industry shared in the boom conditions caused by international
re-armament, and capacity was increased. Japan was the leading
customer of exported pig iron. Between 1923 and 1939 production of
steel ingots had increased eight-fold. But a measure of the impact of the
depression on the Indian economy is the fact that total Indian
consumption of steel, including imports, was still below the 1929 level
in 1939. The engineering industry was less successful. Various
enterprises were set up in and around Jamshedpur to make locomotives,
railway wagons, agricultural implements, tin plate, cables, enamelled
ironware, etc., and much of the industry was granted protection from
1924. But with the possible exception of tin plate, the industry could
not compete with goods imported from abroad. The refusal of
protection to the locomotive industry did not help. The coal industry
benefited from the First World War as imports ceased and all India
had to be supplied from the Bengal coalfields. Coal exports were not
allowed to resume until after 1923 because of the continuing coal
shortage in India. Then serious attempts were made to recapture
markets in South East Asia which had been taken by the South African
coal industry. But more than 96 per cent of Indian coal was consumed
at home. Production was more than 20 million tons in 1924 and
reached 23.8 million tons in 1930. It fell to below 20 million tons in
1933 and did not pass the 1930 level until 1937, reaching its inter-war
peak of 28.3 million tons in 1938. Once again the relative stagnation
of the 1930s is clear. The period 1937 to 1939 was marked by greatly
increased industrial activity and consequent demand for coal. Other
mineral production in India included mica, chromite, woolfram and
manganese, all of which boomed during the First World War but fell
away afterwards. Manganese enjoyed a revival in the late 1930s,
because of the high level of activity in international steel-making in
which manganese was used. Petroleum production from the Punjab and
Assam was insignificant in comparison with that of Burma. Other
Indian industries were the glass industry and the cement industry, the
latter increasing its production from under 1,000 tons on the eve of
the First World War to 1,200,000 tons on the eve of the Second World
War. This success was achieved without protection and imports fell in
consequence. Another successful industry was the match industry, and
India became self-sufficient during the 1930s following the granting of

protection in 1928. Paper-making showed considerable expansion too, assisted by protection in 1925, and chemical production grew after protection was granted in 1931. Leather production increased, after it was discovered during the First World War that Indian hides were suitable for British army boots. This led to more production of boots and shoes in India, and the Bata Shoe Company was set up in the early 1930s.

Apart from these modern industries India continued to have a vast and intricate network of old and traditional industries. Of prime importance was the handloom textile industry which produced a range of cloths from fine sarees to coarse chandar. In 1914 factories produced about the same amount of cloth as the handlooms but by the end of the 1930s the mills produced more than two and a half times as much, despite greater production from the handlooms. Mill yarn had replaced handspun yarn before the turn of the century, and factory cloth increasingly displaced handloom cloth during the inter-war years as fashion dictated a taste for simple standard cloths. The weavers responded to falling prices during the depression by producing more cloth, but between 1928 and 1940 the earnings of handloom weavers plunged, in some cases to less than a third of their previous level. The weavers were driven from the particular countryside districts in which they tended to concentrate, to the towns. There they became dependent on middlemen-employers in whose homes or establishments they worked. The number of looms in Madras increased between 1920 and 1940 but declined in Bengal, and power looms began to be installed particularly around Bombay. Other trades were more closely part of village life, and blacksmiths, carpenters, leatherworkers, potters, oil pressers, rice pounders, basket makers and the rest often received a share of the village crop for their services to the community. This share declined for tradesmen whose products were being displaced by factory goods, potters and oil pressers in particular. What usually happened where factory production ousted hand production is that initially the preliminary processes were supplanted by the factories, as when mill yarn replaced handloom yarn. So dyers used synthetic dyes, smiths used sheet metal and rolled iron, tailors used sewing machines and artisans in general used modern tools. Later the finished products too were driven out. This process could be seen operating all over the developing world in these years. All artisan industry in India was dependent on moneylenders and trader intermediaries, and had high costs and low incomes. As old skills declined new ones developed. For example, as cart making declined there were new jobs in car and bus maintenance. There was also a new demand for urban necessities like locks, cupboards, safes, trunks, furniture, etc. Political support by the Congress Party brought about a revival of cloth woven from handspun thread, and the Village Industries Association helped many otherwise declining industries such as honey making, and handmade paper. Of 15,400,000 industrial workers in 1931 there were 4,100,000 textile workers, of which 2,900,000 were weavers, and there were over 900,000 carpenters, 870,000 potters and 700,000 blacksmiths, besides the multitudes in other trades.

It has been estimated that in 1931 industry and mining produced only 17.7 per cent of the Indian national income despite rapid growth since the beginning of the century. Communications, railways and commerce contributed 15.1 per cent, services and housing 10.4 per cent, government services 4.1 per cent, and agriculture a massive 52.7 per cent. Yet agriculture had grown very little in the previous thirty years. The area under cultivation showed no marked increase or decrease between 1914 and 1939. The main food crops were rice, wheat, jowar and bajra, the area under bajra falling slightly. As the population grew, exports of food grains diminished although they had previously been substantial. Rice was the chief grain crop, but even before 1914 India's rice exports were mainly from Burma. In the three years after the war India imported rice from Burma at an annual average of 512 thousand tons, whilst still exporting 387 thousand tons, a net import of 125 thousand tons each year. By 1938 imports were up to 1,282 thousand tons, while exports were down to 282 thousand tons, a net import of 1,000 thousand tons. Clearly Burma's capacity to increase her rice crop is crucial to understanding how India was able to feed her own growing population in these years. As for wheat India grew just enough for her own needs in the 1920s and in bad years she had to import some. Only in good years such as 1924 was there any left over which could be exported. There were net imports in 1928, 1929 and 1931. An excellent crop was harvested in 1929 but little was sold abroad because of the international glut that year. As the depression took hold duties, which remained in force from 1931 to 1937, were imposed to stop cheap Australian wheat flooding into India. There was no movement of any significance of wheat into or out of India during the 1930s. Cotton and jute acreage showed no discernible trend in these years, but there was a small increase in the area producing oilseeds, especially groundnuts, and also in plantation crops like sugar, tea and rubber. Cash crops like these also seem to have shown increasing yields. Oil seed exports declined in general during the

1920s, except for groundnuts, and they too declined in the 1930s.
Like rice and wheat, oilseeds were being consumed by the growing
population. That Indian peasant farmers were capable of adjusting their
farming practices to grow profit earning cash crops is shown by the
fact that groundnut cultivation in Khandesh and North Gujerat rose
from 4,500 acres in 1912/13 to 310,000 acres in 1926/7. Like the
peasants of West Africa they sought a profit from groundnuts when
they realised it was available. Acreage under sugar increased very
rapidly after 1932 when a protective tariff was imposed against imports
from Java. The number of sugar factories increased from 32 before
protection to 145 by the Second World War, by which time India
had not only become self-sufficient in sugar, but had even begun to
export it. Output of refined sugar rose from 151,700 tons to 1,350,000
tons. Most of the sugar was grown in the United Provinces, the Punjab,
and Bihar and Orissa. Tea production increased during the First World
War, but there was a temporary setback as prices fell after the war.
Then there was further expansion until the depression, which hit the
industry seriously. Because of the restriction scheme agreed in 1933
with Ceylon and the Dutch East Indies, production increased only
moderately in the next seven years. Assam was the major producing
region, although estates in the south were becoming more important.
Another crop in which the south was gaining in importance was rubber,
much of which was grown by peasant smallholders in Travancore,
Madras and Cochin. By 1939 a third of the crop was manufactured in
India. One problem affecting Indian agriculture in this period was the
subdivision and fragmentation of holdings as the population increased;
another was the debt faced by the peasantry during the depression
when prices of food grains fell so severely. Whilst some farmers
benefited from the increase in the area irrigated by government
schemes from 24,287 thousand acres in 1914 to 31,648 thousand acres
in 1938, this was offset by progressive exhaustion of the soil in other
areas. Nearly all agriculturists felt the impact of the depression, but it
was those who were most dependent on cash sales of their crops which
were hit most. The more self-sufficient a peasant was the less affected
he was. The fact that there was no major decline in the consumption of
cotton goods, kerosene, sugar and tea suggest that no undue hardship
was occurring, and this is supported by the fact that population growth
continued. The depression hit India less hard than the famine of 1918.[2]

In Burma economic development after 1914 continued along the
lines established since the middle of the nineteenth century with
peasant rice cultivation expanding, much of it for export. India now

became the main outlet for Burma's rice, not Europe. But a glut of rice production was developing in the world, with greater rice cultivation in Japan and the Philippines and continued expansion in Siam and French Indo-China. Between 1925 and 1929 Burma's exports of rice fell from 3.1 million tons to 2.8 million tons, whilst rice prices declined. Down to Rs 130 for a hundred baskets in 1930, the price collapsed to Rs 75 in 1931. Because Burma was so heavily involved in rice cultivation this price collapse struck at the heart of her economy. Farmers could not pay labourers, or interest on loans, or rents. Many Indian Chettiar moneylenders were forced into bankruptcy when their debtors could not repay loans, making it impossible for them to repay the European banks from which *they* had borrowed. Credit contracted, land was given up and left unfarmed. Prices were even worse in 1933, and although there was then recovery the general price level was only half what it had been in the 1920s. Yet the area under rice was greater in the 1930s than it had been in the previous decade and Burma supplied nearly 40 per cent of the world rice exports. Rice mills increased in number throughout the period, even during the 1930s. Rubber acreage rose from 69,184 acres in 1926 to 106,218 acres in 1936, nearly as much as in India. Petroleum production was 279.7 million gallons in 1920, 253.4 million gallons in 1929 and 251.3 million gallons in 1935, a progress which could hardly be called dynamic. Tin mining became important in this period, and lead, zinc, silver and copper were exported as ore. Coal and iron ore deposits were discovered. Teak was another export industry. There was virtually no modern industry in Burma and apart from her traditional craft industries, Burma had to import her consumer goods, India being a major supplier.[3]

Ceylon's development to a large extent was based on tea, rubber and coconut products. Yet she was by no means a simple plantation economy. If tea was mainly an estate crop, rubber was grown on plantations and by peasant smallholders, and coconuts exclusively by peasants. Tea output grew at 1.8 per cent annually between 1913 and 1929, but declined by 0.9 per cent each year between 1929 and 1939 due to the depression and the increased competition of the Dutch East Indies. Peasant smallholders were increasing their share of tea production and by 1935 there were nearly 70,000 tea smallholdings accounting for approximately 12 per cent of the total area cultivated. Rubber output grew at 13.2 per cent per annum between 1913 and 1929, which was much faster than tea.

In 1929 Ceylon was the third largest rubber producer in the world after Malaya and the Dutch East Indies, and had a tenth of the world's acreage. The depression hit rubber badly, and between 1929 and 1939 rubber output declined by 4.4 per cent annually. As in the case of tea, smallholders had followed the example of the estates and provided over 20 per cent of the acreage in 1936. They weathered the depression better than the estates, for unlike the estates they were not entirely dependent on rubber and could manage perfectly well on their provision crops. Coconuts were the major peasant cash export crop, output growing at 2.8 per cent per annum between 1913 and 1929, but declining by 0.2 per cent between 1929 and 1939. A feature of the 1920s was the emergence of locally owned coconut plantations, a natural development from peasant smallholdings. Many of these were later owned by important local politicians. Ceylon's position in this market was affected by the emergence of the Philippines as the world's major producer. One great advantage of the coconut as a peasant crop is that if prices were unsatisfactory during the depression, the crop could always be eaten. As with other smallholder export production, coconuts were only a part of the peasant economy which depended essentially on home-grown rice augmented by fruit and vegetables. So the peasants were able to adjust to the depression, and as in the case of India, this is revealed by the way the population continued to increase. There was little modern manufacturing in Ceylon other than the processing of export crops. There was a small graphite industry and a minor spice trade. As in other parts of the underdeveloped world the coming of bicycles, cars and buses linked the countryside more closely to the towns and broadened the market for cloth, matches, and kerosene, although these were imported.[4]

Malaya too was strongly influenced by the fortunes of the rubber industry, which between the wars overtook tin mining as the driving force in her development. As in Ceylon, the collapse of rubber prices led to migrant workers being sent home, and peasant smallholders produced almost as much as the estates in 1933. Although they were allowed to supply only just over a third of exports under the restriction scheme, they survived these years by turning to their provision gardens and rice plots. The resilience of rubber-producing peasant smallholders in Malaya, Ceylon and the Dutch East Indies is shown by the fact that in 1939 not far short of half the world's total output came from these small producers. This was a fine example of peasant commercial initiative. Malaya was the world's fifth largest producer of coconut products, which were of course another peasant crop as in Ceylon, the Dutch East Indies and the Philippines. There was expansion in the 1920s and contraction in the 1930s, but of course any surplus was easily absorbed by the peasants themselves. In contrast to coconuts, palm oil was a plantation crop established in the 1930s, a peasant crop of West Africa becoming a plantation crop in Malaya and the Dutch East Indies. By 1940 Malaya supplied 12 per cent of the world's supply. The old staple export of the Malayan economy was tin and Malaya produced a third of the world's supply in these years, despite all the problems of the depressions and the emergence of the Belgian Congo and Siam as producers. The importance of the peasants in the Malayan economy is brought out when it is realised that not only were they important producers of export crops, but also underpinned the economy by their rice and vegetable production. They had never produced enough rice to feed all the immigrant workers, but, when tin and rubber prices fell and immigrant workers returned home, the government encouraged a self-sufficient rice policy now that there were less export earnings to buy imported rice with. This policy of rice self-sufficiency was followed by many rice-importing countries during the depression. But legislation did not prevent the astute peasantry from realising that rubber paid better than rice and they continued to plant it. This is a fine example of peasant resistance to attempts to make them act contrary to their self-interest as dictated by the market. Rubber and tin companies supported the grow-rice policy but would not plant it themselves for exactly the same reason. Modern manufacturing did not make much progress in Malaya, apart from small-scale Chinese enterprises in confectionery, medicines, soap, footwear, cement, bricks, rice milling and oil milling. Even in 1932 the only large factories were a foundry and the Ford assembly plant. Cheap imports forced the British American Tobacco company to close their factory. In 1937 the Bata Shoe Company set up a plant at Klang, Selangor, and two Chinese rubber shoe factories copying Bata's methods were set up nearby.[5]

Like Malaya, the Dutch East Indies made substantial progress during the 1920s with rubber expanding rapidly. Peasant producers were very important and as elsewhere survived the difficult years of the early 1930s and underassessment in the regulation scheme. Smallholder rubber production roughly equaled plantation production by this time and largely accounted for the fact that by 1939 Dutch East Indies rubber exports were greater than those of Malaya. Only sugar, the traditional crop of the Dutch East Indies, was more important than rubber, and peasant production of this was discouraged. Sugar proved very vulnerable to the depression as the major buyers, India, China and Japan, cut back their imports. In consequence the Dutch East Indies was one of the most severely affected countries in these years. Tea expanded during the 1920s and peasants grew about a fifth of the crop, but although production was sustained in the 1930s, price levels were not. Most of the Dutch East Indies' other export crops were hit by the depression and the growth of the palm oil industry was one of the few positive features of the 1930s. Peasant production of rubber, coconuts, tobacco, tea, coffee and groundnuts was important, and the whole basis of the economy was their production of rice, maize and other foodstuffs. When the depression struck, workers returned to their villages in Java from plantations in the Outer Provinces, and land formerly used for sugar was now used for food crops. A policy of self-sufficiency in rice was followed and by 1936 Java had a surplus of paddy. Again the peasant was demonstrating his capacity to survive economically where the plantations could not. Like most countries of Asia the Dutch East Indies had a complex network of traditional industries and crafts to supply the consumer goods and services which her people needed. But after 1914 a few modern factories were established such as a paper mill and a railway wagon works, a cement factory having been started just before the war. In 1922 the first textile mill was set up and in 1925 British American Tobacco opened a cigarette factory. A cotton-wool factory was built in 1926, General Motors built an assembly plant in 1927 and another cement factory opened in 1931. When the depression came the devaluation of the yen in 1931 led to an influx of Japanese goods and the government was forced to abandon its free trade policy of the previous sixty years. So after 1933 import controls were operated. Subsidies were given to establish an aluminium plant and factories to finish the products of small craft producers. Behind the new protective walls several new cotton mills were opened in the 1930s and in 1933 Unilever built a soap factory at Batavia. The Bata Shoe Company opened a leather shoe factory in 1935 and a rubber shoe factory in 1939. Goodyear Tyres began a factory in 1935, and another factory made flash lights and batteries. A second cigarette factory was built. By 1940 there were 3,930 factories in Java and 1,540 in the Outer Provinces, and they employed 324,000 workers, which was three times as many as in 1935. But not all the developments of the 1930s were concerned with domestic food production and factories, for nickel and bauxite mining began in these years and in 1939 petroleum output was up by a half on its 1929 level. Tin output had recovered from the depression by the end of the decade.[6]

Despite the fact that the Philippines, like the Dutch East Indies, was a major sugar producer, it was not as badly affected by the depression. There was expansion in sugar during the 1920s, but whereas the Dutch East Indies lost her markets in Asia as the depression struck, the Philippines continued to have a market for her sugar and other products in the United States. She was the world's second largest producer of coconut products and a major producer of hemp fibre and tobacco. During the 1930s large rubber plantations were established in the Southern Provinces. But the whole economy depended on the rice and food production of her peasants. During the 1920s export crops tended to supplant rice, which was imported from French Indo-China. As in other rice-deficit countries during the 1930s, the government tried to encourage the people to grow enough rice to feed themselves. This policy was fairly successful, rice taking land previously used for export crops, particularly tobacco and hemp. Bananas, mangoes, maize and root crops were also produced in quantity. Gold was the most important mineral product, and as was the case with other gold producers, this helped the country in the depressed years, because of the rise in its value when the dollar depreciated in 1933. In addition chromite and iron ore began to be mined in the 1930s. There were the usual craft industries, but embroidery, button-making and hat-making were particularly prominent and produced to some extent for export. Of modern industries there were by the end of the period three textile mills and eight shoe factories, plus distilleries, foundries, cement factories, brickworks, engineering workshops, boat builders, nickel plating establishments, rice mills, sawmills and plant to process tobacco and coconut products.[7]

Siam was one of Burma's great rivals as a rice exporter and expansion of production and exports continued during the 1920s. The glut of rice which coincided with the depression caused severe problems for her peasant producers, and the situation was made worse by the desire of rice importing countries like Malaya, the Dutch East Indies and the Philippines to become self-sufficient. She had to turn to India, Ceylon, Europe and America instead. Production of rice rose from an annual average of 4.4 million tons in 1921–4 to 4.6 million tons in 1930–4 and 4.8 million tons in 1940–4. Acreage increased by just over a half between 1915–19 and 1935–9. Exports, however, fell during the 1930s and prices fell by a half. The building of railways and various irrigation schemes helped the expansion of rice. Tin expanded in the 1920s but was hit by the depression as everywhere and the teak industry was in continued decline throughout the period. A new development in the 1930s was rubber grown by peasant smallholders.

Sugar production also increased in the 1930s and in 1937 the government built a sugar mill at Lampang. Handloom cotton weaving
continued as the leading craft industry. Imported yarn tended to
displace handspun yarn, but during the depression there was increased
cultivation of cotton by the peasants to spin for their own use. The
army ran a cotton mill but it was unimportant as regards the economy
as a whole. There were seven factories in Bangkok in 1919, including a
cement factory, three aerated-water plants, a soap factory, a cigarette
factory and a leather factory, the cement factory and one of the
aerated-water plants being Thai owned. The Siam Electricity Company
provided electricity and tramcars in Bangkok and there were more than
25 printing companies. Outside Bangkok there were only rice mills and
saw mills. Cement output increased during the 1920s and 1930s and
reached 92,000 metric tons in 1938/9. Tariff revisions were introduced
in 1926, 1931 and 1934, and assisted match, cigarette and tobacco
production. British American Tobacco ran the largest operation,
developing local brand names and marketing a standardised product
countrywide. Other industries were encouraged by the tariff revisions.
A soap factory and the Boon Rawd brewery were built. Several small
Chinese-run sugar factories began operation. In 1936 there were further
tariff changes, from which the tobacco, soap, match, sugar and alcohol
industries all continued to benefit. Of other industrial activity, the
army, having built a paper factory in 1923, started a larger one in 1938
and another textile mill in 1934. Despite these various industrial
enterprises, Siam remained essentially a rice-producing economy, both
for home consumption and export. Given the problem of exports she
seems to have managed reasonably during the depression years, the
peasants living well enough on their rice, fruit and vegetables.[8]

The third great rice-exporting economy of Asia was French Indo-
China. The area under cultivation increased between the wars as
irrigation works extended. Maize became an important crop in these
years, especially in the 1930s. Coconuts were another peasant crop,
and smallholders grew tea, coffee and rubber, but less than was grown
on plantations. As elsewhere in Asia, the production of foodstuffs for
domestic consumption were the basis of the economy, not exports. As
this was only marginally affected by the depression, the people did not
suffer undue hardship. As regards industry, there were the usual
numerous traditional handicrafts, including rice husking, oil pressing,
sugar making and the distilling of alcohol. But the weaving of cotton
and silk were the most important crafts, and there were blacksmiths,
joiners, masons, bricklayers, limeburners and numerous other

tradesmen. The leading modern industry was coal mining, whose
output rose from 501,000 tons in 1913 to 2,308,000 tons in 1937.
There was also tin and zinc mining, zinc declining in the 1930s whilst
tin increased. Wolfram, antimony, graphite and phosphates were mined
in small quantities, and there was a little traditional gold mining in
Upper Tonkin. Of other modern industries, the sole cement factory
was extended in 1926 and by 1929 produced 183,000 tons of which
more than a fifth was exported. Production fell in the early 1930s but
by 1937 it was producing 235,000 tons of which over half was
exported. Of the three cotton-spinning mills in 1913 one was later
closed, but the other two extended. Yarn imports fell from 4,000 tons
a year in 1925 to just over 1,000 tons a year from 1931. Sometimes as
many as 10,000 workers were employed at the mills by 1938. These
mills supplied yarn to the handloom weavers as well as to their own
weaving sheds. Although cotton was grown on family plots all over the
country, the raw cotton for the mills was imported. There were also
two silk-weaving factories in the 1930s, using silk from Chinese mills at
Shanghai and Canton. Modern sugar factories were built, production
rising from 3,000 tons in 1930 to 15,000 tons in 1938. Tobacco and
cigarette manufacture also grew rapidly, 2,800 tons of cigarettes being
made in 1937. Oil processing and soap factories were built in these
years, and beer production increased. There were many rice mills, and
five big distilleries with about 50 smaller ones. There were also
establishments for making bricks, tiles, pipes, glass, china, buttons,
leather, paint, candles, matches, fireworks, paper, rubber goods and
oxygen. In addition there were engineering shops, railway workshops,
an arsenal and shipyards. Electrical power was used more and more.
Some of these industries were helped by the fact that from 1929
Indo-China was able to adopt tariffs to suit her needs. Yet despite all
these developments, industrialisation cannot really be said to have
made much headway and Indo-China was still essentially an economy
of peasant producers.[9]

China's development between the wars was slow and marred by
political warfare in the south from 1922 to 1927, and by the Japanese
annexation of Manchuria in the north from 1932. Exports were only a
very small part of the country's production and the economy was a
vast peasant system in which there was little change in size or structure
in these years. Rice was the main crop and it is estimated that in 1933
it amounted to 232.9 million tons, followed by wheat with 95.2
million tons. Other grains, potatoes, vegetables and fruit were also
grown. Farms were usually small and run by tenants or owner-

proprietors. Indebtedness was a problem as in many parts of Asia and in the early 1930s many tenants gave up the land and went to the towns. Chinese agriculture was not subsistence agriculture, for even part of the staple food crops were sold to the local markets to raise cash for rent, tax and the purchase of manufactures. Cash crops like tobacco, opium, groundnuts, rapeseed, soyabeans and cotton were also raised. It has been suggested that in 1933 79 per cent of the Chinese workforce was in agriculture and 21 per cent in other occupations. Of the workforce 5.4 per cent worked in handicrafts, 0.5 per cent in factories, and 0.3 per cent in mining. Handicrafts overshadowed factory production, which was rather unimportant to the Chinese economy as a whole. It has already been shown in Chapter 3, page 108–9, how Chinese factory cotton cloth replaced imports, but factory cloth was in any case only a small part of the market. In 1924 domestic factory cloth plus imports amounted to 1,044 million square yards, but handloom production amounted to more than three times as much at 3,129 million square yards. In 1936 factory cloth amounted to 1,350 million square yards, but handloom production was nearly twice that at 2,240 million square yards. Chinese yarn from the mills of Tientsin, Tsingtao and Shanghai had replaced imported yarn from India and was used by the handlooms in place of handspun yarns. After the slow progress of the 1920s the Chinese economy experienced great difficulties from 1931 to 1935 due to the disastrous Yellow River floods in 1931 and the depression which particularly affected modern industry in Shanghai and the Coastal Provinces. These industries were more closely connected to the world system than much of China's economy and many factories were foreign owned. The number of modern factories rose from 279 in 1913 to 3,450 in 1933, foreign firms leading in cotton weaving and cigarette manufacture. Chinese firms led in flour milling, the second most important industry after cotton weaving, and in the silk industry. Just over half the cotton-yarn spindles were in Chinese mills and just under half the looms. Chinese firms were also prominent in the production of matches and vegetable oils. Foreign firms controlled the coal industry and the generation of electricity. After the Japanese occupation of Manchuria in 1932 that region's development took on a different shape from that of the rest of China. Japanese investment was made in coal and iron ore mining, and the production of iron and steel. Machine and machine-tool manufacturing expanded, new chemical plants were built and oil shale refining begun. Several large new cotton mills were set up. Japanese enterprise in Manchuria however was partly offset by the withdrawal of Western

companies. China remained at the end of the period much as she had
been at the beginning. What modern industry there was, was confined
to the coastal towns and had little impact inland. The tariffs which
were raised progressively from 1929 gave some encouragement to
modern industry but in no way revolutionised the Chinese economy.[10]

The economic development of Africa was dominated by South
Africa. She had progressed on the basis of gold and diamond mining in
the 1920s although there were serious disturbances known as the 'Rand
Rebellion' in 1922 when white miners rebelled against moves to use
more Africans in the mines. Between 1928 and 1932 the economy was
held back as the effects of the depression were felt. Then the rise in the
sterling price of gold after 1931 and the devaluation of the South
African pound in 1933 gave a new impetus to gold mining. Also in
1933 the first iron and steel was produced at Pretoria from South
African ores. So in the remaining years of the decade progress was
sustained in mining and industry, with foreign capital flowing in and
the number of factories increasing. Agricultural output also expanded
to sustain the growing urban centres to which all races flocked. South
Africa progressed towards being a modern industrial economy whilst
the rest of the world was depressed. Between 1919 and 1939 South
African net national income more than doubled, with an average annual
growth rate of 5.0 per cent between 1919 and 1929 and of 5.8 per
cent between 1929 and 1939. The structure of the economy also
changed, with agriculture in 1911/12 contributing 17.4 per cent,
mining 27.1 per cent and private manufacturing 6.7 per cent. In 1938/9
agriculture had dropped to 12.6 per cent, mining to 20.7 per cent, but
manufacturing had grown to 17.7 per cent. Arable and livestock each
contributed about half of agricultural production, maize being the most
important crop and the staple African food. It was grown by farmers
of all races who supplied it to the miners and industrial workers. Wool
was the leading livestock product and cattle were reared for the
domestic market. Price fluctuations in the 1920s caused the government
to adopt support schemes, but they led to surplus maize stocks
accumulating which had to be sold off abroad at a loss. An artificially
high domestic price had to be charged to cover the export loss.
Tariffs were also imposed to help farmers and there were subsidies and
control boards, because agriculture employed 64 per cent of the
workforce even in 1936 and so was a politically sensitive issue. The
problems of agriculture were counterbalanced in the 1930s by the
near-doubling of the gold price and the fact that gold output increased
two and a half times between 1932 and 1940. New mining areas were

discovered and technical and scientific advances helped the industry, which drove on the economy in these years. The development of the iron and steel industry was a major additional advance. Employment in mining rose by more than a half from 308,000 in 1932 to 475,000 in 1939, and it doubled in manufacturing, construction, electricity, water and gas from 161,000 to 331,000. Altogether about half a million new jobs were created in industry, trade and commerce in these years. Engineering and explosive production developed in association with the mines, and food, drink, tobacco and clothing manufacture expanded to supply the growth of consumer demand. Tariff policy helped, with revenue tariffs being imposed in 1914 and protective tariffs to encourage industry from 1925. This development could not have taken place without the willingness of Africans to migrate to work in the mines and industry. They were peasant farmers who left the farming to the women and children whilst they were away, and returned home every year or so. In this way they gained the benefit of money wages at the same time as they maintained their position in the agricultural community for their old age, and as a safety precaution. Through these migrant workers the benefits of the gold boom were transferred not only to Africans inside South Africa, but also to the many thousands who migrated from surrounding territories like Nyasaland and Mozambique. The employment created on the basis of the mining boom in South Africa provided income to Africans all over southern Africa at a time when agriculture was depressed.[11]

Neighbouring South West Africa was a vast sparsely populated territory. It formed part of South Africa economically, with sheep farming in the south and cattle ranching in the centre, the north remaining an African farming area. Most of the wool and dairy products of the territory went to South Africa and the country had few dealings with any other African territory. In the late 1920s there were wells bored by the government to help the farmers, but the depression and drought in the 1930s put an end to this. Diamond mining was the other important industry, but its fortunes fluctuated with the price of diamonds, which fell drastically during the depression. From the mid 1930s there was recovery as the world began to pull out of the depression.[12]

Mining was the great business of Southern Rhodesia, carrying the mineral belt northwards from South Africa. Gold accounted for four-fifths of the mineral production, followed by asbestos and chrome. Like South Africa, the gold boom of the 1930s brought considerable prosperity and increased employment and the number of Southern

Rhodesian Africans employed in the industry rose from 37,000 in 1912 to 94,646 in 1937. The benefits of the gold boom was also passed on to Africans of other territories, for 149,040 were at work in the country in 1937, 66,700 of them in mining. As in South Africa, African farmers also benefited from the improved demand for food by the miners, particularly maize and vegetables. African crops and livestock accounted for about a third of the country's agricultural production and their acreage increased by more than a sixth between 1924 and 1936. African-owned cattle herds also multiplied. European farmers grew maize and tobacco, but both crops were hit by the depression. As in South Africa, gold sustained the economy when the depression hit its agriculture.[13]

The development of Northern Rhodesia was negligible until the late 1920s when the full potential of her copper reserves was appreciated. The collapse of copper prices during the depression held development back, but from 1932 mining expanded rapidly. By the late 1930s the value of her mineral exports was greater than those of the Belgian Congo, and nearly as much as those of Southern Rhodesia. The European population grew rapidly and Africans migrated to the mines from all the adjacent territories. African farmers closer to the mine-heads were able to benefit from the opportunities of growing food to supply the miners. For the Africans, there was a choice between growing food to supply the mines or working in them. This choice, as elsewhere in Southern and Central Africa, was determined by the fertility of the land and the distance from the mines. The more distant from the mines and the poorer the soil the greater was the incentive to migrate to become a mineworker. Competition from European farmers diminished the returns available to African farmers during the 1930s and led more and more of them to take the then more profitable alternative of work in the mines.[14]

To the east, Northern Rhodesia was connected to Nyasaland and Tanganyika, and beyond them lay Kenya and Uganda. There was no important mining in these territories. Tsetse fly and malaria affected large parts of Tanganyika and Nyasaland. Nyasaland was a major source of migrant workers to the mining belt, as the region was too distant to benefit from the opportunities for supplying food to the mines. Those who remained at home grew tobacco and cotton for cash.[15] In 1935 120,000 men were away at the mines and other jobs, of which 75,000 were in Southern Rhodesia and 25,000 in South Africa. In Tanganyika, where communications with the outside world were better, the Chagga who lived on the southern slopes of Kilimanjaro responded to an opportunity for coffee growing, and between 1922 and 1925 increased their number of coffee bushes from 178,000 to 1,250,000. Other peasants grew cotton as a cash crop. These cash export crops were affected by the depression, but Tanganyika benefited from gold discoveries in the 1930s. Tanganyika also had important sisal plantations and in 1935 there were 220,000 Africans working for wages in the country, of which 112,000 were in agriculture and 24,000 in mining.[16] In Kenya there were plantations of coffee and sisal and these employed Africans. The plantations were hit by the depression and the fall in the price for their crops. Apart from providing labour for the plantations, Africans grew maize both for their own consumption and for export.[17] Uganda developed very much on the basis of her Africans' enterprise, their cotton production spreading to all suitable parts of the country as all-weather roads were built. This provided a cash crop which augmented the production of their own food. The development of cotton in Uganda, like coffee in Tanganyika and cocoa in the Gold Coast, were shining examples of African peasant capitalism.[18]

Mozambique, the Portuguese territory in East Africa, owed its economic importance to the railways which passed through it to the heart of the mining belt in Rhodesia and the Transvaal. From these it derived substantial revenue and it also supplied men to the mines. In 1934 there were 70,000 in the Transvaal and 26,000 in Rhodesia. There were coconut, sugar, and sisal plantations, and peasant crops were groundnuts, millet, maize, and rice grown as local foodstuffs and for exports.[19] Angola, on the other side of Africa, was the remaining Portuguese territory and it too benefited from the railways which passed through to the mining belt. It also had a diamond-mining industry, which suffered like all diamond industries in the depression. Apart from this the economy relied on its indigenous agriculture, maize being an important crop. Dried fish was another African product. There was coffee and sugar from European plantations. Like Mozambique, Angola was an important supplier of labour,[20] in her case to the copper mines.

The heart of the copper belt lay in the Belgian Congo, a vast territory nearly half the size of Europe. Mining of course dominated the economy and in 1934 there were 120,000 Africans in industry, and another 112,000 in agriculture, besides 21,000 in commerce. There were substantial palm-oil plantations which created many of the agricultural jobs. The mining and plantation sector boomed in the 1920s but copper and palm-product prices fell in the depression, to recover from the mid-1930s. Quite apart from the mining and plantation sector, there was vigorous farming by the Africans of foodstuffs for themselves, and provisions for the mines, besides cotton as a cash crop. It is estimated that in 1936 there were 700,000 Africans growing cotton. Production of cotton in Katanga increased from 1,540 tonnes in 1928 to 15,682 tonnes in 1940, rapid expansion taking place in the 1930s. The main agricultural areas were also the populous areas which supplied men to the mines, and farming was so successful that it began to affect the supply of workers to the mines. The adjacent Belgian territory Ruandi Urundi supplied beef on the hoof to the mines.[21]

French Equatorial Africa and the French Cameroons saw development in the inter-war years on the basis of timber and palm produce, although palm-produce prices fell badly in the early 1930s. These were very much areas of peasant enterprise, for the palm produce did not come from plantations as in the Congo. As the crop was a major item in local diet as in West Africa, only a small proportion was actually exported. For this reason the decline in prices during the depression caused little real hardship. There was much experimentation in this period with cocoa, cotton and coffee in search of an additional cash crop.[22]

The other French territories were in West Africa, but in many ways they were similar to the Cameroons and French Equatorial Africa. Their development depended upon peasant cultivation, cocoa and palm products being particularly important. Their exports expanded in the 1920s but fell back in the 1930s because of the fall in primary product prices. The French Government did try to encourage economic specialisation within each local area, with groundnuts predominating in Senegal, cocoa in Guinea, timber and coffee on the Ivory Coast, cocoa and palm products in Togo, and palm products in Dahomey. Attempts to make the region an important producer of cotton were less successful, as the peasants as everywhere refused to follow a course dictated by forces other than the market. Senegal's phenomenally successful groundnut industry was a perfect example of dynamic peasant enterprise in response to market forces.[23]

British West Africa included Nigeria, the second most important trading country in Africa. Peasant production dominated the economy and palm products were very important. In the north groundnut cultivation spread rapidly, the soils being suitable as in Senegal. Cocoa became important in the south. Coal mining to supply the railways began in 1915. Nigeria prospered during the 1920s like other West African countries, but development was checked by the decline in exports during the depression. In the Gold Coast cocoa was the key cash crop, the development of this crop matching the development of cotton in Uganda and coffee in Tanganyika as examples of peasant eagerness to respond to market incentives. Migrant workers were attracted to the cocoa belt to seek work. The Gold Coast also benefited from the rise in gold prices during the 1930s which enhanced the value of her gold production. Sierra Leone was a producer of palm products and she had an important trade with other West African countries in kola nuts, a mild stimulant. In the 1930s there was a rapid expansion of diamond production. Rice was the most import food crop. The Gambia was a producer of groundnuts. West Africa in general held no significant modern manufacturing industry, although there were still many traditional crafts practised to supply the goods and services not imported in exchange for the export of cash crops.[24]

So there appears to have been considerable advance in the developing world during the 1920s in terms of rising *per capita* incomes. Mines and plantations contributed to this, but even in Malaya peasants provided much of the export crop, and they underpinned the economy with their rice and food production. Smallholders were even more important in the Dutch East Indies and the Philippines, whilst in Burma, Siam, and French Indo-China they grew the rice which generated progress there. In Africa too mining and plantations augmented peasant agriculture. But in India and China, where modern factory industry was established in these years, growth of *per capita* income was least. Industrialisation did not create development there. When the depression came at the end of the decade mines and plantations were hit. But as peasant food production remained the basis of the economy in most countries, the people were not too badly affected. The 1930s were a period of survival, not development. Yet in Southern Africa development continued as the gold boom brought prosperity to the mines and migrant workers.

The Depression

There remains the question of the depression. Why did it happen and what part did the developing world play in causing it? It has already been suggested that the development of the 1920s to some extent created the depression. It is well known that the depression was marked by a collapse of commodity prices. Tin and copper prices fell, and so did prices of rubber, cotton, coffee, tea, sugar and rice. The developing world, by increasing its output of these commodities, created the overproduction which forced prices down. Prices began to fall as early as 1925 in many cases and continued to fall slowly until 1929, the year normally assumed to mark the beginning of the depression. Then they collapsed, and remained low until 1933 when recovery gradually took place.[25]

It is worth distinguishing between commodities which are industrial raw materials and those which are basic foodstuffs. Obviously tin, copper, rubber and cotton are raw materials produced to satisfy the demands of industry. The demand forces working on them are different from those affecting foodstuffs. Even among foodstuffs distinction needs to be made between luxury foods such as tea, coffee and sugar, and grains which are essential foods. It seems plausible to argue that underlying the whole structure of demand for commodities was the demand for grains. Only when demand for essential food has been satisfied does demand for luxury foodstuffs and manufactured goods become effective. Only when demand for manufactured goods grows does demand for industrial raw materials increase.

Of essential foodstuffs in the world at large, a disastrous situation developed in the production of wheat from about 1925. There was expansion of production in the United States, Canada, Australia and Argentina, whilst European production recovered after the war. From the mid-1920s there was a series of good harvests, stocks began to rise and prices fell. 1928 saw a bumper crop and the carry-over of stocks was very high as the United States and Canada stockpiled rather than sell at low prices. Just before the 1929 harvest world stocks were still a quarter of the 1928 crop. Although the 1929 harvest was less good it was far from bad and came on top of the heavy carry-over from the previous year. Canada had no more storage space and was forced to sell, bringing prices tumbling down all over the world. Harvests the world over remained plentiful until 1933, the market was glutted and prices remained abysmally low. Farm incomes were correspondingly restricted. Yet farm incomes were vitally important in maintaining the level of demand for industrial goods in the United States, Canada, Australia and many other countries. So it is arguable that the situation in the world wheat market was the fundamental explanation of the depression.[26]

What is less appreciated is that a similar situation was taking place in rice production. There too the 1920s saw expansion in the major exporting countries of Burma, Siam and French Indo-China, and harvests were good. There too prices had begun to fall from the middle

Graph 5.1: World Wheat and Rice Production, 1913–35

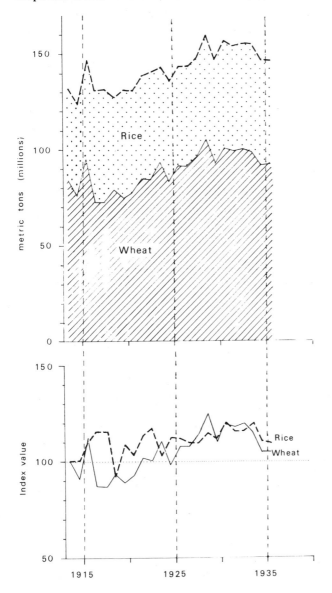

Source: M. K. Bennett, 'World Wheat Utilization since 1885–86' in *Wheat Studies* (12), 1936, p. 392; V. D. Wickizer and M. K. Bennett, *The Rice Economy in Monsoon Asia* (Stanford, Calif: Stanford University Press, 1941), pp. 316–17.

of the decade. Carry-overs were not however a problem, as there were few storage facilities and the crop was consumed before the next harvest. The year 1928 was a bumper one as in the wheat world, both crops being heavily in surplus in the same year. As with wheat 1929 was not such a good year but it was by no means bad. 1930 was an exceptionally good year and production remained high until 1933, just as was the case with wheat. The years 1934 and 1935 were poor for both crops, and as prices moved opposite to production, it was not until then that recovery in prices began. These production figures are shown on Graph 5.1. What seems to have happened is that up to 1927 world rice production and wheat production tended to move inversely, good rice harvests offsetting bad wheat harvests and good wheat harvests offsetting bad rice harvests. But from 1927 the inverse relationship disappeared and production of both grains moved in the same direction, throwing vast quantities of essential foodstuffs onto the world market and forcing down prices. This is shown on Graph 5.1. Rice farmers, like wheat farmers, found themselves in difficulties with their incomes falling. This affected the market for luxury foodstuffs and manufac-tured goods. The Burmese rice farmer was in a similar position to the Canadian wheat farmer, with fixed payments to make on a declining income. It has been put forward elsewhere that rice and wheat were substitutes and formed an integrated market even before the First World War. The depression in grain prices from 1929 bears this out. Certainly merchants in the rice trade in 1929 believed that the fall in rice prices was directly connected to the fall of wheat prices. As wheat was even cheaper than rice, wheat flooded into India from Australia, and into China from Australia and Canada. In these rice-consuming areas wheat was consumed as chapattis or noodles.[27] The ability of the great rice-consuming areas to switch to wheat suggests that if there had been a shortage of rice in 1929 the world surplus of wheat would have been consumed there and prices maintained. Could it be that if the monsoon had failed in 1929 there might never have been a depression?

Notes

1. L. J. Zimmerman, 'The Distribution of World Income, 1860–1960', in *Essays on Unbalanced Growth*, Egbert de Vries (ed.) (s'Gravenhage: Mouton & Co., 1962), pp. 28–55.
2. M. Mukherjee, *National Income of India: Trends and Structure* (Calcutta: Statistical Publishing Society, 1969), pp. 61–71; K. G. Saini, 'The Growth of the Indian Economy: 1860–1960', in *Review of Income and Wealth*, 15 (1969), pp. 247–63; Lars G. Sandberg, *Lancashire in Decline: A Study in*

Entrepreneurship, Technology, and International Trade (Columbus: Ohio State University Press, 1974), p. 183; D. R. Gadgil, *The Industrial Evolution of India in Recent Times, 1860–1939* (Bombay: Oxford University Press, 1971), pp. 207–48, 257–339; Dhires Bhattacharyya, *A Concise History of the Indian Economy* (Calcutta: Progressive Publishers, 1972), pp. 67–121; Vera Anstey, *The Economic Development of India*, 4th edn (London: Longmans, Green & Co., 1952), pp. 490–576; P. J. Thomas, 'India in the World Depression', in *Economic Journal*, 45 (1935), pp. 470–81; George Blyn, *Agricultural Trends in India, 1891–1947: Output, Availability, and Productivity* (Philadelphia: University of Pennsylvania Press, 1966), pp. 94–163.

    3. Gadgil, *Industrial Evolution of India*, pp. 274–5, 280–90, 294–5; Siok-Hwa Cheng, *The Rice Industry of Burma, 1852–1940* (Kuala Lumpur: University of Malaya Press, 1968), pp. 210–12 & c; Michael Adas, *The Burma Delta: Economic Development and Social Change on an Asian Rice Frontier, 1852–1941* (Madison, Wisconsin: University of Wisconsin Press, 1974), pp. 127, 136, 185–9, 223–4, & c; J. S. Furnivall, *Colonial Policy and Practice: A Comparative Study of Burma and Netherlands India* (Cambridge: Cambridge University Press, 1948), pp. 188–90.

    4. Donald R. Snodgrass, *Ceylon: An Export Economy in Transition* (Homewood, Illinois: Richard D. Irwin Inc., 1966), pp. 34–71.

    5. Lim Chong-Yah, *Economic Development of Modern Malaya* (Kuala Lumpur: Oxford University Press, 1967), pp. 50–83, 133–46, 174–7; G. C. Allen and Audrey G. Donnithorne, *Western Enterprise in Indonesia and Malaya: A Study in Economic Development* (London: George Allen & Unwin, 1957), pp. 44, 142–4, 152–61, 261–2.

    6. Allen and Donnithorne, *Western Enterprise in Indonesia and Malaya*, pp. 34–6, 71–2, 84–5, 90–4, 99, 103–4, 120–6, 139–44, 170–8, 256–62; J. S. Furnivall, *Netherlands India: A Study in Plural Economy* (Cambridge: Cambridge University Press, 1944), pp. 428–44; A. N. de Wilde and J. T. Moll, *The Netherlands Indies During the Depression: A Brief Economic Survey* (Amsterdam: J. M. Meulenhoff, 1936); P. H. W. Sitsen, *Industrial Development of the Netherlands Indies* (New York: Institute of Pacific Relations, 1943).

    7. Department of Overseas Trade, *Economic Conditions in the Philippine Islands, 1933–34* (London: HMSO, 1935), pp. 1–19; *Statesman's Year Book, 1941*, pp. 667–8.

    8. James C. Ingram, *Economic Change in Thailand, 1850–1970* (Stanford, California: Stanford University Press, 1971), pp. 36–148; James C. Ingram, 'Thailand's Rice Trade and the Allocation of Resources', in *The Economic Development of South East Asia: Studies in Economic History and Political Economy* (London: George Allen & Unwin, 1964), pp. 102–26.

    9. Charles Robequain, *The Economic Development of French Indo-China* (London: Oxford University Press, 1944), pp. 220–2, 231–84, 305–24.

    10. Albert Feuerwerker, *The Chinese Economy, 1912–1949* (Ann Arbor, Michigan: Michigan University Press, 1969), pp. 1–47; Richard A. Kraus, *Cotton and Cotton Goods in China, 1918–1936* (New York: Garland Publishing Inc., 1980), pp. 3, 167, Table V.1; Frank H. H. King, *A Concise Economic History of Modern China* (London: Pall Mall Press, 1969), pp. 85–6, 113–33; Yu-Kwei Cheng, *Foreign Trade and Industrial Development of China: An Historical and Integrated Analysis through 1948* (Washington D.C.: Washington University Press, 1956), pp. 27–31, 37, 40, 45, 53–4, 67–71, 74, 78, 81, 88, 92–3, 186–92, 199–203, 216, 225–6; G. C. Allen and Audrey G. Donnithorne, *Western Enterprise in Far Eastern Economic Development* (London: George Allen & Unwin, 1954), pp. 175–81.

    11. S. H. Frankel, *Capital Investment in Africa: Its Course and Effects*

180   *Development and Depression*

(London: Oxford University Press, 1938), pp. 106–48; D. H. Houghton, 'Economic Development, 1865–1965', in *The Oxford History of South Africa*, Monica Wilson and Leonard Thompson (ed.), Vol. 2, *South Africa, 1870–1966* (Oxford: Clarendon Press, 1971), pp. 22–35; D. H. Houghton, *The South African Economy* (Cape Town: Oxford University Press, 1964), pp. 15–16, 42–131; M. H. de Kock, *The Economic Development of South Africa* (London: P. S. King & Son, 1936), pp. 82–125.

12. Frankel, *Capital Investment*, pp. 216–25.

13. Ibid., pp. 232–46.

14. Frankel, *Capital Investment*, pp. 247–53; Charles Perrings, *Black Mineworkers in Central Africa* (London: Heinemann, 1979), pp. 89–92, 105–9, 186–94.

15. Frankel, *Capital Investment*, pp. 253–60, 282–9.

16. Frankel, *Capital Investment*, pp. 276–82; J. F. Munro, *Africa and the International Economy, 1800–1960: An Introduction to the Modern Economic History of Africa South of the Sahara* (London: J. M. Dent & Sons, 1976), pp. 138–9.

17. Frankel, *Capital Investment*, pp. 260–9; C. C. Wrigley, 'Kenya: The Patterns of Economic Life, 1902–45', in *History of East Africa*, V. Harlow and E. M. Chilver (eds) (Oxford: Clarendon Press, 1965), Vol. 2, pp. 232–60.

18. Frankel, *Capital Investment*, pp. 272–3; Cyril Ehrlich, 'The Uganda Economy', 1903–45, in *History of East Africa*, Vol. 2, pp. 422–69.

19. Frankel, *Capital Investment*, pp. 367–71.

20. Frankel, *Capital Investment*, pp. 371; Perrings, *Black Mineworkers*, pp. 37–9, 82, 112.

21. Frankel, *Capital Investment*, pp. 289–304; Perrings, *Black Mineworkers*, pp. 144–8, 156–7, 186–7, 194–6.

22. Frankel, *Capital Investment*, pp. 347–8, 352–3; Naval Intelligence Division, *French Equatorial Africa and Cameroons* (London: Geographical Handbook Series, 1942), pp. 390–444.

23. Frankel, *Capital Investment*, pp. 331–47, 354.

24. Frankel, *Capital Investment*, pp. 307–31; Gerald K. Helleiner, *Peasant Agriculture, Government and Economic Growth in Nigeria* (Homewood, Illinois: Richard D. Irwin, Inc., 1966), pp. 5–23; A. G. Hopkins, *An Economic History of West Africa* (London: Longmans, 1973), pp. 216–22; R. O. Ekundare, *An Economic History of Nigeria, 1860–1960* (London: Methuen, 1973), pp. 156–86.

25. W. A. Lewis, *Economic Survey, 1919–1939* (London: George Allen & Unwin, 1966), p. 46; H. V. Hodson, *Slump and Recovery, 1929–1937: A Survey of World Economic Affairs* (London: Oxford University Press, 1938), pp. 34–9; H. W. Arndt, *The Economic Lessons of the Nineteen-Thirties* (London: Oxford University Press, 1944), pp. 10–11; M. T. Copeland, *A Raw Commodity Revolution* (Boston, Mass.: Harvard University Press, 1938), pp. 1, 25, 61; V. P. Timoshenko, *World Agriculture and the Depression* (Ann Arbor: University of Michigan, 1933), p. 66.

26. C. P. Kindleberger, *The World in Depression, 1929–1939* (London: Allen Lane, 1973), pp. 90–4; M. K. Bennett, 'World Wheat Utilization since 1885–86', *Wheat Studies*, 12 (1936), pp. 341, 343; W. Malenbaum, *The World Wheat Economy, 1885–1939* (Cambridge, Mass.: Harvard University Press, 1963), pp. 5–20; Copeland, *Commodity Revolution*, pp. 20–2, 25, 59; Henry C. Taylor, *World Trade in Agricultural Products* (New York: Macmillan, 1943), pp. 110–11; V. P. Timoshenko, *World Agriculture and the Depression* (Ann Arbor, Michigan: University of Michigan Press, 1933), pp. 66–71.

27. V. D. Wickizer, 'Rice and Wheat in World Agriculture and Consumption',

Wheat Studies, 17 (1941), pp. 293, 298; V. D. Wickizer and M. K. Bennett, *The Rice Economy of Monsoon Asia* (Stanford, California: Stanford University Press, 1941), pp. 99 100, 158–9, 161, 332–3; A. J. H. Latham, 'Fluctuations and Responses in the International Rice Market,' unpublished paper to the Mid-Western Economics Conference, Palmer House, Chicago, 7 April 1979; Ahmed Khan, 'International Production and Exchange of Rice with Special Reference to Production, Market Demand, and Consumption of Rice in India and Burma' (University of Wales PhD; Aberystwyth, 1939), pp. xi, 195, 196, 189, 361, 376, 378–82; Food and Agriculture Organisation of the United Nations, *Commodity Bulletin Series 36: The World Rice Economy*, Vol. 2: *Trends and Forces* (Rome: United Nations, 1963), pp. 36, 40, 60, 61, 62, 84; Taylor, World Trade, p. 130; *Interim Report of the Committee Appointed to Enquire into the Rice and Paddy Trade*, Chairman: Thomas Couper (Rangoon, Burma: Superintendent, Government Printing and Stationery, 1931), pp. 14–15.

CONCLUSION

Until the depression the communications revolution continued in the developing world, with railways being built everywhere. Their economic viability was increasingly challenged by the car and truck, which competed first for business in urban areas and then on longer hauls. Gradually roads were improved for them, and even before the depression it was becoming obvious that the greater flexibility of motor transport was going to make it a faster agent of development than the railways. What is more, motor vehicles took transport out of the hands of companies and government and put it in the hands of small private enterprise to the delight of the petty capitalist of the developing world. At sea the steam engine was also being challenged by the internal combustion engine, although the steam turbine was introduced and the triple-expansion engine continued to be used where there was cheap coal because of its greater reliability. The Panama Canal had a more fundamental impact, turning the Pacific at last into a trading ocean by making a direct route from Asia to the industrial regions of the United States. Now the Japanese became an important force in world shipping, and against a world surplus of shipping and national shipping lines the British mercantile marine struggled for survival, a struggle symbolised by the imprisonment of Lord Kylsant of the Royal Mail Company. Great improvements were made in telecommunications with the telephone and radio. The radio was cheap and reliable because it needed no lines which could be cut down during civil disorder. Air transport made its first steps towards regular international services and by 1936 there were regular flights from London to Hong Kong, Cape Town and Lagos.

The international gold standard never really recovered after the war, and although sterling returned to gold in 1925 it was forced off again in 1931. Most of the British territories in the developing world maintained their par with sterling, although South Africa did not follow sterling down until 1933. Even Siam tried to hold her currency against sterling. Other territories followed their metropolitan currency in these difficult years, while French Indo-China pursued its unique 'closed vase' system until 1930. China clung to the old silver standard until 1935 when a Chinese dollar was introduced with a par against sterling. Investment flows to the developing world continued during the

1920s, and although the United States was now the leading world lender, Britain remained the major investor in Asia and Africa. Indian and Ceylon were the main destination for British capital, and in general investment went into transport, mines and plantations. From 1930 Britain became an importer of capital and the flow of funds to Asia and Africa was reversed. So foreign investment in the developing world in 1938 was not much above the 1914 level. Japanese investment in China increased, particularly in Manchuria during the 1930s.

Despite the problems of the inter-war years the developing countries increased their share of world trade. But the complex web of international payments which had grown up in the nineteenth century suffered a severe shock. Even in the 1920s Britain's surplus with the developing world was greatly reduced, making it difficult for her to sustain her deficits with the United States and continental Europe. In the 1930s the surplus disappeared altogether and Britain fell into deficit with all her major trading areas. This was a major weakness in the entire international economic system. One of the main reasons for Britain's declining trade with the developing world was the successful progress of industrialisation in the cotton industry in India and China. Local products displaced those of Lancashire. There was also competition from Japan but this was less important. Rubber became an important export crop in Malaya, Ceylon and the Dutch East Indies during the 1920s as demand for motor tyres increased in the west, but overproduction soon became a problem and international restriction schemes were adopted. They were not very effective and one of their worst effects in the 1930s was that they discriminated against peasant smallholders who had found in rubber an excellent addition to their capitalist activities as cash croppers. Overproduction in tea and sugar also led to restriction schemes. Coconut products were a peasant mainstay which were not subject to restriction schemes although their prices fell, nor was rice, upon which Burma, Siam and French Indo-China depended. Overproduction in the exporting countries and rice self-sufficiency schemes in many of the importing countries pushed prices down to very low levels in the 1930s. Mining in Malaya, the Congo, the Rhodesias and South Africa had developed rapidly in the 1920s but the depression hit tin and copper badly. In South Africa and Southern Rhodesia the rise in the price of gold as currencies depreciated after 1931 stimulated gold production, and their economies boomed at a time when most other economies in the world were in difficulties. Migrant workers flocked to the mines to share in the prosperity. In other parts of Africa plantations and peasants prospered during the 1920s but were hit by the depression. Palm products, groundnuts, maize, cocoa, coffee, cotton and sisal were all affected.

The prosperity of the 1920s brought with it the population explosion. Most countries in the developing world saw their populations grow substantially, but it was in India that the key change was apparent. Normally India had alternate decades of high population growth and low population growth. The second decade of the century had seen low population growth because the famine and influenza epidemic of 1918 had killed so many people. So the high population growth of the 1920s was only to be expected. But on the basis of past experience there should have been low population increase in the 1930s. Instead, the population went on growing rapidly and there was no famine to check it. The depression did not hold back the growth of population. Migration patterns were however upset by the slump, and as it struck, migrant workers in Ceylon and Malaya returned to their homelands in India and China as they became unemployed. Indian workers also returned from Burma where the fall in rice prices brought tension between them and the Burmese. Chinese in Siam and French Indo-China too went home as the rice trade collapsed. Even in the Dutch East Indies migrant workers returned from Sumatra to their home villages in Java as the plantations ran into difficulties. Only in South Africa and Southern Rhodesia did the flow of migrants from other parts of Africa continue to the booming mines. In the late 1930s migrancy to the Copper Belt in Northern Rhodesia and the Congo recovered as mining there picked up.

The depression was to a large extent a consequence of the development of the 1920s. India became a producer of steel in these years, and both India and China saw industrialisation in the cotton industry, but these two countries in fact grew very little because of the stagnation of their agriculture. Industrialisation did not create growth in either country. Other countries like Malaya, the Dutch East Indies, Ceylon and the Philippines advanced rapidly on the basis of their rubber, tea, sugar and coconut products, much of which were produced by peasants. In Burma, Siam and French Indo-China development was founded on peasant rice production. In West Africa and East Africa development was based on agricultural exports many of which were peasant crops. In Southern and Central Africa mining was the basis of development. But all the economies of the developing world were ultimately based on peasant food production. Even where there were mines and plantations they only brought wealth additional to the peasant economy. Only in South Africa was non-peasant food production important, and even there peasant food crops were substantial. Unfortunately, the successful expansion of mines and crops resulted in overproduction which began to make itself felt as early as 1925 and led to the crunch after 1929 in which prices fell drastically. The fundamental explanation of the situation was the collapse in world grain prices. In the West there was vast overproduction of wheat which built up from the mid-1920s. In the East overproduction of rice was also developing. In 1928 both crops had bumper harvests, and when the reasonable crops of 1929 were brought in on top of the stocks held over from the previous year, prices plummeted. As crops remained good right through till 1933 prices stayed down, farm incomes declined, and so did demand for luxuries and manufactured goods. If the rice harvest had failed at this time, the wheat surpluses could have been consumed in Asia, and the price of wheat, farm incomes, and industrial demand would have been maintained. If the wheat harvest had failed the rice surplus would have been consumed in Europe and the west. But both grains in surplus together brought disaster. As agricultural incomes fell and demand collapsed there was a general collapse of prices, and mines and plantations were hit badly. Peasant producers faced with smaller returns from their cash crops were able to get by on the food they grew for themselves. Most of their cash crops they could eat if they could not sell them, except cotton and rubber. That the peasants of the developing world were not hit badly by the depression is shown by the fact that population growth continued during the 1930s. The depression had much less effect in Asia than a monsoon failure would have done. Indeed, the two most striking features of the inter-war years, the depression and the population explosion, seem to have been directly linked. The depression took place because of overproduction of rice at a time when there was a surplus of wheat in the West. A severe harvest failure would normally have been expected in India by the late 1920s as there had not been one since 1918. Instead there was a surplus which forced prices down ushering in the depression. A harvest failure would also have caused starvation and death and held back population growth as in 1918. But there was no harvest failure and the population kept on growing. The depression and the population explosion are both due to the fact that the monsoon did not fail.

Appendix 1: The Cargo Tonnage of the Suez Canal, 1914—39

Year	Northbound tons 000	Southbound tons 000	Total tons 000
1914	12,296	9,039	21,335
1915	9,774	5,365	15,139
1916	7,178	3,415	10,593
1917	5,436	1,339	6,775
1918	6,222	1,610	7,832
1919	10,211	3,762	13,973
1920	10,729	6,318	17,047
1921	10,933	6,576	17,509
1922	13,168	8,192	21,360
1923	15,073	7,704	22,777
1924	16,711	8,818	25,529
1925	17,777	8,801	26,578
1926	15,605	9,804	25,409
1927	18,442	11,082	29,524
1928	20,659	11,963	32,622
1929	21,620	12,896	34,516
1930	19,077	9,434	28,511
1931	17,955	7,377	25,332
1932	17,318	6,314	23,632
1933	19,712	7,203	26,915
1934	20,464	7,984	28,448
1935	17,404	8,924	26,328
1936	16,727	8,829	25,556
1937	22,619	10,157	32,776
1938	21,011	7,768	28,779
1939	17,161	7,517	24,678

Source: D. A. Farnie, *East and West of Suez: The Suez Canal in History, 1854–1956* (Oxford: Clarendon Press, 1969), p. 753.

Appendix 2: Shipping Freight Index, 1920–37 (1898–1913 = 100)

Year	India	Far East and Pacific
1920	498.5	506.5
1921	150.1	174.5
1922	138.4	123.4
1923	122.8	128.4
1924	125.1	127.9
1925	112.6	110.0
1926	114.2	107.1
1927	122.6	128.2
1928	110.1	117.0
1929	112.4	107.0
1930	98.9	80.9
1931	94.6	92.4
1932	91.9	89.7
1933	90.2	87.0
1934	92.9	87.6
1935	94.1	84.2
1936	103.4	97.7
1937	158.5	154.5

Source: *The Economist*, 26 February 1938, p. 484.

Appendix 3: British Trade Balances with Major Regions, 1913–38 (£ million)

Year	Industrial[a] Europe	Africa	Others[b] Asia	India	America	Latin America
1913	−38.7	18.8	12.4	23.3	−82.2	−17.2
1914	−27.9	11.3	−7.1	20.5	−74.0	−31.9
1915	45.6	0.9	−37.8	−15.3	−181.3	−73.7
1916	0.0	5.7	−35.9	−18.0	−227.2	−56.2
1917	0.0	−0.7	−44.2	−6.0	−316.2	−55.1
1918	0.0	−4.1	−26.5	−38.9	−488.6	−76.5
1919	261.4	−26.1	−59.4	−36.2	−476.1	−87.8
1920	154.6	23.9	0.4	88.2	−432.3	−89.8
1921	9.9	10.8	31.8	67.1	−210.5	−51.9
1922	45.4	9.0	25.5	45.7	−144.6	−44.2
1923	22.9	11.4	13.3	20.3	−125.1	−41.8
1924	−6.9	8.8	18.7	12.8	−162.6	−61.2
1925	−24.4	7.7	−10.5	7.1	−162.1	−46.9
1926	−114.0	10.2	−13.5	25.6	−154.0	−59.8
1927	−63.7	11.9	−12.3	20.5	−133.4	−56.6
1928	−50.3	9.7	9.6	20.6	−119.6	−49.5
1929	−59.6	9.2	−2.5	16.5	−133.9	−55.9
1930	−77.6	12.9	−8.9	3.2	−113.6	−41.8
1931	−99.4	12.8	−8.8	−3.6	−77.8	−52.4
1932	−15.8	1.3	−3.2	2.4	−62.8	−50.1
1933	−11.0	7.7	−5.1	−3.3	−49.6	−37.0
1934	−19.7	16.2	−19.6	−4.9	−58.8	−47.4
1935	−22.8	19.3	−17.4	−2.8	−57.4	−41.3
1936	−39.5	18.6	−13.7	−17.3	−56.5	−46.4
1937	−40.3	13.6	−21.1	−25.0	−71.8	−54.7
1938	−39.3	17.4	−20.5	−18.9	−89.2	−33.7

Notes:

[a] Comprises Western Europe and Central Europe, i.e. Netherlands, Belgium, France, Switzerland, Germany, Austria, Wallachia and Moldavia.

[b] Comprises Asia minus India.

Source: B. R. Mitchell and Phyllis Deane, *Abstract of British Historical Statistics* (Cambridge: Cambridge University Press, 1971), pp. 315–27.

Appendix 4: Indian Trade by Sea including Government Transactions, 1913/14 to 1939/40 (rupees × 10 million)

Year	Merchandise exports	Merchandise imports	Trade surplus[a]	Net treasure flow	Net gold flow
1913/14	249.0	191.3	57.6	36.3	23.3
1914/15	182.1	144.9	37.2	16.5	7.6
1915/16	199.5	138.1	61.3	3.7	1.1
1916/17	247.3	160.2	87.1	32.0	13.2
1917/18	244.9	164.3	80.5	44.2	25.1
1918/19	255.3	188.5	66.7	62.3	5.5
1919/20	336.0	221.7	114.3	64.5	35.3
1920/1	267.7	347.5	−79.8	8.5	2.1
1921/2	248.6	282.5	−33.9	12.2	−2.8
1922/3	316.0	246.1	69.8	60.5	41.1
1923/4	363.3	237.1	126.1	49.5	29.1
1924/5	400.2	253.3	146.8	94.0	73.9
1925/6	386.8	236.0	150.8	51.6	34.8
1926/7	311.0	240.8	70.2	39.3	19.4
1927/8	330.2	261.5	68.7	31.7	18.1
1928/9	339.1	263.3	75.7	30.9	21.1
1929/30	318.9	249.7	69.2	22.6	14.2
1930/1	226.5	173.0	53.4	22.8	12.7
1931/2	161.2	130.6	30.5	−58.6	−57.9
1932/3	135.9	135.0	0.9	−67.6	−65.5
1933/4	151.1	117.3	33.8	−63.6	−57.0
1934/5	155.4	134.5	20.9	−58.3	−52.5
1935/6	164.5	136.7	27.8	−38.2	−37.3
1936/7	202.4	137.7	64.7	−14.6	−27.8
1937/8	189.7	177.2	12.5	−15.0	−16.3
1938/9	169.8	155.5	14.2	−11.9	−13.0
1939/40	215.9	168.9	46.9	−34.1	−34.6

Note:

[a] The trade surplus is slightly different from 'exports minus imports' because of rounding.

Source: *Statistical Abstracts for British India.*

Appendix 5: Indian Balances of Private Merchandise Trade By Sea with Major Regions, 1913/14 to 1939/40 (rupees × 10 million)[a]

Year ending 31 March	Britain	Europe	Africa	America	Asia	Australasia	Total[b]
1913/14	−60.2	54.8	3.0	24.0	35.1	4.0	60.9
1914/15	−37.0	28.4	3.5	18.4	22.1	4.0	39.5
1915/16	−5.1	18.9	2.3	21.5	18.1	4.6	60.5
1916/17	−8.7	24.8	6.4	29.2	30.6	5.0	87.4
1917/18	−21.5	13.9	27.9	27.5	29.6	5.5	83.0
1918/19	−6.9	15.2	16.3	28.5	11.5	5.8	70.2
1919/20	−10.2	35.0	3.1	35.7	39.2	1.1	104.3
1920/1	−151.6	16.1	5.1	10.3	17.9	6.3	−95.5
1921/2	−104.8	24.0	0.4	9.1	41.0	−4.7	−34.9
1922/3	−74.1	40.4	6.5	32.2	55.9	5.4	66.4
1923/4	−45.1	62.3	5.3	32.6	60.1	5.9	121.2
1924/5	−35.9	66.2	4.7	35.5	59.9	7.4	138.0
1925/6	−37.5	56.9	7.4	41.2	73.0	7.5	148.6
1926/7	−47.1	19.6	8.4	30.3	51.5	7.4	70.2
1927/8	−41.3	38.5	8.1	31.0	26.9	5.9	69.3
1928/9	−44.2	44.3	8.2	36.3	31.7	0.3	76.8
1929/30	−36.5	33.5	7.4	33.0	30.9	1.5	70.0
1930/1	−9.5	16.1	3.2	13.9	28.7	3.1	55.6
1931/2	−1.9	7.9	1.2	6.2	13.9	2.0	29.5
1932/3	−11.9	3.5	1.1	4.7	−1.4	3.5	−0.3
1933/4	−0.3	10.1	0.8	12.4	5.0	2.4	31.8
1934/5	−5.6	4.6	−0.3	10.3	6.9	2.2	19.3
1935/6	−1.4	7.3	−0.5	12.4	4.6	1.9	26.1
1936/7	15.8	16.1	−0.3	17.5	17.3	2.4	70.8
1937/8	8.8	3.0	−4.7	11.7	−15.8[c]	1.7	7.1
1938/9	9.3	2.9	−3.9	10.2	−13.0	0.8	9.4
1939/40	31.1	2.4	−0.4	19.3	−22.3	3.7	38.6

Notes:

[a] This table is not exactly comparable with that in Appendix 5 of Latham, *The International Economy and the Undeveloped World*, as it no longer includes re-exports which were not disaggregated into regions in this period.

[b] The columns do not add up to the total because of rounding. After 1933–4 the original data were arranged in a different manner, including a figure for 'other' countries not separated into regions as before. This accounts for the even greater disparity between the total and the sum of the columns from that date.

[c] From 1937–8 Burma was no longer part of India and was recorded as part of Asia, distorting the figures accordingly.

Source: *Statistical Abstracts for British India.*

Appendix 6: Indian Balances of Private Merchandise Trade with Asia by Sea, 1913/14 to 1939/40 (rupees × 10 million)

Year ending 31 March	Ceylon	China	Hong Kong	Japan	Java	Straits	Others	Total[a]
1913/14	7.9	3.9	6.6	17.8	−8.8	3.1	4.3	35.1[b]
1914/15	6.7	2.4	3.2	11.2	−6.3	1.6	3.2	22.1
1915/16	8.2	3.4	2.7	10.9	−11.6	1.2	3.1	18.1
1916/17	8.9	4.4	3.2	14.8	−10.4	2.1	7.5	30.6
1917/18	7.2	7.5	2.7	15.8	−9.0	1.3	3.8	29.6
1918/19	7.1	7.6	3.1	−4.3	−7.7	1.4	4.3	11.5
1919/20	8.2	6.9	5.9	27.1	−17.6	1.3	7.3	39.2
1920/1	9.4	8.3	4.7	2.2	−12.7	3.8	1.9	17.9
1921/2	10.1	8.9	4.6	24.5	−19.7	3.3	9.1	41.0
1922/3	10.8	10.7	5.1	25.7	−9.9	3.0	10.3	55.9
1923/4	13.3	7.1	3.4	36.3	−10.4	3.3	6.9	60.1
1924/5	12.2	6.7	2.2	38.0	−12.8	3.1	10.3	59.9
1925/6	12.9	12.8	2.0	38.4	−9.2	4.1	11.8	73.0
1926/7	13.0	7.9	2.0	24.5	−11.4	3.4	11.9	51.5
1927/8	13.3	0.0	1.2	11.1	−12.3	3.2	10.2	26.9
1928/9	11.6	5.1	1.6	16.7	−12.8	2.7	6.6	31.7
1929/30	10.9	8.9	2.2	8.6	−9.4	1.7	7.8	30.9
1930/1	9.6	9.8	0.7	4.2	−7.7	2.2	9.7	28.7
1931/2	6.2	5.0	1.2	0.6	−3.1	1.7	2.1	13.9
1932/3	4.7	0.6	0.9	−6.5	−3.0	0.7	1.0	−1.4
1933/4	4.6	2.3	0.6	−2.8	−1.9	0.5	1.7	5.0
1934/5	5.0	0.5	0.1	3.7	−1.4	0.1	−1.3	6.9
1935/6	5.6	0.0	0.0	0.0	−1.2	0.0	0.1	4.6
1936/7	5.5	−0.1	0.0	8.7	0.3	0.4	2.3	17.3
1937/8	3.6	1.0	0.5	−4.0	0.6	−1.2	−16.4[c]	−15.8
1938/9	3.9	0.7	0.4	−0.8	0.2	−2.0	−15.4	−13.0
1939/40	4.9	5.8	0.3	−5.2	−1.9	−2.2	−24.0	−22.3

Notes:

[a] This table is not exactly comparable with that in Appendix 6 of Latham, *The International Economy and the Undeveloped World*, as it no longer includes re-exports which were not disaggregated into regions in this period. Hong Kong is listed separately from China, not included in it, as in that table.

[b] The columns do not add up to the total because of rounding.

[c] From 1937/8 Burma is included in Asia and no longer regarded as part of India.

Source: *Statistical Abstracts for British India.*

Appendix 7: Imports of Cotton Cloth and Factory Production in India, 1919–35 (millions of square yards)

Year ending 31 March[a]	Imports[a] from Britain	Total imports	Factory production	Imports and factory production
1919/20	828	1,081	1,640	2,721
1920/1	1,498	1,510	1,581	3,091
1921/2	1,182	1,090	1,732	2,822
1922/3	1,507	1,593	1,725	3,318
1923/4	1,519	1,486	1,702	3,188
1924/5	1,726	1,823	1,970	3,793
1925/6	1,546	1,564	1,954	3,518
1926/7	1,668	1,788	2,317	4,105
1927/8	1,766	1,973	2,442	4,415
1928/9	1,631	1,937	1,916	3,853
1929/30	1,489	1,919	2,418	4,337
1930/1	829	890	2,538	3,428
1931/2	428	776	2,891	3,667
1932/3	653	1,255	2,988	4,243
1933/4	522	796	2,777	3,573
1934/5	624	944	3,168	4,112
1935/6	602	947	3,275	4,222

Note:

[a] Calendar year.

Source: Lars G. Sandberg, *Lancashire in Decline: A Study in Entrepreneurship, Technology, and International Trade* (Columbus: Ohio State University Press, 1974), p. 183.

Appendix 8: Chinese Trade Balances, 1913–39[a] (Haikwan taels × 1 million)

Year	Exports	Imports	Trade balance	Treasure[b] flow	Gold flow
1913	403.3	570.1	−166.8	34.5	−1.3
1914	356.2	569.2	−213.0	−26.6	−13.0
1915	418.8	454.4	−35.6	−35.7	−17.3
1916	481.7	516.4	−34.6	−16.8	11.8
1917	462.9	549.5	−86.5	−12.1	8.8
1918	485.8	554.8	−69.0	22.4	−1.0
1919	630.8	646.9	−16.1	94.3	41.1
1920	541.6	762.2	−220.6	75.1	−17.5
1921	601.2	906.1	−304.8	15.9	−16.4
1922	654.8	945.0	−290.1	43.6	4.1
1923	752.9	923.4	−170.4	61.5	−5.6
1924	771.7	1,018.2	−246.4	16.2	−9.7
1925	776.3	947.8	−171.5	61.4	−1.0
1926	864.2	1,124.2	−259.9	45.6	−7.5
1927	918.6	1,012.9	−94.3	63.7	−1.2
1928	991.3	1,195.9	−204.6	112.4	6.0
1929	1,015.6	1,265.7	−250.0	103.8	−1.9
1930	894.8	1,309.7	−414.9	50.4	−16.5
1931	909.4	1,433.4	−524.0	13.3	−32.1
1932	492.9	1,049.2	−556.2	−77.5	−70.1
1933	392.9	863.6	−470.6	−53.7	−44.4
1934	343.8	660.8	−317.0	−197.8	−33.0
1935	369.8	589.9	−220.0	−62.9	−24.8
1936	458.5	604.3	−150.6	−186.2	−26.0
1937	538.3	611.8	−73.5	−293.1	−37.3
1938	490.1	568.8	−78.5	−42.4	−8.9
1939	661.2	855.9	−194.6	−3.4	−2.1

Notes:

[a] Chinese statistics at this time are distorted by the Japanese invasion of Manchuria which affected the figures from the second six months of 1932, and by the outbreak of the Sino-Japanese war which affected figures after 1936.

[b] The treasure series was heavily distorted by smuggling, particularly in the 1930s.

Source: Hsiao Liang-lin, *China's Foreign Trade Statistics, 1864–1949* (Cambridge, Mass.: Harvard University Press, 1974), pp. 22–5, 128.

Appendix 9: Chinese Trade Balance with Major Countries, 1913–39 (Haikwan taels × 1 million)

Year	Britain	India	Hong Kong	Japan	America	Others[a]
1913	−80.5	−42.1	−54.5	−53.8	2.2	61.8
1914	−82.6	−32.3	−73.5	−62.5	−1.0	39.0
1915	−39.6	−32.8	−44.2	−42.5	23.5	100.1
1916	−35.4	−26.1	−33.8	−47.5	18.2	90.1
1917	−25.8	−20.0	−42.7	−115.8	33.8	84.1
1918	−24.6	−19.5	−45.2	−75.4	18.4	77.3
1919	−7.1	−17.3	−22.1	−51.9	−9.1	91.4
1920	−85.9	−23.7	−22.8	−87.2	−76.0	75.1
1921	−119.0	−25.6	−78.2	−38.2	−86.2	42.5
1922	−106.7	−33.3	−69.3	−71.6	−71.4	62.4
1923	−77.1	−42.9	−72.2	−12.5	−27.6	62.0
1924	−75.7	−27.3	−70.7	−33.5	−90.2	51.2
1925	−45.4	−36.0	−61.5	−113.4	0.6	84.3
1926	−60.4	−63.2	−30.6	−125.1	−37.5	57.1
1927	−17.0	−20.1	−42.9	−84.9	−45.0	115.8
1928	−52.6	−28.1	−43.9	−90.6	−78.3	89.2
1929	−44.8	−36.6	−40.9	−66.7	−93.0	32.0
1930	−45.5	−115.2	−60.3	−110.6	−100.5	17.3
1931	−55.4	−67.0	−73.7	−40.9	−201.1	−85.6
1932	−81.6	−6.7	15.9	−40.9	−209.1	−232.9
1933	−67.5	−6.6	46.5	−23.4	−118.2	−301.2
1934	−48.0	−8.8	45.7	−29.2	−113.7	−162.7
1935	−31.2	−9.6	47.8	−36.9	−24.7	−165.2
1936	−29.2	−3.8	56.9	−32.8	0.5	−142.1
1937	−20.0	−0.3	92.2	−42.4	27.2	−130.2
1938	−8.8	2.2	140.4	−59.8	−41.3	−111.1
1939	−8.3	56.9	119.7	−158.3	7.5	−212.2

Note:

[a] The sum of these columns does not equal the Trade Balance of Appendix 8, page 193, because of rounding.

Source: Hsiao Liang-lin, *China's Foreign Trade Statistics, 1864–1949* (Cambridge, Mass.: Harvard University Press, 1974), pp. 22–5, 138–64.

Appendix 10: Imports of Cotton Cloth and Factory Production in China, 1919–36 (millions of square yards)

Year	Imports from Britain	Total imports	Factory production	Imports and factory production
1919	304	816	147	963
1920	453	802	161	963
1921	211	603	212	815
1922	309	746	247	993
1923	235	612	303	915
1924	293	722	322	1,044
1925	173	725	381	1,106
1926	178	806	435	1,241
1927	103	618	496	1,114
1928	187	809	606	1,415
1929	188	793	740	1,533
1930	61	589	759	1,348
1931	81	390	872	1,262
1932	126	356	911	1,267
1933	52	187	1,108	1,295
1934	20	91	1,178	1,269
1935	14	86	1,280	1,366
1936	8	41	1,309	1,350

Source: R. A. Kraus, *Cotton and Cotton Goods in China, 1918–1936: The Impact of Modernization on the Traditional Sector*, PhD dissertation, Harvard University, 1968, Appendix J; Table V-1. See Lars G. Sandberg, *Lancashire in Decline: A Study in Entrepreneurship, Technology and International Trade* (Columbus: Ohio State University Press, 1974), pp. 192–3.

Appendix 11: Trade Figures of Selected Developing Countries, 1913–38

SIAM (Bangkok) (Ticals × 000)

Year	Imports	Index no	Exports	Index no	Balance
1913/14	87,755	100.0	115,433	100.0	27,678
1914/15	74,806	85.9	100,964	87.7	26,158
1915/16	73,838	84.8	105,212	91.4	31,374
1916/17	87,220	100.2	121,153	105.3	33,933
1917/18	96,808	111.2	122,043	106.0	25,235
1918/19	102,977	118.2	160,992	139.9	58,015
1919/20	137,735	158.2	174,957	152.0	37,222
1920/1	145,560	167.2	65,468	56.8	−80,092
1921/2	130,688	150.1	164,345	142.8	33,657
1922/3	129,887	149.1	149,458	129.9	19,571
1923/4	135,185	155.2	170,174	147.9	34,989
1924/5	151,676	174.2	165,333	143.7	13,657
1925/6	157,610	181.1	195,943	170.3	38,333
1926/7	165,193	189.7	196,879	171.1	31,686
1927/8	173.632	199.5	234,174	203.5	60,542
1928/9	159,894	183.6	215,033	186.9	55,139
1929/30	176,121	202.4	178,579	155.2	2,458
1930/1	135,395	155.5	132,011	114.7	−3,384
1931/2	87,954	101.0	96,122	83.5	8,168
1932/3	80,234	92.1	106,111	92.2	25,877
1933/4	82,495	94.7	94,852	82.4	12,357
1934/5	89,711	103.1	117,213	101.9	27,502
1935/6	97,343	111.8	107,019	93.0	9,676
1936/7	96,826	112.2	120.148	104.4	23,322

INDIA (Rupees × 000)

Year	Imports	Index no	Exports	Index no	Balance
1913	1,832,706	100.0	2,411,910	100.0	579,204
1914	1,595,419	87.1	2,075,466	86.0	480,047
1915	1,278,882	69.8	1,802,513	74.7	523,631
1916	1,484,254	81.0	2,264,487	93.9	780,233
1917	1,535,605	83.8	2,344,471	97.2	808,866
1918	1,652,444	90.2	2,442,403	101.3	789,959
1919	1,833,235	100.1	2,898,230	120.2	1,064,995
1920	3,107,148	169.7	2,799,128	116.1	−308,020
1921	2,768,982	151.2	2,168,896	89.9	−600,086
1922	2,395,067	130.8	2,799,027	116.1	403,960
1923	2,219,676	121.2	3,284,746	136.2	1,065,070
1924	2,357,914	128.7	3,705,681	153.7	1,347,767
1925	2,242,790	122.5	3,971,521	164.7	1,728,731
1926	2,360,076	128.9	3,224,271	133.7	864,195

Appendix 11 – continued

INDIA (Rupees × 000) – continued

Year	Imports	Index no	Exports	Index no	Balance
1927	2,480,882	135.5	3,184,858	132.1	703,976
1928	2,498,044	136.5	3,306,405	137.1	808,361
1929	2,502,817	136.7	3,225,371	133.8	722,554
1930	1,879,383	102.6	2,525,876	104.7	646,493
1931	1,361,594	74.3	1,651,894	68.5	290,300
1932	1,327,949	72.5	1,352,870	56.0	24,921
1933	1,147,593	62.6	1,444,376	59.9	296,783
1934	1,252,403	68.4	1,482,789	61.4	230,386
1935	1,342,889	73.3	1,571,221	65.1	228,332
1936	1,223,550	66.8	1,806,076	74.9	582,526
1937	1,594,959	87.1	2,025,860	84.0	430,901
1938	1,502,089	82.0	1,622,424	67.3	120,335

CEYLON (Rupees × 000)

Year	Imports	Index no	Exports	Index no	Balance
1913	185,529	100.0	232,985	100.0	47,456
1914	171,836	92.8	218,352	94.0	46,516
1915	163,289	88.2	273,369	117.8	110,080
1916	209,724	113.3	297,506	128.2	87,782
1917	184,028	99.4	304,161	131.0	120,133
1918	177,717	96.0	211,326	91.0	33,609
1919	239,324	129.3	367,055	158.1	127,731
1920	321,603	173.8	268,462	115.6	−53,141
1921	260,835	140.9	256,600	110.6	−4,235
1922	280,283	151.4	297,753	128.3	17,470
1923	287,803	155.5	377,010	162.5	89,207
1924	302,418	163.4	414,710	178.7	112,292
1925	350,904	189.6	522,238	225.0	171,334
1926	394,758	213.3	532,251	229.3	137,493
1927	406,107	219.5	479,421	206.6	73,314
1928	400,073	216.2	417,619	180.0	17,546
1929	403,004	217.8	422,581	182.1	19,577
1930	302,133	163.2	322,972	139.1	20,839
1931	218,343	118.0	233,129	100.4	14,786
1932	196,049	105.9	188,837	81.3	−7,212
1933	177,147	95.7	200,193	86.2	23,046
1934	194,379	105.0	241,193	103.9	46,814
1935	204,429	110.4	230,041	99.1	25,612
1936	190,277	102.8	244,415	105.3	54,138
1937	220,723	119.2	310,198	133.6	89,475
1938	214,241	115.7	263,535	113.5	49,294

Appendix 11 – continued

SOUTH AFRICA (£ × 000)

Year	Imports	Index no	Exports	Bullion Exports	Exports including bullion	Index no	Balance
1913	40,374	100.0	27,525	37,589	65,114	100.0	24,740
1914	33,916	84.0	17,951	20,544	38,495	59.1	4,579
1915	30,174	74.7	15,028	18,153	33,181	50.9	3,007
1916	37,967	94.0	23,557	39,693	63,250	97.1	25,283
1917	33,583	83.1	28,771	59,910	88,681	136.1	55,098
1918	45,212	111.9	31,128	35,231	66,359	101.9	21,147
1919	46,665	115.5	50,624	47,672	98,296	150.9	5,163
1920	95,931	237.6	46,093	35,547	81,640	125.3	−14,291
1921	53,368	132.1	26,811	34,454	61,265	94.0	7,897
1922	48,098	119.1	29,717	29,313	59,030	90.6	10,932
1923	54,930	136.0	36,368	38,991	75,359	115.7	20,429
1924	63,626	157.5	37,773	40,199	77,972	119.7	14,346
1925	65,509	162.2	45,527	34,329	77,856	122.6	14,347
1926	69,649	172.5	39,734	33,127	72,861	111.8	3,212
1927	69,347	171.7	47,824	28,598	76,422	117.3	7,075
1928	74,159	183.6	48,561	25,815	74,376	114.2	217
1929	77,691	192.4	46,858	35,885	82,743	127.0	5,052
1930	59,945	148.4	32,374	37,084	69,458	106.6	9,513
1931	48,742	120.7	22,402	38,963	61,365	94.2	12,623
1932	31,272	77.4	18,964	47,593	66,557	102.2	35,285
1933	47,525	117.7	23,706	46,416	70,122	107.6	22,597
1934	64,311	159.2	23,935	34,603	58,538	89.9	−5,773
1935	73,006	180.8	28,607	71,440	100,047	153.6	27,041
1936	84,012	208.0	28,808	81,855	110,663	169.9	26,651
1937	100,451	248.8	39,631	82,832	122,463	188.0	22,012
1938	92,620	229.4	29,515	48,069	77,584	119.1	−15,036

DUTCH EAST INDIES (Guilders × 000)

Year	Imports	Index no	Exports	Index no	Balance
1913	463,702	100.0	671,434	100.0	207,732
1914	411,634	88.8	668,953	99.6	257,319
1915	390,077	84.2	770,072	114.7	379,995
1916	419,313	90.5	865,400	128.9	446,087
1917	385,120	83.1	778,222	115.9	393,102
1918	556,049	120.0	676,144	100.7	120,095
1919	739,747	159.7	2,146,337	319.8	1,406,590
1920	1,224,927	264.5	2,228,137	332.0	1,003,210
1921	1,193,983	257.8	1,190,929	177.4	−3,054

Appendix 11 – continued

DUTCH EAST INDIES (Guilders x 000) – continued

Year	Imports	Index no	Exports	Index no	Balance
1922	756,391	163.3	1,142,216	170.2	385,825
1923	642,261	138.7	1,378,481	205.4	736,220
1924	698,178	150.7	1,543,737	230.0	845,559
1925	839,522	181.3	1,801,502	268.4	961,980
1926	894,461	193.1	1,585,105	236.2	690,644
1927	902,212	194.8	1,644,534	245.0	742,322
1928	1,003,492	216.7	1,580,488	235.5	576,996
1929	1,108,216	239.3	1,446,419	215.5	338,203
1930	888,106	191.8	1,160,070	172.8	271,964
1931	592,524	127.9	749,435	111.6	156,911
1932	384,154	82.9	543,711	81.0	159,557
1933	329,379	71.1	470,349	70.0	140,970
1934	290,978	62.8	489,420	72.9	198,442
1935	276,498	59.6	447,446	66.6	170,948
1936	286,855	61.9	539,246	80.3	252,391
1937	498,327	107.6	953,015	142.0	454,688
1938	477,218	103.0	653,210	97.3	175,992

NIGERIA (£ x 000)

Year	Imports	Index no	Exports	Index no	Balance
1913	6,324	100.0	7,097	100.0	773
1914	6,269	99.1	6,420	90.4	151
1915	4,978	78.7	4,941	69.6	−37
1916	5,170	81.7	6,022	84.8	852
1917	5,800	91.7	8,591	121.0	2,791
1918	7,421	117.3	9,510	134.0	2,089
1919	10,791	170.6	14,676	206.7	3,885
1920	20,741	327.9	16,952	238.8	−3,789
1921	10,236	161.8	8,256	116.3	−1,980
1922	10,303	62.9	8,934	125.8	−1,369
1923	10,269	162.3	10,877	153.2	608
1924	10,945	173.0	14,454	203.6	3,509
1925	14,778	233.6	16,957	238.9	2,179
1926	12,755	201.6	16,681	235.0	3,926
1927	14,432	228.2	15,674	220.8	1,242
1928	15,761	249.2	17,075	240.5	1,314
1929	13,216	208.9	17,757	250.2	4,541
1930	12,614	199.4	15,028	211.7	2,414
1931	6,509	102.9	8,772	123.6	2,263
1932	7,194	113.7	9,477	133.5	2,283
1933	6,339	100.2	8,727	122.9	2,388
1934	5,364	84.8	8,874	125.0	3,510

Appendix 11 — continued

NIGERIA (£ × 000) — continued

Year	Imports	Index no	Exports	Index no	Balance
1935	7,804	123.4	11,339	159.7	3,535
1936	10,829	171.2	14,833	209.0	4,004
1937	14,624	231.2	19,436	273.8	4,812
1938	8,632	136.4	9,525	134.2	893

BRITISH MALAYA (Straits Settlements $ × 000)

Year	Imports	Index no	Exports	Index no	Balance
1913	363,557	100.0	339,769	100.0	−23,788
1914	302,253	83.1	299,496	88.1	−2,757
1915	314,374	86.4	413,707	121.7	99,333
1916	391,080	107.5	484,932	142.7	93,852
1917	455,879	125.3	604,148	177.8	148,269
1918	506,290	139.2	578,125	170.1	71,835
1919	629,700	173.2	811,688	238.9	181,988
1920	891,496	245.2	821,260	241.7	−70,236
1921	482,474	132.7	417,605	122.9	−64,869
1922	455,396	125.2	489,100	143.9	33,704
1923	577,568	158.8	669,738	197.1	92,170
1924	653,312	179.7	720,450	212.0	67,138
1925	967,943	266.2	1,281,775	377.3	313,832
1926	1,003,849	276.1	1,262,596	371.6	258,747
1927	990,562	272.4	1,061,729	312.5	71,167
1928	860,643	236.7	845,064	248.7	−15,579
1929	881,171	242.3	925,442	272.4	44,271
1930	706.3	194.2	657.7	193.6	−48.6
1931	453.4	124.7	401.4	118.1	−52.0
1932	376.8	103.6	323.4	95.2	−53.4
1933	350.3	96.3	373.4	109.9	23.1
1934	460.5	126.6	544.0	160.1	83.5
1935	466.7	128.3	570.3	167.8	103.6
1936	503.0	138.3	627.8	184.8	124.8
1937	679.9	187.0	897.1	264.0	217.2
1938	546.6	150.3	569.3	167.5	22.7

PHILIPPINES (Peso × 000)

Year	Imports	Index no	Exports	Index no	Balance
1913	106,626	100.0	95,546	100.0	−11,080
1914	97,177	91.6	97,379	102.4	202
1915	98,624	93.0	107,626	113.2	9,002
1916	90,993	85.7	139,874	147.1	48,881
1917	131,594	124.0	191,209	201.2	59,615
1918	197,198	185.9	270,389	284.5	73,191

Appendix 11 – continued

PHILIPPINES (Peso × 000)

Year	Imports	Index no	Exports	Index no	Balance
1919	237,278	223.7	226,236	238.1	−11,042
1920	298,877	281.8	302,248	318.1	3,371
1921	231,677	218.4	176,231	185.4	−55,446
1922	160,395	151.3	191,167	201.1	30,772
1923	174,999	165.0	241,506	254.2	66,507
1924	216,022	203.7	270,689	284.8	54,667
1925	239,466	225.8	297,754	313.3	58,288
1926	238,598	225.0	273,769	288.1	35,171
1927	231,703	218.6	311,148	327.4	79,445
1928	269,314	254.0	310,109	326.4	40,795
1929	294,321	277.6	328,894	346.1	34,573
1930	246.2	232.2	266,334	280.3	20.1
1931	198.4	187.1	207,944	218.8	9.5
1932	158.8	149.8	190,676	200.6	31.8
1933	134.7	127.0	211,542	222.6	76.8
1934	167.2	157.7	220,807	232.4	53.6
1935	171.0	161.3	188,491	198.3	17.4
1936	202.3	190.8	272,896	287.1	70.5
1937	218.1	205.7	302,533	318.4	84.4
1938	265.2	250.1	231,591	243.6	−33.7

CHINA (Haikwan taels × 000)

Year	Imports	Index no	Exports	Index no	Balance
1913	570,163	100.0	403,306	100.0	−166,857
1914	557,109	97.7	345,281	85.6	−211,828
1915	454,476	79.7	418,861	103.8	−35,615
1916	516,407	90.5	481,797	119.4	−34,610
1917	549,519	96.4	462,932	114.7	−86,587
1918	554,893	97.3	485,883	120.4	−69,010
1919	646,998	113.4	630,809	156.4	−16,189
1920	762,250	133.7	541,631	134.2	−220,619
1921	906,122	158.9	601,256	149.0	−304,866
1922	945,050	165.7	654,892	162.3	−290,158
1923	923,403	161.9	752,917	186.6	−170,486
1924	1,018,211	178.5	771,784	191.3	−246,427
1925	947,865	166.2	776,353	192.4	−171,512
1926	1,124,221	197.1	864,295	214.3	−259,926
1927	1,012,932	177.6	918,620	227.7	−94,312
1928	1,195,969	209.7	991,355	245.8	−204,614
1929	1,265,779	222.0	1,015,687	251.8	−250,092
1930	1,309,756	229.7	894,844	221.8	−414,912
1931	1433.5	251.4	909.5	225.5	−524.0

Appendix 11 — continued

CHINA (Haikwan taels × 000)

Year	Imports	Index no	Exports	Index no	Balance
1932	1049.2	184.0	492.9[a]	122.2	−398.7
1933	863.6	151.4	392.9[a]	97.4	−470.7
1934	660.8	115.9	343.8	85.2	−317.0
1935	589.9	103.4	369.8	91.6	−220.1
1936	604.3	105.9	453.3	112.4	−150.8
1937	611.8	107.3	538.3	133.4	−73.5
1938	568.8	99.7	490.1	121.5	−78.7

Note:

[a] Excluding re-exports.

Source: League of Nations, *International Trade Statistics* (Geneva: League of Nations), 1932, 1934, 1936, 1939; League of Nations, *Memorandum on International Trade and Balances of Payments: Trade Statistics of Sixty-Four Countries* (Geneva: League of Nations), 1928, 1929, 1931.

Appendix 12: Net Migration to Burma, Ceylon and Malaya, 1913–40

Year	Burma	Ceylon	Indians to Penang	Chinese to Malaya
1913	24,900	30,000	+48,493	--
1914	122,200	29,600	−11,856	--
1915	89,800	56,500	+25,003	--
1916	6,500	68,100	+41,087	+121,769
1917	−14,000	15,200	+32,494	+113,885
1918	25,700	20,000	+13,159	+22,836
1919	65,700	78,100	+54,666	+33,322
1920	93,200	18,400	+39,739	+57,694
1921	28,100	29,300	−15,878	+92,057
1922	49,700	28,200	+12,941	+36,017
1923	87,400	41,700	+6,544	+80,898
1924	72,400	25,400	+24,726	+93,681
1925	21,800	5,600	+47,564	+136,772
1926	65,900	−700	+109,009	+228,285
1927	67,100	−11,200	+67,414	+204,064
1928	85,600	300	−28,180	+146,346
1929	33,500	18,500	+37,603	+153,200
1930	−30,700	9,900	−82,621	+74,246
1931	−57,700	−31,900	−81,655	−112,965
1932	11,900	−29,800	−66,767	−97,518
1933	−8,900	−60,100	−12,496	−31,178
1934	29,400	97,600	+61,760	−61,639
1935	39,600	−8,100	+26,799	+90,986
1936	23,900	−8,200	+3,116	+75,801
1937	12,300	9,900	+78,080	+180,502
1938	−40,300	−1,400	−31,272	+53,180
1939	--	−26,400	−18,763	+14,339
1940	--	−33,000	--	+3,322

Source: Siok-Hwa Cheng, *The Rice Industry of Burma, 1852–1940* (Kuala Lumpur: University of Malaya Press, 1968), p. 262; D. R. Snodgrass, *Ceylon: An Export Economy in Transition* (Homewood Illinois: Irwin, 1966), p. 308; J. N. Parmer, *Colonial Labor Policy and Administration: A History of Labor in the Rubber Plantation Industry in Malaya, c. 1910–1941* (New York: J. J. Augustin, 1960), pp. 270–1.

Appendix 13: World Production of Wheat and Rice, 1913–35 (Millions Metric Tons)

Crop year	Wheat[a]	Index No	Rice[b]	Index No	Wheat and rice
1913/14	84.39	100.00	47.61	100.00	132.00
1914/15	76.69	90.87	47.77	100.33	124.46
1915/16	95.28	112.90	52.38	110.01	147.66
1916/17	73.20	86.74	55.34	116.23	128.54
1917/18	72.82	86.28	55.41	116.38	128.23
1918/19	79.14	93.77	44.13	92.69	123.27
1919/20	75.57	89.54	52.35	109.95	127.92
1920/1	78.65	93.19	49.27	103.48	127.92
1921/2	85.45	101.25	54.06	113.54	139.51
1922/3	84.64	100.29	56.07	117.76	140.71
1923/4	93.56	110.86	49.48	103.92	143.04
1924/5	83.38	98.80	53.43	112.22	136.81
1925/6	91.14	107.99	53.12	111.57	144.26
1926/7	91.85	108.83	52.62	110.52	144.47
1927/8	96.58	114.44	52.34	109.93	148.92
1928/9	105.92	125.51	54.54	114.55	160.46
1929/30	93.70	110.03	53.46	112.28	147.16
1930/1	100.53	119.12	57.28	120.31	157.81
1931/2	99.41	117.79	55.27	116.08	154.68
1932/3	100.50	119.08	55.27	116.08	155.77
1933/4	98.08	116.22	56.80	119.30	154.88
1934/5	89.94	106.57	52.62	110.52	142.56
1935/6	90.21	106.89	52.07	109.36	142.28

Notes:

[a] Excluding Russia and China.

[b] Excluding China.

Source: M. K. Bennett, 'World Wheat Utilization Since 1885–86', *Wheat Studies* 12 (1936), p. 392; V. D. Wickizer and M. K. Bennett, *The Rice Economy of Monsoon Asia* (Stanford, California: Stanford University Press, 1941), pp. 316–17.

BIBLIOGRAPHY

Adams, J. Q. III, 'Economic Change, Exports and Imports: The Case of India, 1870–1960', PhD dissertation, University of Texas, 1966

Adas, Michael, *The Burma Delta: Economic Development and Social Change on an Asian Rice Frontier, 1852–1941* (Madison, Wisconsin: University of Wisconsin Press, 1974)

Adloff, R., see: Thompson, V.

Albitreccia, A., see: Wohl, P.

Allen, G. C. and Donnithorne, Audrey, G., *Western Enterprise in Indonesia and Malaya: A Study in Economic Development* (London: George Allen & Unwin, 1957)

Anstey, Roger, *King Leopold's Legacy: The Congo under Belgian Rule, 1908–1960* (London: Oxford University Press, 1966)

Anstey, Vera, *The Economic Development of India*, 3rd edn 1949, 4th edn 1952 (London: Longmans Green & Co., 1952)

Arasaratnam, Sinnappah, *Indians in Malaysia and Singapore* (Bombay and Kuala Lumpur: Oxford University Press, 1970)

Arndt, E. H. D., *Banking and Currency Development in South Africa* (Cape Town & Johannesburg: Juta & Co., 1928)

Arndt, H. W., *The Economic Lessons of the Nineteen-Thirties* (London: Oxford University Press, 1944)

Bagchi, A. K., *Private Investment in India, 1900–1939* (Cambridge: Cambridge University Press, 1972)

Bairoch, Paul, *The Economic Development of the Third World since 1900* (London: Methuen & Co., 1975)

Bauer, P. T., *The Rubber Industry: A Study in Competition and Monopoly* (London: Longmans Green & Co., 1948)

————— *West African Trade: A Study of Competition, Oligopoly, and Monopoly in a Changing Economy* (Cambridge: Cambridge University Press, 1954)

Banerji, A. K., *India's Balance of Payments: Estimates of Current and Capital Accounts for 1921–22 to 1938–39* (New York: Asia Publishing House, 1963)

Bennett, M. K., 'World Wheat Utilization since 1885–86', in *Wheat Studies* 12 (1936), pp. 339–404

————— see: Wickizer, V. D.

Bhattacharyya, Dhires, *A Concise History of the Indian Economy* (Calcutta: Progressive Publishers, 1972)

Blyn, George, *Agricultural Trends in India, 1891–1947: Output Availability and Productivity* (Philadelphia: University of Pennsylvania Press, 1966)

Bogart, E. L., *Direct and Indirect Costs of the Great World War* (New York: Oxford University Press, 1919)

Boeke, J. H., *The Evolution of the Netherlands Indies Economy* (New York: Institute of Pacific Relations, 1946)

————— *Economics and Economic Policy of Dual Societies as Exemplified by Indonesia* (New York: Institute of Pacific Relations, 1953)

Bose, S. C., see: Vakil, C. N.

Bourne, A. M., see: Davies, P. N.

Bowley, A. L., *Some Economic Consequences of the Great War* (London: Thornton Butterworth, 1930)

Broek, J. O. M., *Economic Development of the Netherlands Indies* (New York: Institute of Pacific Relations, 1942)

Callis, H. G., *Foreign Capital in South East Asia* (New York: Institute of Pacific Relations, 1942)

Carr-Saunders, A. M., *World Population* (London: Royal Institute of International Affairs, 1936)

Chaudhuri, K. N., see: *Economy and Society*

Cheng, Siok-Hwa, *The Rice Industry of Burma, 1852–1940* (Kuala Lumpur: University of Malaya Press, 1968)

Cheng, Yu-Kwei, *Foreign Trade and Industrial Development of China. An Historical and Integrated Analysis through 1948* (Washington D.C.: Washington University Press, 1956)

Chilver, E. M., see: *History of East Africa*

Chong-Yah, Lim, *Economic Development of Modern Malaya* (Kuala Lumpur: Oxford University Press, 1967)

Clauson, G. L. M. 'The British Colonial Currency System', in *Economic Journal* 54 (1944), pp. 1–25.

Colonialism in Africa, 1870–1960, Duignan, Peter, and Gann L. H. (eds) Vol 4, *The Economics of Colonialism* (Cambridge: Cambridge University Press, 1975)

Condliffe, J. B., *The Commerce of Nations* (London: George Allen & Unwin, 1951)

Copeland, M. T., *A Raw Commodity Revolution* (Boston, Mass.: Harvard University Press, 1938)

Coquery-Vidrovitch, C., 'Mutation de l'Impérialisme Coloniale Française dans les Années 30', in *African Economic History* 4 (1977), pp. 103–52.

Cowan, C. D., see: *The Economic Development of South East Asia*

Croxton, A. H., *Railways of Rhodesia: The Story of the Biera Mashonaland and Rhodesia Railways* (Newton Abbot: David & Charles, 1973)

Davis, Kingsley, *The Population of India and Pakistan* (Princeton, New Jersey: Princeton University Press, 1951)

Davies, P. N., *The Trade Makers: Elder Dempster in West Africa, 1852–1972* (London: George Allen & Unwin, 1973)

——— and Bourne, A. M., 'Lord Kylsant and the Royal Mail', *Business History* 14 (1972), pp. 103–23

Davies, R. E. G., *A History of the World's Airlines* (London: Oxford University Press, 1964)

Deakin, B. M. and Seward, T., *Shipping Conferences: A Study of their Origins, Development and Economic Practices* (Cambridge: Cambridge University Press, 1973)

Department of Overseas Trade, *Economic Conditions in the Philippine Islands, 1933–34* (London: HMSO, 1935)

Deolalkar, P. V., see: Vakil, C. N.

D'Erlanger, Emile, B., *The History of the Construction and Finance of the Rhodesian Transport System* (London: Burrup Mathisson, 1938)

Dewey, Clive, 'The End of the Imperialism of Free Trade: The Eclipse of the

Lancashire Lobby and the Concession of Fiscal Autonomy to India', in *The Imperial Impact*, pp. 35–67.

——— 'The Government of India's "New Industrial Policy" 1900–1925: Formation and Failure' in *Economy and Society*, pp. 215–57

——— see: *The Imperial Impact*

——— see: *Economy and Society*

Dhekney, M. R., *Air Transport in India: Growth and Problems* (Bombay: Vora & Co., 1953)

Donnithorne, Audrey, G., see: Allen, G. C.

Duignan, Peter, see: *Colonialism in Africa*

Durand, J. D., 'The Population Statistics of China AD 2–1953', in *Population Studies* 13 (1959–60), pp. 209–56

Dutta, Amita, 'The Economy of Inter-War Ceylon: A Neo-Classical Model of Trade and Migration', in *Indian Economic and Social History Review* 7 (1970), pp. 1–23

Economic Development in a Plural Society: Studies in the Border Region of the Cape Province, Houghton, D. H. (ed.) (Cape Town: Oxford University Press, 1960)

Economic Development in the Long Run, Youngson, A. J. (ed.) (London: George Allen & Unwin, 1972)

Economy and Society: Essays in Indian Economic and Social History, Chaudhuri, K. N., and Dewey, Clive (eds) (Delhi: Oxford University Press, 1979)

Ehrlich, Cyril, 'The Uganda Economy, 1903–45' in *History of East Africa*, Vol 2, pp. 422–69

Ekundare, R. O., *An Economic History of Nigeria, 1860–1960* (London: Methuen & Co., 1973)

Empire Marketing Board, Survey of *Oilseeds and Vegetable Oils*, Vol. 1, *Oil Palm Products*, Vol. 2, *Coconut Palm Products* (London: HMSO, 1932)

Essays on Unbalanced Growth, de Vries, Egbert (ed.) (s'Gravenhage: Mouton & Co., 1962)

Fairplay (London)

Farnie, D. A., *East and West of Suez: The Suez Canal in History, 1854–1956* (Oxford: Clarendon Press, 1969)

Fayle, C. E., *A Short History of the World's Shipping Industry* (London: George Allen & Unwin, 1933)

de Fellner, F. V., *Communications in the Far East* (London: P. S. King & Son, 1934)

Feuerwerker, Albert, 'Materials for the Study of the Economic History of Modern China' in *Journal of Economic History* 21 (1961), pp. 41–60

——— *The Chinese Economy, 1912–1949* (Ann Arbor, Michigan: University of Michigan Press, 1968)

Food and Agriculture Organisation (FAO), *Commodity Policy Studies No. 7: The Stabilization of the International Trade in Rice, A Report on Possible Measures* (Rome: United Nations, 1955)

——— *Commodity Bulletin No. 36: The World Rice Economy*, Vol. 1, *Selected Papers*, Vol. 2, Trends and Forces (Rome: United Nations, 1962 and 1963)

——— *Commodity Bulletin No. 39: The Economic Relationships between Grains and Rice* (Rome: United Nations, 1964)

Frank, A. G., 'Multilateral Merchandise Trade Imbalances and Uneven Economic Development' in *Journal of Economic History*, 5 (1976), pp. 407–38

Frankel, S. H., *Capital Investment in Africa: Its Course and Effects* (London: Oxford University Press, 1938)

Furnivall, J. S., *An Introduction to the Political Economy of Burma* (Rangoon: Burma Book Club, 1938)

────── *Netherlands India: A Study of Plural Economy* (Cambridge: Cambridge University Press, 1944)

────── *Colonial Policy and Practice: A Comparative Study of Burma and Netherlands India* (Cambridge: Cambridge University Press, 1948)

Gadgil, D. R., *The Industrial Evolution of India in Recent Times, 1860–1939*, 5th edn (Bombay: Oxford University Press, 1971)

Gann, L. H., *A History of Northern Rhodesia: Early Days to 1953* (London: Chatto & Windus, 1964)

────── *A History of Southern Rhodesia: Early Days to 1934* (London: Chatto & Windus, 1965)

────── see: *Colonialism in Africa*

Garratt, G. R. M., *One Hundred Years of Submarine Cables* (London: HMSO, 1950)

Gayer, A. D., see: *The Lessons of Monetary Experience*

Ghosh, A., 'The Trend of the Birth Rate in India, 1911–50' in *Population Studies*, 10 (1956–7), pp. 53–67)

Glass, D. V., and Grebenik, E., 'World Population, 1800–1950' in *The Cambridge Economic History of Europe*, Vol. 6, pp. 57–138

Gould, P. R., *The Development of the Transportation Pattern in Ghana* (Evanston, Illinois: Northwestern University, 1960)

Greaves, I., *Colonial Monetary Conditions* (London: HMSO, 1953)

Grebenik, E., see: Glass, D. V.

Gunasekera, H. A. de S., *From Dependent Currency to Central Banking in Ceylon: An Analysis of Monetary Experience, 1825–1957* (London: G. Bell & Sons, 1962)

Gupta, Ranajit Das, 'Factory Labour in Eastern India: Sources of Supply, 1855–1946: Some Preliminary Findings' in *Indian Economic and Social History Review*, 13 (1976), pp. 277–330

Gurtoo, D. N., *India's Balance of Payments, 1920–1960* (Delhi: S. Chand & Co., 1961)

Habakkuk, H. J., see: *The Cambridge Economic History of Europe*

Harlow, V., see: *History of East Africa*

Helleiner, G. K., *Peasant Agriculture, Government and Economic Growth in Nigeria* (Homewood, Illinois: Richard D. Irwin, 1966)

Hieke, Ernest, *G. L. Gaiser, Hamburg-Westafrika, 100 Jahre Handel mit Nigeria* (Hamburg: Hoffman und Campe Verlag, 1949)

Higham, R., *British Imperial Air Routes, 1918–1939* (London: G. T. Foulis, 1960)

Hill, M. F., *Permanent Way*, Vol. 1, *The Story of the Kenya and Uganda Railway*, 2nd edn (Nairobi: East African Railways and Harbours, 1961)

────── *Permanent Way*, Vol. 2, *The Story of the Tanganyika Railways* (Nairobi: East African Railways and Harbours, 1962)

Hill, Polly, *The Migrant Cocoa Farmers of Southern Ghana: A Study in Rural Capitalism* (Cambridge: Cambridge University Press, 1963)

History of East Africa, Harlow, V., and Chilver, E. M. (eds) (Oxford: Clarendon Press, 1965)

Ho, Ping-ti, *Studies on the Population of China, 1368–1953* (Cambridge, Mass.: Harvard University Press, 1959)

Ho, Ping-yin, *The Foreign Trade of China* (Shanghai: The Commercial Press Ltd, 1935)

Hodson, H. V., *Slump and Recovery, 1929–37: A Survey of World Economic Affairs* (London: Oxford University Press, 1938)

Hopkins, A. G., *An Economic History of West Africa* (London: Longmans, 1973)
——— 'Innovation in a Colonial Context: African Origins of the Nigerian Cocoa-Farming Industry, 1880–1920' in *The Imperial Impact*, pp. 83–96
——— see: *The Imperial Impact*

Horowitz, R., 'The Restriction of Competition between Road Motor Transport and the Railways in the Union of South Africa' in *South African Journal of Economics*, 5 (1937), pp. 145–63

Hou, Chi-ming, *Foreign Investment and Economic Development in China, 1840–1937* (Cambridge, Mass.: Harvard University Press, 1965)

Houghton, Hobart, D., *The South African Economy* (Cape Town: Oxford University Press, 1964)
——— 'Economic Development, 1865–1965' in *The Oxford History of South Africa*, Vol. 2, pp. 1–48.
——— see: *Economic Development in a Plural Society*

Hsiao, Liang-lin, *China's Foreign Trade Statistics, 1864–1949* (Cambridge, Mass.: Harvard University Press, 1974)

Hubbard, G. E., *Eastern Industrialisation and its Effect on the West, with Special Reference to Great Britain and Japan* (London: Oxford University Press, 1935)

Huybrechts, André, *Transports et structures de développement au Congo: Étude du progrès économique de 1900 à 1970* (Paris: Mouton et IRES, 1970)

Hyde, F. E., *Shipping Enterprise and Management, 1830–1939: Harrisons of Liverpool* (Liverpool: Liverpool University Press, 1967)

Ingram, J. C., 'Thailand's Rice Trade and the Allocation of Resources' in *The Economic Development of South East Asia*, pp. 102–26
——— *Economic Change in Thailand, 1850–1970* (Stanford: Stanford University Press, 1971)

Interim Report of the Committee Appointed to Enquire into the Rice and Paddy Trade, Chairman: Thomas Couper (Rangoon, Burma: Superintendent, Government Printing and Stationery, 1931)

Islam, Nural, *Foreign Capital and Economic Development: Japan, India, and Canada: Studies in Some Aspects of Absorption of Foreign Capital* (Rutland, Vermont: Charles E. Tuttle Co., 1960)

Jackson, R. N., *Immigrant Labour and the Development of Malaya* (Kuala Lumpur: Government Press, 1961)

Jasny, N., *Competition Among Grains* (Stanford, California: Stanford University Food Research Institute, 1940)

Jewsiewicki, B., 'The Great Depression and the Making of the Colonial Economic System in the Belgian Congo' in *African Economic History*, 4 (1977), pp. 153–76

Jones, David, *The Time Shrinkers: The Development of Civil Aviation between Britain and Africa* (London: David Rendel Ltd, 1971)

Kahn, A. E., *Great Britain in the World Economy* (London: Sir Isaac Pitman & Sons Ltd, 1946)

Katzenellenbogen, S. E., *Railways and the Copper Mines of Katanga* (Oxford: Clarendon Press, 1973)
——— 'The Miners' Frontier' in *Colonialism in Africa, 1870–1960*, Vol. 4, *Economics of Colonialism*, pp. 360 426

Keith, A. B., *The Belgian Congo and the Berlin Act* (Oxford: Clarendon Press, 1919)

Keynes, J. M., *The Economic Consequences of Mr. Churchill* (London: Hogarth Press, 1925)

Khan, Ahmed, 'International Production and Exchange of Rice with Special Reference to Production, Market Demand, and Consumption of Rice in India and Burma',(PhD thesis, University of Wales, Aberystwyth, 1939)

Kidron, Michael, *Foreign Investments in India* (London: Oxford University Press, 1965)

Kiewiet, C. W. de, *A History of South Africa: Social and Economic* (Oxford: Clarendon Press, 1941)

Kindersley, R. M., 'British Overseas Investments in 1931' in *Economic Journal*, 43 (1933), pp. 187 204
——— 'British Overseas Investments in 1935 and 1936' in *Economic Journal*, 47 (1937), pp. 642 62

Kindleberger, C. P., *The World in Depression, 1929 39* (London: Allen Lane, Penguin Books Ltd, 1973)

King, Anne, see: Zwanenberg, R. M. A. van

King, Frank, H. H., *Money in British East Asia* (London: HMSO, 1957)
——— *A Concise Economic History of Modern China, 1840 1961* (London: Pall Mall Press, 1969)

de Kock, G., *A History of the South African Reserve Bank, 1920 1952* (Pretoria: Van Schaik, 1954)

de Kock, M. H., *The Economic Development of South Africa* (London: P. S. King & Son, 1936)

Koh, S. J., *Stages of Industrial Development in Asia: A Comparative History of the Cotton Industry in Japan, India, China and Korea* (Philadelphia: University of Pennsylvania Press, 1966)

Kraus, Richard, A., *Cotton and Cotton Goods in China, 1918 1936* (New York: Garland Publishing Inc, 1980)

Kuczynski, R. R., *A Demographic Survey of the British Colonial Empire*, Vol. 1, *West Africa*, Vol. 2, *East Africa* (London: Oxford University Press, 1948 and 1949)

Kuznets, Simon, *Economic Growth of Nations: Total Output and Production Structure* (Cambridge, Mass.: Harvard University Press, 1971)

Landon, K. P., *The Chinese in Thailand* (London: Oxford University Press, 1941)

Latham, A. J. H., *The International Economy and the Undeveloped World, 1865–1914* (London: Croom Helm Ltd, and Totowa, New Jersey: Rowman and Littlefield, 1978)
——— 'Multilateral Merchandise Trade Imbalances and Uneven Economic Development in India and China' in *Journal of European Economic History*, 7 (1978), pp. 33 60
——— 'Fluctuations and Responses in the International Rice Market', Paper to Mid-Western Economics Conference, Palmer House, Chicago, 7 April 1979

Lawford, G. L. and Nicholson, L. R., *The Telecon Story* (London: The Telegraph Construction and Maintenance Co. Ltd, 1950)

League of Nations, *Memorandum on International Trade and Balances of Payments: Trade Statistics of Sixty-Four Countries* (Geneva: League of Nations, 1928, etc.)

———*International Trade Statistics* (Geneva: League of Nations, 1932, etc.)

———*World Economic Survey* (Geneva: League of Nations, 1932, etc.)

———*The Course and the Phases of the World Economic Depression* (Geneva: League of Nations, 1931)

———*The Network of World Trade* (Geneva: League of Nations, 1942)

———*International Currency Experience: Lessons of the Inter-War Period* (Princeton: League of Nations, 1944)

———*Industrialisation and Foreign Trade* (Geneva: League of Nations, 1945)

Leduc, Michel, *Les Institutions Monétaires Africaines des Pays Franco-phones* (Paris: A. Pedore, 1965)

Leubuscher, Charlotte, *The West African Shipping Trade, 1909–1959* (Leyden: A. W. Sythoff, 1963)

Lewis, Cleona, *America's Stake in International Investments* (Washington D.C.: Brookings Institute, 1938)

Lewis, W. A., *Economic Survey, 1919–1939*, 8th imp. (London: George Allen & Unwin, 1966)

———'World Production, Prices and Trade, 1870–1960' in *Manchester School of Economics and Social Studies*, 20 (1952), pp. 105–38

Lin, Cheng, *The Chinese Railways: A Historical Survey* (Shanghai: China United Press, 1935)

Liu, Ta-chung and Yeh, Kung-chia, *The Economy of the Chinese Mainland: National Income and Economic Development, 1933–1959* (Princeton: Princeton University Press, 1965)

Loynes, J. B., *The West African Currency Board, 1912–1962* (London: West African Currency Board, 1962)

Macpherson, W. J., 'Economic Development in India under the British Crown, 1858–1947' in *Economic Development in the Long Run*, pp. 126–91

Malenbaum, W., *The World Wheat Economy* (Cambridge, Mass.: Harvard University Press, 1953)

Malik, M. B. K., *Hundred Years of Pakistan Railways* (Karachi: Ministry of Railways, 1962)

Maluste, D. N., see: Vakil, C. N.

Manning, Patrick, *Slavery, Capitalism and Economic Growth in Dahomey, 1640–1960* (Cambridge: Cambridge University Press, 1981)

Marx, Daniel, Jr, *International Shipping Cartels: A Study of Industrial Self-Regulation by Shipping Conferences* (New Jersey: Princeton University Press, 1953)

McLachlan, D. L., *The Conference System since 1919: Business History*, 4 (1961), pp. 54–63

Mehta, S. D., *The Cotton Mills of India, 1854–1954* (Bombay: The Textile Association (India), 1954)

Meyer, R. H., *Bankers Diplomacy: Monetary Stabilisation in the Twenties* (New York: Columbia University Press, 1970)

Middleton, P. H., *Railways of Thirty Nations: Government versus Private Ownership* (New York: Prentice Hall, 1937)

Mikesell, R. F., see: *US Private and Government Investment Abroad*

Miles, John, 'Rural Protest in the Gold Coast: The Cocoa Hold Ups, 1908–1938' in *The Imperial Impact*, pp. 152–70

Moggridge, D. E., *The Return to Gold, 1925: The Formulation of Economic Policy and its Critics* (Cambridge: Cambridge University Press, 1969)

Mukherjee, M., *National Income of India: Trends and Structure* (Calcutta: Statistical Publishing Society, 1969)

Moll, J. T., see: de Wilde, A. N.

Morris, M. D., 'South Asian Entrepreneurship and the Rashoman Effect, 1800–1947' in *Exploration in Economic History*, 16 (1979), pp. 341–61

Munro, J. Forbes, *Africa and the International Economy, 1800–1960: An Introduction to the Modern Economic History of Africa South of the Sahara* (London: J. M. Dent & Sons, 1976)

Murray, M., *Union Castle Chronicle, 1853–1953* (London: George Allen & Unwin, 1953)

Myers, R. H., 'Cotton Textile Handicrafts and the Development of the Cotton Textile Industry in Modern China' in *Economic History Review*, 18 (1965), pp. 614–32

Naval Intelligence Division, Admiralty, *French Equatorial Africa & Cameroons* (London: Geographical Handbook Series, 1942)

———*The Belgian Congo* (London: Geographical Handbook Series, 1944)

Newman, R. K., 'Social Factors in the Recruitment of the Bombay Millhands' in *Economy and Society*, pp. 277–98

Nicholson, L. R., see: Lawford, G. L.

North, D. C., 'International Capital Movements in Historical Perspective' in *US Private and Government Investment Abroad*, pp. 10–43

Onselen, C. van, *Chibaro: African Mine Labour in Southern Rhodesia, 1900–1933* (London: Pluto Press, 1976)

Palmer, Mabel, *The History of the Indians in Natal* (Cape Town: Oxford University Press, 1957)

Papers on Malayan History, Tragonning, K. G. (ed.) (Singapore: Journal of South East Asian History, 1962)

Parmer, J. N., *Colonial Labor Policy and Administration: A History of Labor in the Rubber Plantation Industry in Malaya, c. 1910–1941* (New York: J. J. Augustin, 1960)

Perkins, D. H., *Agricultural Development in China, 1368–1968* (Chicago: Aldine, 1969)

Perrings, Charles, *Black Mineworkers in Central Africa: Industrial Strategies and the Evolution of an African Proletariat in the Copper Belt, 1911–1941* (London: Heinemann, 1979)

Pim, Alan, Sir, *The Financial and Economic History of the African Tropical Territories* (Oxford: Clarendon Press, 1940)

———*Colonial Agricultural Production: The Contribution made by Native Peasants and by Foreign Enterprise* (London: Oxford University Press, 1946)

Postan, M., see: *The Cambridge Economic History of Europe*

Purcell, Victor, *The Chinese in Malaya* (London: Oxford University Press, 1948)

———*The Chinese in South East Asia* (London: Oxford University Press, 1951)

Radius, W. A., *United States Shipping in Transpacific Trade, 1922–1938* (Stanford: Stanford University Press, 1944)

Railway Year Book (London) 1914, etc. sec: *Universal Directory of Railway Officials*

Rajaratnam, S., 'The Ceylon Tea Industry, 1886–1931' in *Ceylon Journal of Historical and Social Studies* July–Dec 1961, pp. 169–202

Rees, G., *The Great Slump: Capitalism in Crisis, 1929–33* (New York: Harper & Row, 1970)

Remer, C. F., *Foreign Investments in China* (New York: Macmillan, 1933)

Robequain, C., *The Economic Development of French Indo-China* (London: Oxford University Press, 1944)

Robertson, C. J., 'The Rice Export from Burma, Siam and French Indo-China' in *Pacific Affairs*, 9 (1936), pp. 243–53

Robinson, H., *Carrying British Mails Overseas* (London: George Allen & Unwin, 1964)

Royal Institute of International Affairs, *The Problem of International Investment* (London: Oxford University Press, 1937)

Saini, K. G., 'The Growth of the Indian Economy, 1860–1960' in *Review of Income and Wealth*, 15 (1969), pp. 247–63

Sandberg, L. G., *Lancashire in Decline: A Study in Entrepreneurship, Technology, and International Trade* (Columbus: Ohio State University Press, 1974)

Sandhu, K. S., 'Some Preliminary Observations of the Origins and Characteristics of Indian Migration to Malaya, 1786–1957' in *Papers on Malayan History*, pp. 40–72

Sanyal, N., *Development of Indian Railways* (Calcutta: University of Calcutta, 1930)

Sarkar, N. K., *The Demography of Ceylon* (Colombo: Ceylon Government Press, 1957)

————'Population Trends and Population Policy in Ceylon' in *Population Studies*, 9 (1955–6), pp. 195–215

Sastry, N. S. R., *A Statistical Study of India's Industrial Development* (Bombay: Thacker & Co., 1947)

Saul, S. B., *Studies in British Overseas Trade, 1870–1914* (Liverpool: Liverpool University Press, 1960)

Seward, T., see: Deakin, B. M.

Simmons, C. P., 'Indigenous Enterprise in the Indian Coal Mining Industry, c. 1835–1939' in *Indian Economic and Social History Review*, 13 (1976), pp. 189–218

————'Recruiting and Organising an Industrial Labour Force in Colonial India: The Case of the Coal Mining Industry c. 1880–1939' in *Indian Economic and Social History Review*, 13 (1976), pp. 455–86

Sitsen, P. H. W., *Industrial Development of the Netherlands Indies* (New York: Institute of Pacific Relations, 1943)

Smith, E. C., *A Short History of Naval and Marine Engineering* (Cambridge: Babcock & Wilcox, 1937)

Smith, H. L., *Airways Abroad: The Story of American World Air Routes* (Wisconsin: University of Wisconsin Press, 1950)

Snodgrass, D. R., *Ceylon: An Export Economy in Transition* (Homewood, Illinois: Richard D. Irwin, 1966)

Staley, Eugene, *War and the Private Investor* (Chicago: University of Chicago Press, 1935)

Statistical Abstracts for the British Colonies (London: HMSO)

Statistical Abstracts for the British Dominions and Protectorates (London: HMSO)

Statistical Abstracts for the British Empire (London: HMSO)

Statistical Abstracts for British India (London: HMSO)

Studies in American Demography, Willcox, W. F. (ed.) (Ithaca, New York: Cornell University Press, 1940), pp. 22–5

Sturmey, S. G., *British Shipping and World Competition* (London: Athlone Press, 1962)

Svennilson, Ingvar, *Growth and Stagnation in the European Economy* (Geneva: United Nations, 1954)

Tawney, R. H., *Land and Labour in China* (London: Allen & Unwin, 1932)

Taylor, H. C., *World Trade in Agricultural Products* (New York: Macmillan, 1943)

The Cambridge Economic History of Europe, Habakkuk, H. J. and Postan, M. (eds) Vol. 6. *The Industrial Revolution and After* (Cambridge: Cambridge University Press, 1965)

The Economic Development of South East Asia: Studies in Economic History and Political Economy, Cowan, C. D. (ed.) (London: George Allen & Unwin, 1964)

The Economist (London) 16 Feb. 1938, p. 484

The Imperial Impact: Studies in the Economic History of Africa and India, Dewey, Clive and Hopkins, A. G. (eds) (London: Athlone Press, 1978)

The Lessons of Monetary Experience: Essays in Honor of Irving Fisher, Gayer, A. D. (ed.) (London: George Allen & Unwin Ltd, 1937)

The Oxford History of South Africa, Wilson, Monica and Thompson, Leonard (eds) 2 Vols, (Oxford: Clarendon Press, 1971)

The Statesman's Year Book (London: Macmillan, 1921, etc.)

The Statist (London) 2 Sept. 1939, pp. 282–8, 'British Capital Invested in India'

Thomas, P. J., 'India in the World Depression' in *Economic Journal*, 45 (1935), pp. 469–83

Thompson, Leonard, see: *The Oxford History of South Africa*

Thompson, V. and Adloff, R., *French West Africa* (London: George Allen & Unwin, 1958)

Thornton, R. H., *British Shipping*, 2nd edn (Cambridge: Cambridge University Press, 1959)

Timoshenko, V. P., *Wheat Prices and the World Wheat Market* (Ithaca, New York: Cornell University Press, 1928)

——— *World Agriculture and the Depression* (Ann Arbor, Michigan: University of Michigan, 1933)

——— 'Monetary Influences on Post-War Wheat Prices' in *Wheat Studies*, 14 (1938), pp. 263–318

Tomlinson, B. R., 'Monetary Policy and Economic Development: The Rupee Ratio Question, 1921–1927' in *Economy and Society*, pp. 143–62

——— 'Britain and the Indian Currency Crisis, 1930–32' in *Economic History Review*, 32 (1979), pp. 88–99

Tomlinson, J. D., 'The Rupee/Pound Exchange in the 1920's' in *Indian Economic and Social History Review*, 15 (1978), pp. 133–50

——— 'The First World War and British Cotton Piece Exports to India' in *Economic History Review*, 32 (1979), pp. 494–506

Tregonning, K. G., see: *Papers on Malayan History*

United Nations, *International Capital Movements during the Inter-War Period* (New York: Lake Success, 1949)
———*Demographic Yearbook* (New York: United Nations, 1956)
Universal Directory of Railway Officials and Railway Year Book (London: 1933, etc.)
US Private and Government Investment Abroad, Mikesell, R. F. (ed.) (Eugene, Oregon: University of Oregon Books, 1962)
Utley, F., *Lancashire and the Far East* (London: George Allen & Unwin, 1931)
Vakil, C. N., Bose, S. C. and Deolalkar, P. V., *Growth of Trade and Industry in Modern India: An Introductory Survey* (Calcutta: Longmans, Green & Co. Ltd, 1931)
Vakil, C. N. and Maluste, D. N., *Commercial Relations between India and Japan* (Calcutta: Longmans, Green & Co., 1937)
Van Der Horst, Sheila, T., *Native Labour in South Africa* (London: Oxford University Press, 1942)
Venkatasubbiah, H., *The Foreign Trade of India: 1900–1940: A Statistical Analysis* (Bombay: Oxford University Press, 1946)
Vries, Egbert, de, see: *Essays on Unbalanced Growth*
Walker, G., *Traffic and Transport in Nigeria: The Example of an Underdeveloped Tropical Territory* (London: HMSO, 1957)
Weiner, Lionel, *Les Chemins de Fer Coloniaux de l'Afrique* (Bruxelles: Geomaere, 1930)
Westwood, J. N., *Railways of India* (Newton Abbot: David & Charles, 1974)
Wickizer, V. D., 'Shipping and Freight Rates in the Overseas Grain Trade' in *Wheat Studies*, 15 (1938), pp. 47–120
———'Rice and Wheat in World Agriculture and Consumption' in *Wheat Studies*, 17 (1941), pp. 261–314
———'Coffee, Tea and Cocoa: An Economic and Political Analysis' (Stanford, California: Stanford University Press, 1951)
———and Bennett, M. K., *The Rice Economy of Monsoon Asia* (Stanford, California: Stanford University Press, 1941)
Widjojo, Nitisastro, *Population Trends in Indonesia* (Ithaca, New York: Cornell University Press, 1971)
Wilde, A. N. de and Moll, J. T., *The Netherlands Indies during the Depression: A Brief Economic Survey* (Amsterdam: J. M. Meulenhoff, 1936)
Willcox, W. F., 'Population of the World and its Modern Increase' in *Studies in American Demography*, pp. 21–51
Williams, David, 'London and the 1931 Financial Crisis' in *Economic History Review*, 15 (1962–3), pp. 518–25
Wilson, Francis, *Labour in the South African Gold Mines, 1911–69* (Cambridge: Cambridge University Press, 1972)
Wilson, Monica, see: *The Oxford History of South Africa*
Wohl, P. and Albitreccia, A., *Road and Rail in Forty Countries* (London: Oxford University Press, 1935)
Wolfe, M., *The French Franc between the Wars, 1919–1939* (New York: Columbia University Press, 1951)
Woodruff, W., *Impact of Western Man: A Study of Europe's Role in the World Economy, 1750–1960* (New York: St Martin's Press, 1960)
Wright, S. F., *China's Struggle for Tariff Autonomy, 1843–1938* (Shanghai: Kelley & Walsh, 1938)

Wrigley, C. C., 'Kenya: The Patterns of Economic Life, 1902–45' in *History of East Africa*, Vol. 2, pp. 232–60

Yates, P., Lamartine, *Forty Years of Foreign Trade: A Statistical Handbook with Special Reference to Primary Products and Underdeveloped Countries* (London: George Allen & Unwin, 1959)

Yeh, Kung-chia, see: Liu, Ta-chung

Youngson, A. J., see: *Economic Development in the Long Run*

Zachariah, K. G., *A Historical Study of Internal Migration on the Indian Sub-Continent, 1900–1931* (Bombay: Asia Publishing House, 1964)

Zimmerman, L. J., 'The Distribution of World Income, 1860–1960' in *Essays on Unbalanced Growth*, pp. 28–55

Zwanenberg, R. M. A. van, with King, Anne, *An Economic History of Kenya and Uganda, 1800–1970* (London: Macmillan, 1975)

INDEX

Accra 52
Adidjan 37
Africa: agriculture, peasant 18; income, national and *per capita* 20; population 19, 20; railways 15, 23, 24 (map), 25 & 26 (tables); trade 17, 87, 88 (tables); *see also* individual countries
African and Eastern Trading Corporation 49
African Steamship Company 50
Agreement system 47
agriculture *see* peasant agriculture, plantation agriculture; prices, falling 128, 175–6, 178, 183, 185; *see also* individual crops, countries
Ahmedabad 157
air transport 52–3, 79, 182; *see also under* individual countries
alcohol 18
America *see* Latin America, North America, South America
Amsterdam 49, 52
Angola: agriculture, peasant 173; plantation 38, 173; coffee 38, 125, 173; currency 66; depression 173; exports 125; fish 125, 173; ivory 18; maize 125, 173; migrant workers 148–9, 173; population 149; railways 38, 84, 173; rubber forest 18; sugar 125, 173; telecommunications 51
Anstey, Vera 97
antimony 168
Antwerp 49
areca nuts 115
Argentina: financial crisis (1931) 58; wheat 176
Arnhem 116
asbestos 124, 171
Asia: income, *per capita* 20; population 19; railways 15, 23, 24 (map), 25 (table); trade, exports and imports 17, 87; *see also* individual countries
Assam: petroleum 158; rice 134–5; tea 19, 21, 134, 161

Australia: air transport 52; shipping lines 43; tin dredging 76; wheat 176; exports 160, 178
Austria: banks 57; financial crisis (1931) 57; shipping lines 46

Babington Smith Committee 59
baht 61
bajra 160
Baltimore 39
Bamako 37
bananas 125, 166
Bandoeng 52
Bangka 142, 144
Bangkok 117–18, 144, 167
Bank: Chartered, of India, Australia and China 63; of Communications 63; of England 56, 59; of Indo-China 61–2, 77; of the Belgian Congo 65; *see also* Banque
Banningville 53
Banque d'Afrique Occidentale 65
Barclays DCO 64
Barotse province 148
Basra 52
Basutoland 147
Bata Shoe Company 159, 164–5
Batavia 165
Bathurst 52
Bauchi Light Railway 35
bauxite 165
Bechuanaland 147
beef on the hoof 174
beeswax 124
Belgian: currency 65–6, 82; franc 65–6
Belgian Africa *see* Belgian Congo and Ruandi Urundi
Belgian Congo: African wage workers 173–4; agriculture, peasant 174; air transport 52–3; cash crops 174; cement 125; cotton, raw 174; currency 65–6; depression 173; economic development 125, 173–4; investment, from abroad 16, 17, 71 (table), 82–3, in mining and

217